### David Long

Loan Consultant | NMLS #2174899
M: 206-940-2180 | O: 425-979-5277
loansbydavidlong.com
David.long@caliberhomeloans.com

DAVID LONG
MORTGAGE FINANCING

# MAX OUT MINDSET

**www.mascotbooks.com**

*Max Out Mindset: Proven Strategies that Prepare You and Your Team for Battle in Business, Sport, and Life*

**For more information, please contact:**
Mascot Books
620 Herndon Parkway #320
Herndon, VA 20170
info@mascotbooks.com

Library of Congress Control Number: 2020912182

CPSIA Code: PRFRE0820A
ISBN-13: 978-1-64543-718-5

Printed in Canada

*As of this writing, my wife Julie and I just celebrated our thirtieth wedding anniversary and have been together since I was eighteen and she was sixteen. Our first date was thirty-eight years, one month, and nine days ago. I will keep it simple. She is thoughtful, kind, selfless, creative, and beautiful from the inside out. I have had several nicknames for her over the years. There is only one that has stuck with her, and it says everything about how I feel: LOML. Love of My Life.*

# THE 15 POWERS

# MAX OUT MINDSET

## WHEN IT MATTERS THE MOST

PROVEN STRATEGIES THAT PREPARE YOU AND YOUR
TEAM FOR BATTLE IN BUSINESS, SPORT, AND LIFE

### LARRY WIDMAN, M.D.

**HIGH PERFORMANCE MINDSET COACH**

**FOREWORD BY DR. TOM OSBORNE**

Former University of Nebraska Head Coach and Five-Time
NCAA Football National Champion

# TABLE OF CONTENTS

# FOREWORD

## COACH TOM OSBORNE

OVER A THIRTY-SIX-YEAR PERIOD of coaching football at the University of Nebraska, I observed many changes. The most profound change that I observed was the shift in family stability. Early on we saw very few of our athletes coming from broken or unstable backgrounds. With the passage of time, things changed, and today over half of our young people grow up without both biological parents. Many are fatherless, and this lack of family stability leaves coaches and teachers in a much different place than they were a generation or two ago. There was a time when a coach could make decisions such as what position an athlete played, how much playing time the athlete received, and what training activities were employed without much question or opposition.

Today, there is little a coach does that goes unquestioned. Where the coach at one time was seen as the ultimate authority, today parents and advisers are often critical of every move the coach makes and often encourage transferring to another school or another sport when things don't go exactly according to their plan for the young athlete. Some have gone so far as to believe that everyone in a race or a competition should receive a medal or a ribbon. The promotion of self-esteem in the 1980s and the advent of social media in the 1990s has led to a very different coaching environment than the one that Vince Lombardi or Bear Bryant experienced.

There have been many innovations in the world of athletics over the last fifty years. At one time it was believed that weightlifting made an athlete "muscle bound," and then strength training evolved into a basic pillar of athletic training. Next came advances in nutrition, and now every major college and professional athletic team has someone supervising the nutritional needs of athletes. Also, coaching seminars, webinars, and clinics have led to much more information available to coaches regarding fundamentals, offensive and defensive strategies, and skill development. All of these changes have led to a large number of athletes who are physically more advanced and better coached than athletes were previously. Still, some teams are better than others; the playing field has been leveled some, but it is not entirely even. The most recent frontier in athletics is not focused on physical development or even coaching strategies. Rather, it consists of focus on the mental, emotional, and even spiritual elements of athletics. I remember Phil Jackson, coach of the Chicago Bulls in the 1990s, using some unusual team-building strategies and talking about mental imaging. Since that time the value of sports psychology has taken off and has become more and more crucial.

Taking a group of young people who have often been raised in unstable environments and who live in a "me first" culture and helping them develop into a cohesive, unselfish unit willing to put team accomplishment and the welfare of others ahead of self-interest is difficult and is something of an art. I was fortunate to experience the importance of an excellent sports psychologist in the 1990s, Dr. Jack Stark. I could care about our players; I could see to it that they were well trained and well fed and that they possessed strategies that gave us a good chance to succeed on the field—but I would not be the one they would come to when their girlfriend broke up with them, when they were homesick, when they flunked a test, or when their confidence was shaken. Since I was their coach, they would not want me to see their hurts, their insecurities, and their problems with others on the team. They wanted me to see them at their best, as I would decide who would play and who would not. However, they would drop their mask with Jack and would enable him to deal with their hurts and their insecurities. We were able to develop strategies that enabled players from very different backgrounds to come together and to begin to put team accomplishment ahead of personal accomplishment—something that is rare in our culture. Jack was a big part of whatever success we had during that time.

So, that brings me to Dr. Larry Widman. I got to know Larry when I was athletic director at Nebraska from 2007 through 2012. Larry worked with our women's volleyball team and was very helpful to Coach John Cook. John, like me many years before, realized that young people were very gifted athletically but that their lives were more complex and that there were many forces interfering with team chemistry. John credits Larry with helping create a stronger sense of trust within his team and helping him develop strategies to better relate to his athletes. John has won four national championships and multiple conference championships, but he continues to grow and strive toward higher levels of performance, and relying on Larry Widman and others has been instrumental in his success. The time of the coach who thinks he or she has everything figured out and is resistant to change is past.

Larry also worked with our women's bowling team at Nebraska and was very helpful in their winning several national championships. The mental game is certainly as important as physical skills in bowling, and our coach, Bill Straub, used Larry's skills in compiling an amazing record during his career at Nebraska. Larry also worked extensively with Nebraska's women's gymnastics program and helped Coach Dan Kendig accomplish an amazing record of conference championships and high national rankings. He guided gymnasts with their ability to focus and remain poised and confident in highly pressured environments where one slip or one misstep could ruin an individual or even a team performance.

Larry has also helped Kirsten Booth and the Creighton University volleyball team as they won six straight Big East Conference championships and had some excellent runs in the national volleyball tournament. Kirsten is very complimentary of the role Larry has played in helping her build a very strong volleyball program in a state with a far lower population than most of the states in the Big East Conference.

And Larry has not limited his work to elite teams, professional athletes, and Olympians. He has also worked with high school athletes and youth sports teams. His twenty-plus years of work in developing excellence in the athletic arena has carried over to work with many business leaders who are seeking strategies to improve cohesiveness and performance within their organizations.

Larry is unique in the field of sports psychology, as most sports psychologists have advanced degrees in psychology but have not gone to medical school. Larry is a licensed psychiatrist, so he is able to combine his knowledge of psychology as it applies to all types of peak performance, but he also has the advantage of seeing things from the perspective of his medical training. I find his book very insightful and practical. He is not writing from an ivory tower perch that is long on theory and short on experience. He has been involved in performance at the ground level, where competition is fierce and the margin between success and failure is often razor thin. I think the reader will catch a glimpse of what Larry pursues with his teams, an elite mindset, as they try to climb Performance Mountain.

Tom Osborne
Lincoln, Nebraska
April 27, 2020

# INTRODUCTION

## PREPARING FOR BATTLE

I AM WRITING THIS BOOK for many reasons. I've been blessed over the past twenty years to work with some of the best teams, coaches, athletes, and other high performers in business, sport, and life. I want to be able to share what I've taught many of them as well as share what I have learned from them. Throughout the book, the goal will be to highlight experiences to help individuals gain insight into what goes into creating elite performance.

I often choose to work with young people because I find it rewarding to help empower young men and women to grow up into healthy adults who have great self-esteem, know how they want to be treated by others, have learned to build deeper relationships, and feel like they can accomplish anything they set out to do in this world as adults.

Many of the stories are intentionally specific to the coaches, athletes, and teams that I have worked with over the years. I've chosen to do it this way for authenticity but also to highlight the struggles and accomplishments, the highs and the lows, and all that goes along with pursuing the edges of elite. It is done so with their blessing and/ or the stories have already been shared in a public format such as in the newspaper or on TV. I believe the lessons learned from these experiences are universal.

From an early age I knew I was going to be a physician and fairly certain that I was going to be a surgeon. For a variety of reasons, my path changed, and I made the decision to practice psychiatry because I believed that it was the best way for me to help others through healing of the mind and the accompanying issues created by the mind-body connection.

I found out at the onset of my medical career, due to outside forces that influenced day-to-day practices, that the role of the psychiatrist in the 1990s was starting to change. We were asked to diagnose and treat mental illness, generally treating with pills, but were expected to leave the growth, insight, and evolution of people to the therapists. While I believe strongly about the role of medications for those who need them for their mental health, I could never fully accept that my main role was as a "pill pusher." Luckily, two events happened early on that changed the trajectory of my career.

First, my employer at the time, Trinity Health (located in Minot, North Dakota), bought out a competing hospital, including its residential addiction-treatment unit. It was in the addiction world that I had my first opportunity to work with high performers. Though their addiction was holding them back at the time, I witnessed many of them blossom; they were able to get back to doing great things in their personal as well as professional lives once they were able to manage their addiction.

The Minot Air Force Base, located about eight miles north of town, provided my hospital with a unique group of patients with roots all over the country. The air force base is called a dual nuclear-capable wing base because it is home to the Fifth Bomb Wing, an element of the Global Strike Command—one of only two bases in the world to maintain and operate B-52 bombers with nuclear weapons capability.

The other group to call Minot home is the Ninety-First Missile Wing. Its mission is to maintain the Minuteman III nuclear missiles located in three main silo fields surrounding the base. This means that there were nuclear weapons in the ground in missile silos as well as those carried by the B-52 bombers.

I had built some goodwill and great relationships with the military through helping out their dependents. Thus, the second event, 9/11, presented me the opportunity to help top-ranking air force personnel, including B-52 pilots. Many of the air force psychiatrists were being deployed, and as you can imagine, the stress levels there were very high at that time. I was contacted by the military and asked to be of service. The good news was that I was told I could not use any medications to help with stress and anxiety. The bad news was that I was told I couldn't use medications! Yikes! I realized I had come to rely on medications for reasons previously stated. Yet this was my opportunity to use my skill sets to help with such things as anxiety, confidence, concentration, and composure by teaching high-performance mental skills and strategies. I have shared this phrase many times, due in part to my experiences with the air force:

*If mental skills training and strategies work for those in a stressful environment such as combat, they will work in any other aspect of business, sport, or life.*

After gaining confidence from my Minot experiences, I started working with other elite performers, athletes, and business leaders. In 2006 we made the decision to move back to our home state when an opportunity presented itself in Lincoln, Nebraska. In 2007, while working for Bryan Hospital, a college athlete who was having a mental health crisis was admitted there. I collaborated extensively with Dr. Lonnie Albers, who was the head of Athletic Medicine for the University of Nebraska (UNL), concerning this athlete during his hospital stay. As a result, Dr. Albers asked me to come on board as a consultant with the UNL Athletic Department. It was this chance meeting that led to the opportunity to work with individual athletes and eventually collaborations with a few coaches and teams at UNL.

I've been blessed to collaborate with coaches and teams at the Division I level that have won five national championships, numerous conference championships, and in the case of women's gymnastics, several Super Six National Championship appearances, as well. I have worked with numerous Olympic and professional athletes. There is a different sense of accomplishment when you know that you've played a role in making their professional dreams come true—and for some to be set financially for life. As of the writing of this book, more than two hundred million dollars have been earned at the professional level by athletes for whom I provided support.

Over the past couple of years, there has been the opportunity to work with wonderful high school athletes and teams that have won state and conference championships or have maxed out in their own right. These teams include Omaha Westside Football and the following volleyball teams: Skutt Catholic, Waverly, Papillion La Vista, Clarkson-Leigh, and Fillmore Central. The youngest athlete I've worked with is a thirteen-year-old gymnast aspiring to make it to the highest level of her sport!

At the Division I level, it became clear to me that the big separator in performance was those athletes who developed the strongest mental game and those teams that developed the best culture and team chemistry. Michael Jordan may have summed it up best: **"Talent wins games, but teamwork and intelligence win championships."**

I have worked with three teams at UNL and one team at Creighton University over an extended period of time. At UNL the teams are women's volleyball, women's bowling, and women's gymnastics. At Creighton it is women's volleyball. There are two common denominators among these four teams: (1) each team had seasoned coaches who were elite, and (2) each team had slight decreases in performance just prior to their coaches reaching out for assistance with mindset training and team dynamics.

One example will shed just a little light on how fine a line there is between great and elite. Bill Straub's bowling team had won its third national championship in 2009. However, from 2010 to 2012 they failed to make the national championship match, finishing third or fourth in the country each year. Early in the 2013 season, while being ranked near the top again and after winning a big tournament, I ran into Coach Straub at the North Stadium, where many of the student-athletes train and recover, and congratulated him on his recent victory. Surprisingly, he told me that the team needed some help if it was going to compete for a national title that year, and that led to a fruitful three-year collaboration with his team from 2013 to 2015.

During those three years, several ingredients identified with Coach Straub and worked on by his teams contributed to their winning two national championships and a runner-up finish. The self-awareness from that coach and the understanding of what his team needed, even when they were near the top, were so critical and a reminder of what a fine line there is between great and elite. We'll discuss those ingredients in this book.

In the summer of 2013 a mutual friend, Tim Clare, introduced me to Commander Jack Riggins, a Navy SEAL who was still on active duty stationed in Germany. It was clear early on that we shared similar philosophies about how to help individuals and teams optimize performance. Jack brought instant credibility because of his SEAL training and his leadership expertise in the most rugged of environments. In the fall of 2013, he started helping me with the Husker volleyball team and Coach John Cook. Some of our best work was done in this environment; some of it is documented in Coach Cook's book *Dream like a Champion.*

In writing this book I have tried to organize my thoughts, philosophies, and beliefs based on my years of experience in working with top coaches, athletes, and teams and also based on work with businesses through our company Performance Mountain that was cofounded with Jack Riggins in 2016. Our team now includes former NFL player Danny Woodhead, Lauren Cook West (Coach John Cook's daughter), and Coach Tom Osborne. My hope is that the book can be used in its entirety or that individual chapters, each representing a different "power," can be selected to help an individual, group, or team with the lessons necessary to put them in the best position to max out when it matters the most.

The first few powers are my foundational beliefs and philosophies; thus, they are best suited for the introduction, as they set the tone for what is necessary to optimize performance. These are the Power of the Space, the Power of Positive Psychology, and the Power of the Four Legs of Elite Performance.

## 1  THE POWER OF THE SPACE

Dr. Viktor Frankl (1905–1997) was an Austrian-born neurologist and psychiatrist, a Holocaust survivor, and the author of *Man's Search for Meaning.* He originated logotherapy, a school of psychology and a philosophy based on the idea that we are motivated to live purposeful and meaningful lives—and that we do so by responding authentically and humanely to life's challenges. Dr. Frankl has also articulated many transcendent ideas, including one of my favorites, which also happens to be one of my guiding philosophies, the Power of the Space:

> *Between stimulus and response there is a space. In that space is the power to choose our response; in our response lie our growth and our freedom.*

Well, what does this mean? First, we need to briefly go back to the animal world and understand that due to the lack of a well-formed frontal lobe of the brain—that separates man from animals—the fight-or-flight response is the main driver of behavior when there is stress or fear in an animal. Animals simply react to events—by fighting or fleeing as a primary survival mechanism. Humans are wired similarly, but due to a couple of factors, the full fight-or-flight response can often be attenuated or avoided altogether. Thankfully, most humans today rarely encounter threats like being chased by a lion or any of the other multitude of dangers that humans faced while trying to survive daily life in centuries past.

Human beings, due to having well-formed frontal lobes that assist in thinking, planning, and emotional regulation, have a window or "space" in which we can decide how to respond to most situations. Today there are many events that trigger the fight-or-flight response, contributing to the mind-body stress response that can cause burnout and sickness—common things like traffic (road rage comes to mind!), watching a sporting event, receiving an upsetting email or text, having a challenging conversation with a peer/boss/ significant other, dealing with a teenager, and so forth. How we handle these everyday, often mundane stimuli, events, or circumstances is more crucial than most of us realize.

We can train the brain using high-performance mental skills and other strategies to expand this "space" even more. I fully believe that this is the overriding factor in the genesis of mental and physical well-being and elite performance in business, sport, and life.

Dr. Frankl, in part due to his experiences in the Holocaust, said, "Everything can be taken from a man but one thing: the last of the human freedoms—to choose one's attitude in any given set of circumstances, to choose one's own way."

In fact, Dr. Frankl interviewed hundreds of inmates who had been treated in camp hospitals. He identified that those who survived illness and mistreatment almost always had a deeper meaning or purpose in their lives. In Frankl's own case, he was determined to survive to be reunited with his wife, the love of his life. He stated that this drove him to dig frozen Earth, endure countless beatings, and fight off the scourges of malnutrition and tetanus for four years:

> *I recognized that I could not control how much I suffered, but I could control my inner response to my sufferings. I could manage my own inner state . . .*

Frankl's observations are quite powerful about the role that purpose, meaning, and passion have as they relate to overcoming adversity in life and having the staying power to achieve elite performance.

## 2  THE POWER OF POSITIVE PSYCHOLOGY

*Positive psychology* is a term coined by Abraham Maslow in the 1950s that later became a school of thought pioneered by Martin

Seligman in 2002. It is defined as the study of positive emotions and the "strengths that enable individuals and communities to thrive." Seligman, born in 1942, is known for using scientific exploration to explore human potential, looking at things such as resiliency, optimism, gratitude, and hope as well as pessimism and learned helplessness. All of these factors can either enhance or be a barrier to elite performance in all aspects of life.

Let's look at some of the key ingredients that enhance elite performance.

> Optimism is a mental attitude reflecting a belief or hope that the outcome of some specific endeavor, or outcomes in general, will be positive, favorable, and desirable . . . Being optimistic, in the typical sense of the word, is defined as expecting the best possible outcome from any given situation.

Optimists believe that negative events are temporary, limited in scope, and manageable. Optimists recover from disappointing outcomes more quickly. Optimists react to problems with a sense of confidence and high personal ability. One of the things we have clearly observed in the high-performance world and then spend considerable time training and coaching is the ability of the high performer to move on to the next point, the next play, and the next situation—and to stay in the present moment.

*Elite performers do this better than others; thus, learning and training optimism becomes a huge competitive advantage.*

Being optimistic leads to enhancements to our immune systems, prevents chronic disease, and leads to decreased anxiety, depression, and stress. Can you train optimism? Luckily, the answer is clearly yes, both in the research world and in real time, as we have shown repeatedly with the mental skills training of high performers. One study, called the Penn Resiliency Program, helped train adolescents over twelve sessions and looked at things like how to change negative self-talk and the thoughts that go along with a pessimistic exploratory style, such as seeing events as internal, unchangeable, and pervasive. In both the short-term and long-term follow-ups to this training, the outcomes showed overall more optimism and at least a 20 percent decrease in the rates of depression, anxiety, and stress as compared to the control group.

Later, when we explore grit and its role in elite performance, we'll learn that one of the key psychological aspects for grit is hope—or the expectation that tomorrow will be a better day. And hope, too, can be modeled and trained by coaches, mentors, teachers, and business leaders.

Harvard Medical School says this about gratitude: " . . . a thankful appreciation for what an individual receives, whether tangible or intangible. With gratitude, people acknowledge the goodness in their lives . . . As a result, gratitude also helps people connect to something larger than themselves as individuals—whether to other people, nature, or a higher power."

Gratitude also overlaps with appreciation. Persons who practice gratitude have increased energy and increased enthusiasm as well as decreased self-centeredness, narcissism, and negative emotions. As it relates to high performance, gratitude leads to an increased desire to build and strengthen relationships. Admiring good characteristics of other persons encourages us to get closer to others. Reflecting upon the good another has done for us elevates the mood of all participants in the group. All of these things lead to building deeper relationships, which I feel is a critical ingredient for elite group performance. It is why I ask teams to spend so much energy doing team-building exercises and other activities to build these deeper relationships, including learning to be vulnerable, and to do exercises that focus on gratitude and appreciation.

A barrier to positive psychology is pessimism, and the remedy for this is to train optimism. You can do this by having important persons in your life model optimism for you—people such as coaches, bosses, teachers, parents, teammates, and friends.

One of the areas studied by Seligman was *learned helplessness*.

*Learned helplessness is behavior that occurs when the subject—person or animal—endures repeatedly painful or otherwise aversive stimuli which it is unable to escape from or avoid.*

Seligman subjected two groups of rats to electric shocks. (Animal lovers, don't shoot the messenger here!) One group had control over stopping the shock by pushing a lever. The other group depended on the first group to stop the shock for them since their lever didn't work, leading the second group of rats to learn that they had no control over the situation. When placed in a different box that allowed them to escape by jumping over a small barrier, the first group figured it out fairly quickly, while the second group never even tried to escape, despite the shock stimulus. This is what *learned helplessness* looks like in the research setting.

Similarly, as it relates to human beings and performance, it is the feeling of lack of control over a negative stimulus—like the berating from a coach, boss, or teacher—that leads to this helpless-feeling state. It can lead to depression, giving up, not looking for solutions to problems, decrease in confidence and self-esteem, and in the end to a significant deterioration in performance. It is why, in my opinion, coaches who had a period of success (such as Bobby Knight) ultimately had a downturn in their careers with their teams eventually underperforming in part due to the effects of learned helplessness.

Coach Tom Osborne, best known for his twenty-five-year head football coaching career at the University of Nebraska, never won less than nine games in a season. In the last five years of his career, his teams went 60–3 and won the 1994, 1995, and 1997 national championships. More importantly, Coach Osborne is a selfless man and a mentor to more people than anyone I've ever known. While he generally seemed composed as a coach, there was nobody who was more competitive than he was. He had an innovative offensive mind, but he also evolved over time into a master motivator, much of this based in positive psychology. One of my favorite quotes from Coach Osborne that clarifies what I am talking about regarding positive psychology is the following:

> *The best way to change behavior was to catch somebody doing something right and reinforce that.*

Wow! How simple to do, yet how many do it? How many times does one blow the whistle in practice just to tell the team or an individual player what they did right? Imagine what that might do for team morale and confidence! Yet many coaches and leaders spend an inordinate amount of time telling those they lead what they did wrong. How much energy does one spend criticizing somebody's thoughts or ideas in a brainstorming or planning session? What does that do to persons on your team? One thing this does for certain is create fear, leading me to introduce an important concept called *psychological safety*.

When people feel psychologically safe on a team, members are more willing to take risks, voice opinions, and ask judgment-free questions. A coach or manager has to create this safe zone where members of the team can let down their guard, and then the stage is set for creativity, innovation, and fearlessness. And ultimately, elite performance can take place. Psychological safety is necessary for the development of elite team dynamics. As Coach John Wooden, former UCLA basketball coach and arguably the best coach in NCAA basketball history, has said, **"Young people need models, not critics."**

The theme of modeling behaviors for those you lead will be seen throughout this book. Coach Wooden was right about what young people need, but adults need positive modeling as well! Ultimately, the head coach or the leader of a business team must find a way to get their team to perform when it really matters, even if under pressure.

What are you doing to train this in the persons you lead? What are you willing to do to model the behaviors of resiliency, optimism, gratitude, and hope to put yourself or those in your charge in the best position to be successful when it matters the most? The University of Nebraska women's bowling team has been national champion ten times! Their coach, Bill Straub, has stated, **"It's all about being able to handle the physical and emotional demands in crunch time. If you can't do it when it counts the most, what is the point?"**

## 3 THE POWER OF THE FOUR LEGS OF ELITE PERFORMANCE

The final core philosophy is understanding the concept of the four legs of the elite performance stool: mental, physical, technical, and tactical. As you know, if one leg of a stool is weaker than the rest, the stool becomes unsteady, or it may even fall over. Thus, if you want to be elite, you need to maximize your skill sets in all four of these domains.

Most of my attention will be on the *mental* side of elite performance, detailing mental skills and strategies, but with any endeavor, there are important overlaps. However, before I focus on the elite mental skills, it is important to mention that one must take care of his or her overall mental health first. High performers are not immune to the biological/psychological/social factors that can contribute to depression, anxiety, PTSD, eating disorders, addictions, and a whole host of other mental conditions. Human beings have about a 40–50 percent chance of developing a mental health condition in their lifetime, women somewhat more likely than men. While there is still a stigma to a certain degree, fortunately we live in times where high performers in all aspects of life are much more open and willing to share their stories on social media and other outlets about how they have dealt with their mental issues and hardships. Please get help if you're suffering from a mental health condition. They are treatable, and obviously it is necessary to be mentally well if you want to continue the pursuit of an elite mindset.

Core *physical* ingredients include elements such as sleep, nutrition, alcohol intake, preventive health care, and exercise. For athletes, it also includes rest/recovery, strength and conditioning, physical therapy, and so forth. *Technical* factors include the nuts and bolts, or the skill sets you need to do your craft. *Tactical* factors are often guided by the head of the family unit, your boss, or your coach. Tactical factors include goal setting, strategy sessions and game planning, or watching film of yourself or your opponents.

One core theme from the mental leg of elite performance, taken from what I've learned from *SEAL Team*, is the focus on these two controllable factors: ***attitude*** and ***effort***. It is simple, trainable, yet elusive for many to maximize attitude and effort, especially under stress or when things aren't going one's way. However, being able to "own your space" further optimizes your ***attitude*** and ***effort,*** which then fuels positive energy—all of which sets the stage for elite performance.

Before we delve into the world of high-performance mental skills training, I need to go back to that first chance meeting in 2013 with Commander Jack Riggins at the US Senior Open golf tournament in Omaha, Nebraska. Prior to meeting Jack, I had never personally met a Navy SEAL. However, I had been showing a video that I found online to teams and businesses about how Navy SEALs train. A number of excellent SEAL candidates failed to complete training successfully, in part due to the difficult underwater swim test. During this test, the candidates are subjected to chaos by the instructors with frequent cutting off of their underwater breathing apparatus, among other things. They were taught specific techniques for every problem they would encounter, yet due to the chaos and the superfear of drowning, processes were often forgotten. If a SEAL candidate surfaced too early, he would fail; if it happened again, his dream of being a Navy SEAL was over. The navy asked neuroscientists and psychologists if they could come up with a mental game plan that would help otherwise-qualified SEAL candidates improve their pass rate.

**They devised what they called the Big Four Mental Skills: goal setting, self-talk, visualization, and arousal control.**

These were the exact same mental skills that I had been training with my own high performers for years! It turns out that by incorporating a mental skills program into SEAL training, the pass rate significantly improved on the underwater test. If it weren't for this video, I probably would not have struck up a meaningful conversation with Jack, and it also confirmed what was already known: there are mental skills that can be trained that enhance performance in a very meaningful way when the pressure is on and when it matters the most.

# PART I

# MAX OUT
# YOUR MIND

# 1

## THE POWER OF HIGH-PERFORMANCE MENTAL SKILLS

### GOAL SETTING

Human beings love to set goals. Most of us set goals at a minimum of one time per year right around the beginning of the year, notably called New Year's resolutions. These types of goals are what are known as outcome goals: I want to lose weight, I want to get in shape, I want to spend more time with my family, I want to save more money, and so forth. Amazingly, by February 1, between 60 percent and 90 percent of New Year's resolutions have been given up on by those who set them. Why is that? Setting goals with a focus only on the outcome generally leads to failure. There are several steps, however, that one can take to dramatically increase the chances of being successful with a given goal.

We like to use the term **SMART** when doing elite goal setting.

SPECIFIC
MEASURABLE
ACHIEVABLE
RELEVANT
TIME BOUND

A common New Year's resolution is weight loss. "I want to lose weight." From a SMART goal perspective, more detail is needed. How much do you need to lose? Is it realistic to reach the goal in the time you've given yourself? Do you *need* to lose weight?

A weight-loss SMART goal may look like this: "I want to lose twenty-five pounds in three months, as my doctor told me that I may have to take medication for my blood pressure if I don't lose the weight." The SMART goal remains just an outcome goal, which is a necessary first step. The key to achieving your goal is spending the majority of your time setting all the process goals, or ingredients that will put you in a position to reach your goal. There could be five processes (or more) for weight loss:

- Attend Weight Watchers, follow the prescribed number of points per day, and attend the weekly accountability sessions.
- Walk sixty minutes per day, six days per week.
- Eat all meals in a mindful way (no TV or smart devices in use).
- Get eight hours of sleep per night.
- Meditate twenty minutes per day.

Now that we have the ingredients we believe will lead to success, what else can one do to become an elite goal setter?

## 1   WRITE OUT YOUR GOALS

This may amaze you, but did you know that just by *writing down your goals and placing them in a visible place* to look at every day, you increase your chances of success by *40-100 percent*? That's right—something that simple. Have an accountability buddy, or a "battle buddy" as Jack Riggins likes to talk about, and one's chances of success improve even more. We love it when athletes post their goals in their lockers or when business leaders have them posted on their smart tablet weekly calendar!

Other things you can do to improve the likelihood of success include the following:

## 2   BREAK YOUR GOAL INTO MANAGEABLE COMPONENTS OR "CHUNKS," AND BE FLEXIBLE

Be ready to adapt and change your process goals if progress toward your goal is not on target. Without this mindset of being able to adapt, most of us get frustrated when things aren't going as planned, and we often give up on that goal. Now, we must be honest with ourselves and look at why the results aren't going as planned. There are times when, if we are being honest, we are not completely following our process goals that we agreed upon. If that is the case, we have to decide if we're going to recommit to what we said we were going to do and get back on track. Otherwise, we become one of the majority of people who give up on the goal by the thirty-day mark.

However, there are many times when we are following all the processes we set forth and still aren't making the progress we hoped to be making. Let's say at the one-month mark we are only down four pounds, but we're doing everything we said we would do. We have a choice: get frustrated and quit, keep doing things as we have been doing, or change our processes. For example, we may need to increase the intensity of our exercise, or we may need to talk with Weight Watchers staff and decrease the number of points per day or adjust the time at which we're eating. This is also a time to determine if the goal we set is achievable. There is nothing wrong with changing up our outcome goal as well after a thorough assessment. Losing twenty-five pounds can seem daunting, but setting up weekly goals, like being down three pounds in a week and ten pounds in a month, can seem much more manageable with the way most humans are wired. When I ran my first and only marathon in 2008, part of my mantra was *one mile at a time.* There were also times when I would just run to the next crack in the road, and then get to the next crack, and so forth. Mentally, that helped me get through the challenging portions of the marathon.

## 3  AN EXAMPLE THAT IS OFTEN OVERLOOKED BUT CAN BE CRITICAL TO ACHIEVING YOUR GOAL IS UNDERSTANDING YOUR *WHY*

Why haven't I done this already? Why do I feel the need to do this now? I will leave you with these thoughts about how your **WHY** can be so powerful. In another weight-loss example, what is likely the bigger **WHY?** Wanting to lose fifteen pounds so that you can look a bit better in a bathing suit this summer, or losing seventy-five pounds because your doctor told you that losing this weight is necessary if you want the best chance to be alive to walk your daughter down the aisle on her wedding day? It doesn't mean you can't be successful in both circumstances, but which **WHY** is more powerful? The most important thing is to know your **WHY** and make sure it is strong enough to help you when the going gets tough—as it usually does—when you are trying to lose weight, make the starting lineup of your high school team, make the Olympics, get your dream job or promotion, and so forth.

Since I mentioned the Olympics, there was one female student-athlete who stood out to me in college in her ability to set elite goals. Her name is Kayla Banwarth. Her overall story is incredible in part because she went from a walk-on libero at the University of Nebraska in 2007 to starting libero for the US Women's Volleyball national team. Kayla helped them win a gold medal in 2014 at the FIVB World Championship and a bronze medal in the 2016 Olympics—and I can promise you that elite goal setting was part of her success. I remember sitting down with her before her senior year at Nebraska and listening to her articulate her goals. She referenced them again at the end-of-year banquet, and I remember how proud she was of feeling like she did everything process-wise she set out to do with regard to her goals, even though not all of the outcome goals of her team were met.

Similarly, one male football player I had crossed paths with at the University of Nebraska, Will Compton, set some amazing goals that he wrote out in July 2013 when he was at training camps trying to secure a spot on the roster with the Washington Redskins. He laid out the reality of his situation. He was the seventh out of seven linebackers at camp, and he was an undrafted free agent, so the odds were stacked against him. He laid out his vision: Who are YOU? "I am a linebacker for the Washington Redskins." He laid out his process goals that included working on his mind: "Your mind is your most powerful weapon. The Law of Attraction is real. The way you believe, along with your intentional action, will do wonders your mind can't even fathom at this moment ... Write shit down, backtrack on what that example of a person looks like, then take action and discipline to achieve it. THEN bring others along!"

He identified a one-year and a five-year vision. He identified what he called his Prizefighter Day and the ingredients for that day. He had two quotes: "Some people wait for fate; others create their own destiny" and "We are what we repeatedly do."

He was vulnerable enough to share the goals that he had come up with in 2013 four years later on Twitter for all of his followers to see. Will became a master at setting his process goals and then doing everything in his power to accomplish them. Should it surprise you that he became a full-time starter in the 2015 and 2016 seasons for the Washington Redskins and was named a defensive captain in 2016? As of this writing, he remains in the NFL, living his dream—and master goal setting contributed to his success.

## SELF-TALK

Henry Ford said, **"Whether you think you can or whether you think you can't, you're right."**

What we say to ourselves is powerful, and words matter! Believe it or not, we have up to fifty thousand individual thoughts per day. The average person has three times as many negative thoughts as positive thoughts. It is believed that we are hard wired for negative thoughts as an inborn survival mechanism from centuries ago, when it paid to be leery, suspicious, and on guard. There are certainly other factors, like individual genetics or the modeling effects from our parents, parent figures, mentors, and coaches, that shape how we learn to behave and think. What we do know is that elite performers learn how to flip the script and have three times as many positive thoughts on average compared to negative ones. For most people this does not come naturally, and it simply needs to be trained like any other skill.

So, how do we change our self-talk? First, we have to recognize that it is normal for most of us to have internal chatter and much of it negative. We have to accept that most of us are wired for negativity and that it does have an impact on how we feel, think, and behave. We have to learn strategies to erase and replace our self-talk with positive words, motivational words, or performance/instruction-al-based words.

I will be the first to admit that my first foray into learning about someone who used positive self-talk made me a bit nauseous! Stuart Smalley was a fictional character on *Saturday Night Live* in the early 1990s and was portrayed by Al Franken. His daily affirmation always included the positive mantra **"I'm good enough, I'm smart enough, and doggone it, people like me!"** I have since learned that positive mantras can be very effective for some people, but for others an alternative approach is needed. Motivational self-talk can be helpful when we want to psych ourselves up for something challenging. It can be as simple as "I know I can do this" or "You've got this next one."

When I think of the athlete who best used a combination of positive and motivational-based talk, I think of Muhammad Ali. His press conference leading up to the George Foreman fight in the 1970s—a fight that most gave him no chance to win—was a great illustration of what I am talking about. George was undefeated at the time and thought by many to be the greatest fighter of all time. Here is just a sampling of what Ali said: "I'm bad. Only last week I murdered a rock, injured a stone, hospitalized a brick. I'm so mean I make medicine sick." And my favorite: "Fast, fast, fast. Last night I cut off the light in my bedroom, hit the switch, and was in bed before the room was dark!" He concluded with this: "And you, George Foreman, all you chumps are going to bow when I whoop him, all of you. I know you got him, I know you got him picked, but the man's in trouble. I am going to show you HOW GREAT I AM!" Nobody had more belief in self than Ali, and he used words like these to help fortify that belief.

Most perfectionists do not like to use statements like "I'm the hardest worker I know" or "I'm the best wide receiver in the league" or "I'm the most powerful attacker in the country." This can feel silly, stupid, or disingenuous to some people. That being said, there is plenty of room for positive self-talk replacement with simple motivational statements to include things like "You've got this" or "I can get it done" or "Let's go!" Like I stated at the beginning of this chapter, "I can" instead of "I can't" completely changes mindset.

One volleyball player at the University of Nebraska, Kelsey Fien (2012–2015), came up with a clever thought-replacement strategy. Earlier in her career she had trouble at times moving on to the next point after an error. You could see her body language change for the worse, which is almost always a sign of negative self-talk. One of her errors was hitting the ball long in her role as an outside hitter. She used to beat herself up mentally or worry that the coach was going to pull her out of the game, both of these situations taking her out of the present moment. She came up with this statement: "That is just Husker Power," referencing the famous strength and conditioning program at Nebraska as the reason that she hit it long, as a way of replacing her negative self-talk. That didn't stop her from making technical adjustments if necessary and taking corrections from the coaching staff or her setter, but it did allow her to lighten up on herself and stay more present, and she eventually learned to move on to the next point more quickly. She didn't become a full-time starter until late in her junior year. I'm happy to say that she continued to progress her senior year, and in the national title game in 2015 she played with abandon, not allowing an error here or there to affect what was about to happen next. Also, on a play called specifically for her, she provided a monster kill on the last point to help Nebraska win the national championship! To this day, it is the best example of thought replacement I've ever heard!

Another favorite example of mine comes from one of the most popular and outgoing football players at Nebraska in recent history—Kenny Bell. He had big hair and an even bigger personality. He was also a darn good wide receiver. Before his senior year, during the intense grind of the summer, he started to tweet out something that I've never forgotten:

### RISE & GRIND!!! #1000 #$YEAR

Summer conditioning can be brutal, physically and emotionally draining, and it would be so easy to start each morning at six o'clock with a negative attitude, especially when you're tired and sore. Yet each day Bell started with this positive mantra. The alternative thoughts could be many, including these:

- I'm tired today.
- I don't want to do this at six in the morning.
- I hurt.
- I just want to stay in bed.
- What's the point? I'll never play this year anyway.

Kenny chose to have a positive mantra, and it reflected in his daily preparation and attitude. He is also one of the most appreciative and grateful persons I've ever seen and often shares his thoughts on social media.

Jaali Winters (2015–2018) from Creighton University was one of the toughest volleyball competitors I've been around. As her self-talk skills evolved, she shared with her teammates that she had learned to talk to herself like she would talk to a good friend. What a powerful way of thinking about positive self-talk! It can be amazing how hard elite performers—especially women who are perfectionists—can be on themselves. When we do an exercise in which we go around the room and openly talk about the words/phrases we say to ourselves, it is always a stark reminder of how cruel we can be to ourselves. It made me finally appreciate the words of Stuart Smalley of *Saturday Night Live* fame, as it is more common to say something opposite: "I'm not good enough; I'm not smart enough; I'm not pretty enough; I'm not funny enough; I'm not thin enough." So Jaali's plan to only talk to herself like she would talk with a good friend was brilliant! This is just one of the many skills Jaali developed that helped her to be considered as one of the best female athletes in Creighton history.

What many high performers do now is use performance-based words, instructional words, or cue words. In golf, they may call them swing thoughts. It is simply one or two words that are the key ingredients for that skill to be achieved successfully. The body often follows the mind's instructions, and it is simply a cue or brief reminder. For example, I worked with a top-level left tackle in football whose job it is to protect the "blind side" for the QB. He would have cue words for each type of play. It may be simply words like *step back*, *hands*, or *inside hands* to remind him of the importance of hand placement to the success of that blocking scheme. This strategy has helped him make millions in the NFL—but it has also helped some great high school players we know as well. A volleyball server may use the word contact or elbow as a cue about what the key ingredient is for success for their serve.

Using these words also serves the purpose of helping a performer stay in the present moment; contrary to some persons' beliefs, you can't have two thoughts at once. Thus, performance words can keep our mind from starting to worry about the past or what is about to happen, both of which can lead to deterioration in performance.

The best performers stay in the present moment better than others, and the use of these types of words is one strategy to help stay in the present moment.

In the business world, the best teams have been shown to have a positive feedback-to-criticism ratio of five to one. Average teams are about two to one, and poor teams have an inverted ratio of one to three, similar to the positive/negative self-talk ratio of the typical person.

In the marriage world, one of the more fascinating findings comes from Dr. Gottman, who for thirty-five years studied more than three thousand couples who were preparing to get married. He was able to predict with over 90 percent accuracy which couples were going to be divorced after five to ten years just by the way they interacted with each other during the time he observed them together. That still blows me away! What he discovered was that couples who went on to have successful marriages had positive-to-negative interactions of five to one and that they handled conflict in a gentle manner like they would with a good friend. The key findings for those couples who ended up getting divorced was a positive-to-negative ratio of 0.8/1 or worse, and criticism was directed at the partner's personality, often using contemptuous statements that reflected a relative position of authority.

I know a lot more goes into a successful marriage, but if you just talk nicely to each other and work through conflict in a gentle way, you're almost guaranteed to succeed. However, we have to be able to talk to our own selves in a healthy way first if we expect to be able to do so with other persons in our lives.

One of my favorite athletes, Jamie Schleppenbach (2011–2014), was a perfectionist in the truest sense of the word, much like many of the elite female athletes I've known. She also decided to participate in the sport that I feel requires the most mental resilience and physical toughness—women's gymnastics. The failure rate is high when learning and perfecting new skills, and even after mastery has been mostly achieved, it is very hard to be perfect on apparatus like the balance beam that is only four inches wide! Female gymnasts are also unique in the sense that they often start training for their sport by the age of five or six for up to twenty or thirty hours per week. Often, due to the time requirements necessary to master their sport, they don't participate in many other activities. Jamie had the added pressure and excitement of being one of the few Lincoln, Nebraska, kids to ever get a college scholarship to the University of Nebraska.

We always say there are benefits and costs to perfectionism. The attention to detail and the willingness to practice until one gets things right is an obvious benefit. One of the costs is the mental anguish that often goes along with adversity—manifested by intensely negative self-talk.

One day, during a difficult period, Jamie told me the following when asked about her practice: "It started terrible and went downhill from there." Oh boy! Interestingly, however, after she reported an early struggle with a skill on the balance beam, she went on to tell me about each event in which she actually did some very good things, but that one negative event overshadowed her thought processes. A game plan was devised, along with her assistant coach on balance beam, Heather Brink (now the current head coach), to do written success logs in real time during practice. It was awkward at first, but the goal was to train her brain to focus first on what went well and write it down, and then write down something she could improve upon with a defined action plan. Also, each evening she had to think about her day and write down as many things she could think of that went well, whether it was in school, with friends/family, or in the gym. She then could only write down a couple of things that she needed to improve—since a perfectionist could fill up pages if not given a limit! The key step was again to get into solution-focused mode and come up with an action plan for each area that she needed to improve. The outcome goal was the skill she needed to improve while the action plan was the process goal. Jamie also started to take control of her self-talk, especially as it pertained to her balance beam routine. She used performance words such as *breathe*, *patience*, and *legs* for each of her seven skills to remind her body what to do and, just as important, to keep herself in the present moment and not allow negative talk or doubt to enter her brain.

Later during her sophomore season, Nebraska was competing on the road against the University of Utah—ranked number seven in the nation—where their crowd was in excess of fourteen thousand (the biggest crowd in the country). The meet was high level and intense, with the teams going back and forth with big-time routines. In the end, it all came down to one routine as Jamie was last up—on the balance beam, of all things—and she needed to stick a big routine for Nebraska to win. She scored 9.9, a career high at the time, and not only did she win the first all-around title of her career, but Nebraska pulled out a major win on the road!

In the words of Vince Lombardi, the former Green Bay Packers coach, "Gentlemen, we are going to relentlessly chase perfection, knowing full well we will not catch it, because nothing is perfect.

But we're going to relentlessly chase it because in the process we will catch excellence."

Jamie caught excellence that evening, and she was able to deliver under pressure when it mattered the most, in part due to the growth of her mindset allowing her to stay composed, confident, and focused.

Jamie had a major setback her junior year when she tore her Achilles tendon. This is not an easy injury to recover from either physically and mentally. When an athlete is injured, it is easy to get depressed and feel disconnected from their teammates as well. Jamie worked through this very tough period and made a comeback. Her nemesis, the balance beam, gave her some difficulties late in the regular season of her senior year. This time she had strategies in place to fight through the adversity better than ever. In the postseason at the national championships, she scored a 9.9 again on the balance team. Her team pulled off a miracle by scoring 49.425 on the balance beam to pass Utah and UCLA (who were competing on their best apparatus—vault and floor respectively), and advanced to the Super Six Finals! There will be more to this story in a later chapter.

Jamie's career had a storybook ending, as on the last day of Nationals she competed on the balance beam in the individual finals and scored an incredible 9.8875 to finish third in the nation! She went out on top—and it was her hard work in the gym and on her mental game that put her in a position to be successful in the biggest moments. Jamie identified one main ingredient that helped her be successful: confidence. As we will explore in more depth later, one of the most important and least recognized ingredients of confidence is what we say to ourselves—something Jamie learned to master.

## AROUSAL CONTROL

Regulating our physiology and managing the stress response, in my opinion, are the most important steps one can take to be healthy and successful in all aspects of life. The fight-or-flight response (or the stress response), managed by the sympathetic nervous system, was wired into humans as a survival mechanism to respond to danger. When it is activated (especially when there is a false sense of danger), it can affect our central nervous system negatively in the following three ways: physiologically, mentally, and behaviorally. Our body is activated physiologically for action, with changes that include increased heart rate, increased breathing, and diversion of blood/oxygen from the GI tract to the muscles. Muscles can get too tight to perform movements the way we want, even though we have practiced the movements for thousands of hours. Mentally we can get hyperfocused, but we can also get very tense/anxious and prone to having our mind "go blank" or have very negative thoughts. Behaviorally, some of us get quiet, while others may start to talk very rapidly and seem very out of sorts with alterations in body language and facial expressions. There are many other negative consequences of the stress response, including more proneness to getting sick, poor decision-making, difficulty regulating our emotions, decreased reaction time, deterioration in fine motor control, and difficulty bouncing back from adversity. Not one of these is helpful for high performance in the boardroom, at home, or while playing your sport.

We know there are at least three main ways to regulate our physiology and "reset" the fight-or-flight system:

- Breathe.
- Take a twenty- to forty-minute power nap.
- Practice mindfulness.

While it may seem initially obvious, the question of why we breathe needs to be answered. There is also something relatively unique about our breathing system. Do you know what that is?

First, we can go weeks without eating, days without water, but only five to six minutes without oxygen. We generally breathe about twenty-five thousands times per day, using our upper chest and almost always on "autopilot." (And 25 percent of our oxygen needs go to our central nervous system and predominantly the brain.) Also fairly unique about our ability to breathe: it is one of the few body mechanisms that has both an automatic portion and an ability to allow its conscious control (eye blinking is another that comes to mind).

That being said, have you ever wondered why you have been told to breathe when you need to calm down? Why not bang your elbow on a table or hit your head against a wall? Well, there is science behind the power of breathing to calm the nervous system. The diaphragmatic technique is very different in that it requires you to take full control of your breathing, sometimes called a belly breath. Using your diaphragm (the muscle used to expand your chest) allows for a couple of important things to occur. First, you are able to get more oxygen to the lower lobes of your lungs and into the rest of the body. The other thing that occurs requires just a little more explanation regarding our anatomy and understanding the science.

The nerve that allows the diaphragm to work is called the phrenic nerve. However, there is another nerve, called the vagus nerve, that passes through the diaphragm. The vagus nerve is responsible for a number of bodily functions and is very important in the calming part of the nervous system, or the parasympathetic nervous system. When the diaphragm gets engaged with deep breathing, it causes the vagus nerve to be "tugged on" and sends signals back to the portion of the brain that calms our nervous system. Simply stated, when we learn to take control of our breathing, we can calm ourselves down, which puts us in a position to perform at our best when it matters the most.

There are several ways in which we can learn performance breathing, or what a Navy SEAL calls tactical breathing. I like to teach four-to-six breathing, meaning to take a deep inhalation though the nose, engage the diaphragm for four counts, followed by a slower exhalation though the mouth for six counts. The actual time in/out will be dependent on the individual, but generally it is about four seconds in and six seconds out. The Navy SEALs do what they call four-by-four breathing. They breathe in deeply through the nose for a count of four, hold the breath for a count of four, exhale through the mouth for a count of four, hold for a count of four, and repeat as needed. The SEALs do this literally as the "bullets are flying." One can use these breathing techniques anytime there is recognition that one's arousal level is too high. We also recommend developing a breathing plan in which you practice deep breathing for three to five minutes per day to help prevent the fight-or-flight system from kicking off as strongly when there is a trigger in the future. There are also several other ways to learn high-performance breathing; yoga, progressive muscle relaxation, guided visualization with breathing, and mindfulness meditation are just a few examples.

It makes me think of a couple of videos that we love to show involving two elite NBA basketball players. The first is a very short video in which LeBron James is shown sitting on the bench when the team is in the huddle talking to the coach. LeBron has his eyes closed, taking slow, deep breaths. What you don't know is that this is in 2012 during game three of the NBA finals. I often ask people, "Why is LeBron breathing in this fashion at this moment in time?" My answer is simple: "He has complete self-awareness and knew in that moment that he needed to calm his nervous system down—manage his arousal, if you will—so that he could put himself in the best position to succeed." LeBron explained in his Train Your Mind series on the Calm app why he was meditating for thirty seconds on the bench this way: "I was gathering my thoughts, checking my emotions, so I could approach the moment with a clear mind."

The second video was from an interview with Ron Artest right after the Los Angeles Lakers captured the 2010 NBA championship, in part because his three-point shot late in the game helped secure the victory. It may be the only time that a professional athlete has openly thanked his psychiatrist on national TV. He said, "I want to thank my psychiatrist. She really helped me relax a lot . . . it's so difficult to play with so much commotion going on in the playoffs. She helped me relax." Here's the deal: high performers need to be aware of where their nervous system functions best. Some need to be very calm; others need to be hyped up a bit, and so forth. On a scale of one to ten, with one being as calm as can be and ten being as amped up as one can be, one athlete may function best at a seven, another at a four. The problem arises when an athlete who functions best at four feels like his nervous system is at an eight. In that situation, he may be feeling anxious, muscles tight, mouth dry, heart rate increased, butterflies, and the like. If strategies aren't employed fairly quickly, there will most likely be suboptimal performance, like hitting a volleyball serve long or overthrowing an open receiver by five yards. The athlete will say that he choked, but in reality he didn't take control of his nervous system. While it may not be realistic to get down to a four in the biggest of moments, one may be able to get it down to a five or a six, leading to an increased chance of success.

I can give one personal example that forces me to reveal one of my strange talents. Back in the 1970s/1980s, Putt-Putt golf was very popular, and it even had a professional tour with decent prize money. During high school I became a fairly high-level player. At that time there wasn't any specific training for high-performance mental skills such as arousal control and self-talk. That being said, I was naturally good at these skills, especially arousal control—until I wasn't! I was in a tournament in Omaha (which I won) and in "the zone." In fact, after fifteen holes, I'd had fourteen holes in one! I then overheard one of the spectators say that I had a great chance to break the long-standing course record of twenty-one. Do the math: I needed to finish the last three holes with two holes in one. Well, my nervous system went into overdrive when I heard this—and I had no strategies to deal with it. My mind went from being in "the zone" or completely in the present moment to thinking about the future and seeing my name on the lighted scoreboard for everybody to see forever—making it more likely that I would underperform. Also, nobody had taught me how to breathe or how to use some mindfulness strategies. I just remember trembling, my hands shaking, and my muscles feeling so tight. Needless to say, I was able to manage only one hole in one in the final three holes, and I tied the course record. To this day, especially with what I now know about how to manage arousal control, it pains me that there were mental strategies that could have helped put me in the best position to max out when it mattered the most.

One more story comes to mind. As mentioned earlier, I had the pleasure of working with the University of Nebraska bowling team. In 2015 there was an athlete, Melanie Crawford (Epperson), who transferred from Stephen F. Austin State University. She was always attentive, had great energy, and was an active participant in our team meetings. That being said, you never know how much any individual buys into working on the mental skills—and like my story, sometimes you don't realize you need to do so. One thing that is unique to NCAA bowling is that most of it is done in relative obscurity during the regular season and postseason, only to find the team on ESPN "under the bright lights" if the team makes it to the national championship match. Also, as Coach John Cook has often said, it is the Elite Eight match in volleyball with the winner advancing to the Final Four that holds the most pressure for a team. Similarly, the round that leads up to making it on national TV for bowling brings on an incredible amount of pressure as well.

How does this relate back to Melanie? I traveled with the team to St. Louis that year for the eight-team national championship tournament. We had a couple of team meetings during that time, but on the evening of April 10, 2019, I received a call from Melanie; she told me she had really struggled with her ability to stay calm during one of the preliminary matches and that it had affected her performance. She was anxious about the next day, since the winner of the morning match would go on to play on national TV for the national title. Melanie recognized that the familiar strategies she used to maintain the proper level of arousal were not working given the intensity of the competition. We employed some breathing strategies that night and during the morning matches to follow. She also used visualization/imagery skills, which will be discussed in the next chapter. She performed well, and her team advanced to the national championship match against her former team, Stephen F. Austin. The title match was nerve racking for all the competitors. Melanie had trouble finding the strike zone early but managed to pick up every one of her spares, which was critical for her team. She remained composed throughout the evening on national TV, and when it mattered the most, she helped the team by striking on both occasions in the deciding match—and the University of Nebraska become national champions!

The second strategy to help with managing one's arousal level is the power nap. It is simply a period of twenty to forty minutes that helps to recharge the mind/body and resets the nervous system. Taking a time-out to sleep during the day does much more than just give us a quick energy boost. It gives us serious cognitive and health advantages as well.

It is interesting that 85 percent of all mammalian species sleep more than once a day, but this does not include most humans. It's clear that one-third of all humans are not getting enough sleep. Power naps can help to alleviate our so-called sleep deficits, but they can also boost our brains, including improvements in multiple learning modalities to creative problem solving and our reaction times. Naps improve our mood and feelings of sleepiness and fatigue. Naps are also good for our heart, blood pressure, stress levels, and weight management.

A power nap is a sleep session that happens during the day (ideally between 1:00 p.m. and 4:00 p.m.) lasting between ten and forty minutes. Any longer and you run the risk of developing "sleep inertia"—that unpleasant groggy feeling that takes a while to shake off. Some sleep scientists, like University of California, Riverside's Sara Mednick—author of *Take a Nap! Change Your Life*—says that naps of different durations result in different benefits. For example, a ten- to twenty-minute nap will provide a quick boost of alertness while mitigating the onset of sleep inertia: "You reset the system and get a burst of alertness and increased motor performance. That's what most people really need to stave off sleepiness and get an energy boost."

A 1995 NASA study looked at the effects of napping on 747 pilots. Each participant was allowed to nap for 40 minutes during the day, sleeping on average for 25.8 minutes. Nappers had vigilance-performance improvements of 34 percent and improved alertness by 54 percent. Planned naps have been shown to improve alertness and performance in emergency department physicians and nurses along with first-year medical students. What's more, the effects of napping extend a few hours into the day. Companies and professional teams are starting to catch on by providing time and proper space for restorative naps.

Finally, a 2008 study showed that naps are *better* than caffeine when it comes to improving verbal memory, motor skills, and perceptual learning.

Mindfulness is something that we feel is so powerful for high performance in business, sport, and life that it will be examined much more deeply in its own chapter. What I will say as it relates to the story I just shared, or for any high-performance endeavor, is the following:

> *One of the great separators between average and elite performers is the ability to stay in the present moment. And one definition of mindfulness is simply the ability to spend a prolonged period of time in the present moment.*

## VISUALIZATION/IMAGERY

Our central nervous system can't differentiate between real and imagined events. This is one reason that the skill of visualization is so powerful. In the real world, if we attached an EMG machine (which measures muscle activity) to a downhill skier, the report would be strikingly similar if she were actually skiing or if she just imagined in her mind that she was skiing. Visualization is simply the act of picturing in your mind exactly how you want to perform a skill. Imagery is an advanced form of visualization in which you use all the senses—

sight, smell, hearing, touch, taste—to picture yourself performing, generally with the goal of doing it in a perfect manner. What we do know is that visualization/imagery helps with confidence, composure, and concentration, which are all ingredients of elite mindset. We also know that mastering this skill allows us to create grooves or deeper tracks in our neuromuscular system, otherwise known as "muscle memory." In essence, practicing imagery is just like getting additional reps or practice. I've looked at all the data, and depending on how efficient one is in doing visual reps, one minute of visualization can equal up to seven minutes of real-time practice! Think about it: by incorporating visualization for just five minutes a day, one can get up to an equivalent of thirty-five minutes of practice each day!

There are many examples of how the skill of visualization/imagery has been studied in the applied research setting. One example, a study conducted by Dr. Biasiotto at the University of Chicago, placed free throw shooters of similar skill in three groups after a baseline test. One group then did nothing for a month, one group practiced free throws for thirty minutes per day, and one group only visualized shooting free throws for thirty minutes per day. The first group—the one without any practice—did about the same or just a bit worse at the end of the month with their free throw performance. The second group, which practiced their free throw shooting, improved by about 24 percent. Now what about the group that used visualization only? They also improved by nearly 23 percent—without taking any reps!

One of the more fascinating studies regarding the use of mental training to improve physical strength was done at the Cleveland Clinic. Subjects were placed in three groups similar to the free throw study. They then measured pre and post strength in the muscle of the little finger as well as elbow flexion. The control group that did nothing showed no gains or mild losses, as one would expect. The active group for finger strength and elbow flexion improved by 53 percent and 30 percent respectively. What about the group that did only visualization? Without doing any physical activity, there was improvement of 35 percent and 13 percent in strength for the respective muscles!

Similar experiments at Ohio University and University of Washington have shown the same findings. Arnold Schwarzenegger has stated in the past that visualizing his muscles growing and the way he wanted them shaped played a big role in his winning Mr. Universe competitions.

Jack Nicklaus, arguably the best golfer of all time and eighteen-time Majors winner, stated, "I never hit a shot, not even in practice, without having a very sharp in-focus picture of it in my head."

Jordan Burroughs, a former University of Nebraska wrestler, has gone on to be one of the most decorated wrestlers in the world, winning both world championships and an Olympic gold medal. I asked him once, around 2015 when he was visiting with one of the teams that I worked with at the time, what he learned from a mental standpoint as an Olympian. He said that he learned to become a master visualizer. He told me an amazing story about the 2013 World Championships. About one month prior to the competitions, he fractured his ankle during conditioning exercises and underwent surgery that required a plate and five screws. There was supposed to be a recovery process of six to eight weeks, but he was able to return to the mat about eleven days before the event. What was his hidden ingredient? You guessed it. He used the skill of imagery to picture every opponent and every move, using all of his senses—sight, hearing, smell, taste, and touch. That was a big factor in helping him to win another World Championship and overcome his physical injury and loss of training!

In the business world, this same skill can be used to picture yourself making the perfect presentation or speech, interviewing for a promotion, or even playing through your mind a challenging conversation that you may need to have with your boss or someone that you lead. Mental rehearsal activates very similar parts of the brain, so that when it gets to be time to do the real thing, you feel like you've done it before! When one gets really good at this skill, different scenarios—even difficult ones—can be played out in the mind, allowing one to get into solution mode and be ready for any situation that may occur. The Navy SEALs use imagery, mental rehearsal, or some combination of these before every mission. Even better, when you combine the mental skills such as visualization, arousal control, and self-talk, your confidence to make the perfect play or give the perfect presentation goes up exponentially, especially in crunch time or when it matters the most.

Back to Jaali Winters. In 2017 her goal was to get an invitation to play for one of the US women's collegiate national volleyball teams. In an *Omaha World-Herald* story about the invitation, she told the reporter that she trained hard physically but said the visualization she did was just as important. Jaali stated she was always a fan of the method but that it became much more a part of her preparation after her arrival at Creighton. She talked about some of the scenarios that she would visualize. Game point with the ball in her hands? No problem. She'd already been through that situation hundreds of times in her mind. Jaali was a guest on my podcast, *Max Out Mindset*, in May 2020, and she shared that she had been struggling with a blocking move that she needed to improve prior to the national team tryouts. She visualized every night doing this blocking move perfectly and confirmed that she had her best blocking performance ever at those tryouts.

In the *Omaha World-Herald* she went on to say, "Imagine where you are going to stay calm where most people would fold or crumble."

Several times a week before bed, Jaali pictured herself having her best performances at the tryout. While she was waiting to hear if she'd made the team, she would tell herself, "Don't worry. You are going to Europe." She would even see herself opening the email with the good news. Not even thirty seconds after giving herself that message, Jaali said her phone lit up and she was told she had made a team. The power of self-talk and visualization!

Similarly, on the podcast called *Conversation with the Cooks*, Episode 5 (December 16, 2019), part of the discussion was about mindfulness and other mental techniques. Lauren Cook (Coach Cook's daughter and an All-American setter for Nebraska 2010–2012) hosts the podcast with her father and went into great detail about how she used visualization techniques before matches to help her performance. She commented, " ... This is going to sound crazy, but it's almost like what would play out as the match went on is what I visualized ... you feel like you've already done this and you knew what to expect, and it all goes smoothly." Coach Cook responded to what she said: "Yeah, that's having a quiet mind, so we try to eliminate as much interference as we can when we perform, and that's the whole key to performing at the highest level that you can." As I will mention a couple of times, a big part of my WHY is to help empower young men and women to grow up into healthy adults who have great self-esteem, know how they want to be treated, and feel like they can do anything they set out to do in this world as adults. Lauren Cook is a shining example of a young lady who was a tremendous student-athlete, faced adversity head-on, and has now grown into a healthy, empowered adult!

# EXERCISES

## SMART GOAL EXERCISE

- Come up with one SMART outcome goal for either business, sport, or life.

- Come up with at least three to five process goals to help you reach your outcome goal.

- Write down your process/outcome goals, and remember to look at them every day.

- Be ready to be flexible and adapt.

- Identify WHY the goal is important to you.

- Share your goal with one person who will be your accountability buddy.

# SELF-TALK EXERCISE

- Identify your most common negative self-talk statements.

- Come up with your positive self-talk replacement strategies by using some combination of positive mantras, motivational words, and performance words.

# 2

## THE POWER OF MINDFULNESS

JON KABAT-ZINN, ONE OF the leading experts on mindfulness today, defines mindfulness as follows:

> *Mindfulness means paying attention in a particular way: on purpose, in the present moment, and non-judgmentally.*

Simply, mindfulness equals awareness of one's physical, mental, and emotional state in that moment in time. In the high-performance world—which includes endeavors such as being an athlete, a musician, an actor, or a surgeon—self-awareness is critical for self-regulation, which is one of the key ingredients of being successful when it matters the most. Also, notice the words *present moment* again. As Michael Gervais, one of the best high-performance psychologists, stated, **"Mindfulness is a defining feature of elite athletes. So if you want to get better, best practice would suggest do what the best do."**

Here is a quote from Kobe Bryant, who recently passed away: **"It's not about the number of hours you practice; it's about the number of hours your mind is present during practice."**

Before we get into the discussion of developing a mindfulness practice, I want to introduce the concept of three mind states: positive mind, negative mind, and quiet mind. Another way of thinking about quiet mind is with terms such as *the zone*, *present*, or *mindful*. When I think of *the zone*, I picture elite performers in a relaxed, focused state doing exactly what they have trained hundreds or thousands of hours to do without thinking and just doing. As Yoda says, "There is no try, only do." Most high performers would do anything to get into the zone—as that is usually when moments of best performance take place.

That being said, it is not easy to get there, as the mind and other distractions get in the way. If one is in negative mind, which is primarily fueled by negative self-talk or negative talk from our coaches/bosses/teammates/coworkers, there is virtually no chance of ever getting to quiet mind. If that is the case, and quiet mind can often be elusive, I implore high performers to hang out in positive mind. Positive mind is primarily fueled by positive self-talk, what our coaches/bosses/teammates/coworkers say to us, and other factors such as body language, facial expressions, eye contact, and getting external. Great things can and will happen in positive mind even if quiet mind is elusive. In fact, top performances will take place often by only being in positive mind. That being said, if you hang out in positive mind long enough, occasionally you will switch right into quiet mind, and as mentioned, that is where the opportunity for the most elite-performance moments take place.

It is harder than ever today, for a variety of reasons, to stay present. One of the reasons is part of the human condition, as articulated by Eckhart Tolle: **"Most humans are never fully present in the now because unconsciously they believe that the next moment must be more important than this one."**

The best strategy I know to overpower the unconscious is to develop a mindfulness practice. What does a mindfulness practice look like? Well, there are formal ways to train mindfulness, and there are activities one can do that often lead to a mindful state. Let's first talk about common mindful activities, although individual preferences are widely varied. Personally, the activity in my adult life that put me completely in a mindful state—completely present—was when I coached my son's flag football team. Both at practices and at games, I recognized that I was fully engaged, never thinking about the past or the worries of the future. It took me a while to explain why I enjoyed coaching so much. Sure, it was about coaching my son, teaching young men how to compete and be good teammates—but it was that full engagement in an activity that so many adults I know can relate to that led to a joyful or content state of mind.

What a blessing to have periods where the brain isn't actively thinking about work or family concerns or any other of life's issues! For some, it is having a great conversation with a friend at a coffeehouse, where time gently flows by and before you know it a couple of hours have passed. Other activities such as yoga, running, swimming, biking, surfing, or rock climbing can be extremely mindful activities. The key is to focus on the activity and not spend the time while you're doing them thinking about the past or the future. I have often noticed that those who choose to do extreme sports such as surfing or scaling rocks/mountains have had life circumstances or natural wiring that make it hard to stay present or have a quiet mind. In a sense, these activities force the mind to be present, as a lack of focus while doing them can lead to very bad outcomes—and I do think it is one of the reasons some people choose these types of endeavors.

Other mindful activities that adults do are things such as gardening, mowing the lawn, and sometimes motorcycle repair. There was even a book called *Zen and the Art of Motorcycle Maintenance*! The key in any of these ventures is choosing to focus on the activity. If you are in the garden, then have your mind focused on the garden. If the mind drifts to actions of the past such as an argument with your boss or you worry about a project at work due the next day, then the key is to bring the mind back to the activity. Being present is the only way to actually make it a mindful activity.

Interestingly, when I did an exercise with the University of Nebraska women's gymnastics team, having them use the whiteboard to name all possible mindful activities that they could do, adult coloring books garnered their interest the most. Many of them chose this as their mindful activity the night before a meet; the key was to have coloring within the lines as their focal point. And as I am about to discuss in much more detail, when the mind naturally drifts over and over again from the focal point, the goal is just to bring the mind back to focusing on coloring inside the lines. Another example: In 2013, Coach Heather Brink (balance beam coach, University of Nebraska) had the team all lie on their stomach in a circle, facing inward at a candle that was lit in the center. The team initially used the light of the candle as their focal point and had to stare at it for ninety seconds, focusing on the light and then refocusing on it when their mind drifted. Eventually, her team would visualize their balance beam routine during those ninety seconds while staring at the candle.

I will never forget the hour in the gym before the Big Ten Championships that year. While other teams were milling about—some distracted, some nervous—the Nebraska team got in their circle and did their mindfulness activity like they did at every meet. The reason I will never forget it is that one of the assistant coaches for the University of Illinois came over and made a sarcastic comment, smirking about our doing something "kum-ba-yah." In that moment I was so proud to be a part of a team that was willing to think outside the box instead of finding ways to make fun of our team like this coach was doing. It was even better when Nebraska pulled off a minor upset over the University of Michigan and crushed the rest of the field with one of the highest scores in Nebraska history to win the Big Ten Championship!

The formal training of mindfulness involves the act of meditation. There are several types of meditation: mindfulness meditation (which is what I teach), transcendental meditation, chakra, loving-kindness, and body scan, to name a few. All share the concept of having a focal point. For mindfulness meditation, the focal point is often the breath. For transcendental meditation, it is a mantra. For body scan, the muscles are the focal point.

The first thing you need to know is that mindfulness requires practice just like any other form of training. The second thing is that the mind literally has a mind of its own and will wander repeatedly. It is just the nature of the brain. It's also the reason so many give up, because they feel they aren't doing it right. With regard to doing a mindfulness meditation, it is important to find a relatively quiet place if possible, sit in a comfortable position (although some choose to lie down), and close your eyes. The goal is to just focus on the breath. One can focus on the breath as it comes in/out through the nose. My preference is to count my breaths. Even now I rarely make it to ten before my mind starts to drift, and that's okay. The mind will wander to all types of things—the past, the future, worries, unsolved problems, or simple things like what's for dinner. That's normal. The goal is simply to nonjudgmentally bring your mind back to the breath and do so over and over. If you think about it, we are training the brain to focus (breath, mantra, etc.) but also, just as importantly, training the art of refocusing.

I always tell people that one of the things high performers do better than others is focus. While that's absolutely true, another real secret to high performance is the ability to refocus. In sport, the loss of focus may be due to a bad call or an unforced error. In the business world, it could be the boss poking a hole in an idea in the middle of a presentation. In surgery, it could be an unexpected complication in the middle of the procedure. All of these events can lead to distraction, but how quickly we can refocus and get on to the next play, the next point we are trying to make, or the next step in the surgery while staying calm and composed—that's one of the keys to elite performance. To be clear, meditation helps one train the skill of focus/refocus. For beginners, many like to use a guided meditation. There are several apps today, such as Calm and Headspace, that have guided options and help you with your journey to mindfulness.

There is nothing that has had a bigger impact on my physical and mental well-being in the past five years than the development of a mindfulness practice. It took me a long time to believe in the powers of mindfulness. It took getting very ill on September 9, 2014—when the shingles virus attacked my left facial nerve, leaving me with facial paralysis, vertigo, and the most intense pain of my life—to make me actually start my own mindfulness practice. It was important to understand the science of mindfulness, given the scientist in me. What I learned was simply amazing.

In 2011 Harvard Medical Center did a study looking at subjects who participated in eight weeks of mindfulness meditations for just under thirty minutes per day. The results were astounding! They actually showed that a couple of structures in the brain changed in size. The hippocampus—an area of the brain that helps with emotional regulation, compassion, and self-awareness—grew in size. The amygdala—an area responsible for survival instincts, signaling the brain for the fight-or-flight response/fear response, anxiety, and stress—became smaller in size. These changes also correlate with many of the positive changes we see in those who meditate. It certainly explains, in part, why those in the Eastern world have used meditation for thousands of years for physical/mental well-being. Duke University, in conjunction with the Center for Koru Mindfulness, also showed that college students who participated in mindfulness meditations for as little as ten minutes three times per week had decreases in stress, depression, and anxiety while showing improvements in sleep, compassion, and GPA. The goal is twenty to forty minutes daily, but even a few minutes per day can have benefits.

Before we move on, let's look at the overall benefits of mindfulness. Physically, it can help lower blood pressure, decrease chronic pain, alleviate GI distress, and improve sleep. Mentally, we see improvements in depression, anxiety, substance abuse, eating disorders, and PTSD. Overall life satisfaction improves, and we are more likely to savor the pleasures of life as they occur. There is a greater capacity to handle adverse events. We are less likely to get caught up in the worries of the future or regrets of the past. We are more likely to form deeper connections with others. More importantly, we can relearn to be fully engaged in activities.

A fascinating study came out in 2014 looking at unintended injuries on the playground in kids under five years old. The study looked at the years 2005–2012 and found that injuries increased by 10 percent over that time period. The timing coincided with—you guessed it—the introduction of the first smartphone. Two things come to mind: (1) it is obviously sad that young children were getting injured, and (2) what's even sadder is the lack of engagement of parents and their kids on the playground. In years past, parents used to go to the playground and engage with their kids, letting them explore but also participating with them. With the advent of the smartphone, often the first thing parents do is sit on the park bench and start scrolling through the phone, completely missing out in being engaged with their children.

This can also happen when playing a board game or any other activity with your child. Are you fully engaged, or are you in the past/future or looking at your phone each time it beeps? That's a decision each of us will have to make. A mindfulness practice makes it much more likely that one will spend more time being present and engaged. Remember, as Kobe Bryant said, "It is not about the number of hours you practice; it's about the number of hours your mind is present during practice." You can replace the word *practice* for anything in your life. "It is not about the number of hours you spend with your children; it is about the number of hours your mind is present when you spend time with your children." When you think about it that way, it becomes a lot more powerful.

Here are a few final thoughts—and if you remember nothing else from this chapter other than these thoughts, you will be more likely to give mindfulness a chance. When looking at the hundreds of studies out there on mindfulness, here are the four big benefits that tend to show up repeatedly:

- Stronger focus
- Ability to stay calm under stress
- Improved memory
- Increased kindness

These four benefits are often why I get buy-in from high performers. Similarly, the fact that mindfulness trains the skill of focus and refocus is another reason that high performers become interested. It is hard to argue that you won't do better in school, sport, business, or life with improvements in these four areas. In a world that is often divided over politics and religion, among other things, increased kindness alone is well worth developing a mindfulness practice.

Kobe Bryant said this about mindfulness meditation: "It's like having an anchor. If I don't do it, I feel like I'm constantly chasing the day as opposed to being in control."

Lastly, when I got sick in 2014, I put my money where my mouth was and recognized that I needed to make a change; I decided to incorporate the skills that I teach. I set SMART goals to get my facial nerve to work again. I was told that I had a 50 percent chance of regaining the use of the nerve, so my positive mantra became "The right side of fifty." I took my anatomy books out, visualized the regrowth of the facial nerve, and practiced five minutes every day. Finally, I started my mindfulness practice, learning both mindfulness and transcendental meditation, and I continue to practice it a minimum of twenty minutes per day. What I know is that I have never been calmer. I can manage "the space" much better because my fight-or-flight response doesn't kick off nearly as strongly as it used to for similar stimuli, giving me just a little bit longer to decide how to respond to an event. My ability to focus and stay present has never been better. I am a kinder and more compassionate person. In the end, I am a better leader, better parent, better husband, better friend, and better doctor/mindset coach because of the power of mindfulness.

# EXERCISES

## PRACTICING MINDFULNESS

- Identify one informal mindfulness strategy, such as using an adult coloring book, and commit to doing this for ten minutes, one time per week.

- Identify one formal mindfulness strategy, such as mindfulness meditation, and commit to doing this a minimum of ten minutes three times per week.

# 3

## THE POWER OF MINDSET

DEVELOPING AND TRAINING AN elite or high-performance mindset is where most of my energy is spent these days when working with individuals and teams. We train mindset by incorporating many of the skills discussed previously in this book. Before we delve into this in more detail, I want to discuss briefly the concepts of fixed mindset and growth mindset. Carol Dweck, PhD, wrote a wonderful book called *Mindset: The New Psychology of Success* where she discusses fixed and growth mindset at length. Here are a couple of her thoughts in this regard:

> Believing that your qualities are carved in stone—the fixed mindset—creates an urgency to prove yourself over and over. If you have only a certain amount of intelligence, a certain personality, and a certain moral

character—well then, you'd better prove that you have a healthy dose of them. It simply wouldn't do to look or feel deficient in these basic characteristics.

This belief that talent and intelligence are fixed leads to issues such as fear of failure, fear of rejection, and, as noted, a constant need to prove yourself to others.

In contrast, Dweck talks about another mindset in which "the hand you're dealt" is just the beginning of one's development:

This growth mindset is based on the belief that your basic qualities are things you can cultivate through your efforts. Although people differ in every which way—in their initial talents and aptitudes, interests, or temperaments—everyone can change and grow through application and experience.

This mindset leads to a passion for learning and acceptance that failure is necessary for growth and that we should embrace challenges that allow us to grow. It's a mindset that is absolutely necessary to master the ingredients that lead to elite mindset—and for the development of grit, another power crucial for high performance. This will be delved into further in a later chapter.

I believe there are four main ingredients that, if mastered, lead to the development of an elite mindset:

- Commitment
- Confidence
- Concentration
- Composure

While each of these ingredients is independent to some degree, there is enough overlap that being deficient in one area can make it very difficult to master some or all of the other ingredients of elite mindset. We first need to define what each word means as it relates to performance in any aspect of life.

## COMMITMENT

When I think of **commitment,** two words come to mind: *all in.* Keep in mind that when I get together with individuals, groups, or teams, nearly everyone raises their hand or nods affirmatively when I ask, "Are you all in?" I honestly think that most of them believe it, but the truth is that some have no idea what it means or the effort that's required to actually fulfill this notion of being "all in." Jay Wright, Villanova head basketball coach, said this about one of his recent players, Jalen Brunson: "It's his consistent commitment to health, hydration, strength training, ball handling skills, shooting every day, watching film. He gets the proper amount of rest. He's a great student. Mentally, he's the toughest guy I've ever had." It shouldn't surprise you that he was a member of two national title teams, was named NCAA Player of the Year on one occasion, and has made it to the NBA.

The other challenge for many persons is to stay motivated over the long haul, particularly when under stress. As Inky Johnson, motivational speaker and former college football player, has stated, **"Commitment means staying loyal to what you said you were going to do, long after the mood you said it in has left you."**

We have to go back to the four legs of elite performance to explain what is required. To review, certain mental, physical, technical, and tactical components need to fully develop in order to consider ourselves truly committed to the process of being great. On the mental side, we has to take care of our mental health as well as work on the trainable mental skills; this takes a lot of effort. On the physical side, you may remember that many are fully within one's control and need great attention: sleep, hydration, nutrition, recovery, exercise, alcohol consumption, and so forth. Research over the past ten years regarding the impact of sleep on athletic performance had some fascinating findings:

- A University of California study on adolescent athletes showed injuries were 1.7 times higher for athletes who slept less than eight hours versus those who got more than eight hours of sleep.
- For college basketball players at Stanford University, free throw success increased by 9 percent. Three-point field goals increased by 9.2 percent. Sprint time decreased by 0.7 seconds in timed tests for baseline/half court/back to baseline/full court and back in those athletes who slept on average 8.5 hours versus 6.5 hours.

On the technical side, ongoing skill mastery, growth, ability to adapt, and lifelong learning become necessary and are often a merger of the boss/employee, coach/athlete, teacher/student ideas and interactions. On the tactical side, this is about mastering goal setting, being active in business strategy sessions, being attentive to game plans, and/or watching film of opponents to gain an advantage by finding mismatches and weaknesses, to name a few. It takes a tremendous amount of effort to develop the commitment part of an elite mindset. I think we all know it, though, when we see somebody who is that way.

I used to joke that if everybody were like Rex Burkhead (former Husker football player and now playing for the New England Patriots), I wouldn't have a job. While I had brief conversations and interactions with him when he was at Nebraska, I can't say that I really knew him; yet just from observing the way he carried himself and went about his business, I knew that he was fully committed to the process of being great. Ironically, I remember an athlete commenting to me that he even saw Rex reading a book called *The Mental Edge* on the team plane one day. So even for those who naturally appear to have mastered the mental game, there are always ways to continue to improve. I remember thinking he was a steal as a late-round NFL draft pick, and it was not surprising to me at all that he has ended up playing for what could be considered the best professional franchise of any type in history—one that values mental resilience.

Another athlete that comes to mind is Marysa Wilkinson, Creighton volleyball player who graduated in 2017. I watched her play in high school after I heard she was going to Creighton, and I thought to myself that Coach Booth had a "recruiting miss" as she didn't appear to have Division I skills. She graduated from Creighton with numerous awards, including honorable mention All-American! Well, what did I miss besides not being a recruiting expert? I had no idea that she would be one of the most committed athletes I've ever observed with growth in all areas—physically, mentally, technically, and tactically. In 2017, in a story on the White & Blue Review website, Brad Schmidt, the team's head athletic performance coach, noted that Marysa was in the top ten of the hardest-working athletes he has ever been around—improving her vertical jump by seven inches since her freshman year while being the strongest woman on the team. Her teammate, Lydia Dimke, said in 2017, "She has such an awesome work ethic. We lift at 6:30 a.m. every day during the summer, and she's always in there working her butt off. Whether she's injured, whether she's fatigued or tired, she's always setting a good example of how to work hard. I think she's always so encouraging of those around her to get them to work hard as well. She definitely leads by example."

In the same White & Blue Review story, it was noted that Marysa had to make changes nutritionally and with her workout efforts and had a genuine commitment to altering her lifestyle. "We were a good team my freshman year, but it takes the little things to make a great team, and I think nutrition, motivating yourself, and having a hundred percent effort during the workouts is another thing that adds on to it . . . I really like fried food, so I tried to cut back on that . . . my teammates helped me with that, too. If we all do something together, it's a lot easier." It wasn't long before she showed tremendous improvement on the court as well and became a dominating middle blocker/right side hitter. In the 2016 postseason run to the Elite Eight, she had forty-nine kills and hit .342 as well as having her share of blocks. Nobody worked harder in the off-season to add to or perfect her hitting or blocking skills. As her career progressed, she mastered getting on to the next point and maintaining great body language even under stress. It's always rewarding to watch persons fully buy into the process of becoming great and then having their dreams come true!

## CONFIDENCE

When I think of **confidence,** the thought that comes to mind is a staunch belief in one's own ability as a result of the effort that has been put in over a long period of time. I also believe that confidence can be fragile—thus the need to train confidence in such a way that one can get back to a confident state fairly quickly, especially under duress and when it matters the most. Over time, I have formulated six ingredients that I believe are critical to developing a confident mindset. I will list them in general order of importance, although there certainly can be differences among individuals.

## 1  PREPARATION/HARD WORK

Without a doubt, being confident begins with putting in the preparation for whatever your endeavor may be. For this reason alone you can already see that having a high level of commitment is necessary in developing confidence. What I have found, however, is that many individuals often don't know what it really means to work hard—or the mind gets in the way, leading to not pushing themselves to the necessary degree. In the movie *Facing the Giants*, there was a scene in which one of the athletes was asked to do the death crawl—wearing a blindfold. With encouragement and his mind out of play due to the blindfold, he was able to crawl farther than he ever imagined. Jack Riggins, my partner and retired Navy SEAL commander, has often told teams that the mind will give out way before the body. It has also been stated: "The US Navy SEALs have a theory that no matter how bad we feel or how tired we get, we're actually nowhere near the limit of what we can achieve; the brain is deceiving us to save the body from pain. In fact, they think we're only 60 percent there. It's a way of saying that by drawing on our mental strength, we can push through any situation. When the chips are down, tell yourself you have at least 40 percent left in the tank." Whether there is actual science to back up this exact percentage is up for debate, but not the fact that we have to learn to prepare mentally so that we can push through to necessary levels of work to earn the right to be confident.

In the business world you don't have to look any further than the work ethic of Warren Buffett and his ability to study for hours the minutest details concerning individual businesses. This trait, evident from the time he was a very young man and coupled with his meticulous preparation, gave him the confidence to buy parts of these businesses, known as stocks, as part of his portfolio. That earned him the reputation of being considered the best investor in the world over the past fifty years. Preparation is generally the most important factor for those who have the highest GPAs, those who are able to defend their business proposal, or those who max out in the sporting arena as an individual or part of a collective team.

As Muhammad Ali famously said, **"The fight is won or lost far away from witnesses—behind the lines, in the gym, and out there on the road, long before I dance under those lights."**

## 2 SELF-TALK

Assuming that you are willing and understand the mechanics of what it means to put in the preparation/hard work at the highest level, I believe that self-talk is the hidden ingredient for maximizing confidence.

Michael Gervais, an exceptional high-performance psychologist whom I had the pleasure of meeting and spending a day with, shares a similar viewpoint. He has said the following:

> Confidence is the cornerstone of great performance, and it comes from just one place: what we say to ourselves. It must be grounded in credible conversations with yourself, which means you have to have a disciplined mind to focus on when you've been successful

in the past and to bring that success into the present. Part of the training is being mindful, on a moment-to-moment basis, of whether you're building or taking away from confidence. The second part is being able to guide you back to the present moment and adopt a positive mindset about what is possible. So confidence comes from what you say to yourself, and becoming aware and mindful of your inner dialogue is really at the center of being able to grow, to be able to develop, to be able to pursue potential. And it's a skill that we can teach; it's a skill that we can develop.

Think about it. How can we be confident in the moment if we are telling ourselves things like, "I'm not good enough. I don't belong. I suck. I can't do anything right. I screwed up again. She is just better than me"? As a trained observer, all I need to do is look at somebody's body language—the window into their self-talk—and know what is going on inside their head. Facial expressions and poor eye contact also often give away what we are thinking or saying to ourselves. As discussed earlier, there are several strategies to help one master self-talk in a positive manner. It is also under one's full control—and not dependent on anybody else.

## 3  WHAT OTHERS SAY TO US—COACH/BOSS/ TEAMMATES

If you're part of a group or team, this ingredient is on par with mastering your own self-talk. I know most leaders don't put much thought into whether they are helping or hurting the confidence of those they lead, especially on an individual basis and when under stress.

In fact, over the years when I've spent time observing a practice or match at the request of a coach, during the debriefing I will often ask, "Do you want Mary to be confident?" The answer is always yes. The follow-up is often something like this: "When you say to Mary after a couple of mistakes, 'I should pull your scholarship' or 'You'll never see the court again playing like this,' do you think you're helping or taking away from her confidence?" Now, I am not suggesting that leaders shouldn't hold those they lead accountable for their actions, but there is no question that the best way to effect change over time is to spend more energy catching somebody doing something correctly and giving praise. When giving constructive criticism, it's critical to make sure it is not made personal but is said with a focus on technical/tactical corrections.

I once observed a coach yell out during a drill in practice, "That was sure a dumb blonde moment." The athlete had accidentally interfered with the drill because the assistant coach had stopped her to make a correction. That one comment not only hurt the athlete's confidence but broke the trust that this coach and athlete had been working so hard to build. Bosses, managers, teachers, and parental figures carry so much power that it's important to talk to those they lead in a positive way to add to their confidence. The "Bobby Knight" method, coaching out of fear, at times can give short-term gains, but it will rarely lead to long-term success with athletes or to a team playing fearlessly when it matters the most.

Team members play a huge role in helping or hurting each other's confidence with both verbal and nonverbal communications. The best example that I can think of where a communication exercise would have benefited teammates earlier in their career was an issue between an All-American setter and an All-American outside hitter in volleyball who had played together for a couple of years. When the outside hitter made an unforced error such as hitting the pin, the setter would always say, "That was on me" or "My bad." It used to infuriate and cause stress for the outside hitter because she knew it was her mistake, but she never told the setter how she felt. The setter was just trying to make her feel better and keep her confidence levels up and had no idea that it was backfiring. Once the outside hitter was honest and told the setter that all she needed from her was a comment like "I'm coming right back at you," the setter knew what to do. A team member with the right words can be huge in helping another work out of a stressful situation in real time, and the opposite is clearly true as well.

This is one of the exercises that many teams I work with do, usually in the preseason: players go around the room and say what they need from their teammates and coaches when they are stressed during practice or competition to help bring them out of it as quickly as possible. Some need a positive affirmation such as "You're the best setter in the country." Others need "You got this; I am coming right back to you." Still others need someone to give them a high five or make them laugh. Each person on the team has very different needs, but often these are never communicated to one another. One athlete told the team during this exercise that she doesn't like to be touched after a mistake, but previously nobody knew this about her. One of the freshmen had been patting her on the shoulder or on the back, thinking she was being supportive of her teammate. There are no unacceptable requests, and for me there is only one thing that is non-negotiable: shutting down and not communicating with your team is not allowed. If that is the way some players have previously dealt with stress, they know they need to learn a different strategy and have their teammates/coaches help them if they want to stay on the court.

I listed this as number three because self-talk is under one's full control, but players do not have full control over what teammates and coaches ultimately say to them. I tell them it is their responsibility, however, to let others on the team know what types of comments help their confidence and similarly what types of comments hurt their confidence.

## 4  PAST SUCCESS

While I agree with Dr. Gervais that self-talk is very important to confidence, past successes can play a big role, as well. It is hard to have absolute confidence if you have not previously been successful in that endeavor. Preparing for an extended time while waiting for your opportunity to shine, whether it is getting your first start with your team or getting to play your first solo with the symphony, can give you confidence that you're ready for this moment. I think most will agree that there is another level of confidence that comes with having successes over a period of time and under a variety of circumstances. I have past success as number four because there are times when successes haven't occurred for a while, and yet one still needs to be able to access the strategies in this arena to remember successes from the past.

The best strategy I know is the use of the mental skill of imagery/ visualization that has already been discussed. I often suggest making a highlight reel of best performances to watch and remind people why they have the right to be confident. This highlight reel can also be used to assist with visualization. Use of imagery to help with confidence can get very specific. The example from my experience that best illustrates this comes from the world of women's gymnastics. I was working with an athlete at the University of Nebraska, Brittnee Habbib, who at times warmed up poorly on the uneven bars during the allotted period before the actual competition. The team was competing against the University of Florida, which was one of the top teams in the country. Unfortunately, Brittnee warmed up poorly again and the coach considered pulling her from the lineup. Luckily, she ended up scoring in the 9.9 range (out of 10) and won the bar competition that day!

A few meets later, a similar situation occurred at a critical competition—Brittnee warmed up poorly again. In the time between warm-ups and the competition, I pulled her aside and had her watch her performance against Florida on video and then visualize that performance for a few minutes, using all of her senses. I wanted her to remember the feeling of how she had previously overcome the poor warm-up with a championship performance, to give her the confidence that she needed to perform under pressure again when it mattered the most. Was this the sole reason that she again nailed her performance? Of course not. That being said, it was a helpful strategy that added to her confidence levels at a time when her confidence otherwise could be shaken.

## 5 FAMILY/FRIENDS

Family, especially parents, can have a big impact on helping or hurting one's confidence levels. Parents generally want the best for their kids, and it is rare that they would intentionally try to do them harm. However, parents are often oblivious to the impact of their words during and after games. Yelling at the refs, shouting out instructions, or loud commentary after a mistake during a game can cause quite a bit of distress and lead to a deterioration of confidence. It is important to empower athletes to address with their parents what types of things they say that help or hurt the confidence. It is also important for athletes to talk to their parents when they don't get the role that they want. Parents today, often trying to be supportive and well meaning, will say things like, "You're the best at that position; Coach is just playing favorites." Not only does this put doubt into the athlete's mind, but it can also undermine the coach.

Sometimes parents will start to tell other parents what they think, and it can eventually lead back to the team; nothing good comes of this type of situation. I will suggest to the team that if one of their parents says something negative about the role they have been given, say this to that parent: "I am supportive of the coach's decision and will do everything I can to win the spot that I want, and I need you to not keep saying these things to me or other parents." I have seen parents in tears when they learned about the negative impact of their words in these types of situations, and they quickly made the changes needed.

People generally want to say things they think their friends want to hear. Example: when a team is highly ranked preseason, especially if ranked number one, friends can talk about how exciting it will be when the team wins the state championship. If enough people continue to say things like this, it can lead to unnecessary and unhealthy pressure/expectations that can disrupt a team's confidence, especially after a loss or setback.

I have this at number five because, on average, the impact on confidence from family/friends is not as great, but it can be challenging to talk to parents and tell them how you feel. That being said, I try to get athletes to understand that it is their responsibility to let family/friends know how they feel, especially if confidence is being impacted. While I have observed a large number of supportive families, one in particular stands out to me. Jessie DeZiel was on the University of Nebraska women's gymnastics team from 2012 to 2015. Her parents, Craig and Jean, and sister Brittany (who was also a college gymnast), helped give Jessie confidence. Her father had the gift of knowing just what to say, with a near-perfect balance of love and accountability. Jean always had a way of providing just the right amount of emotional support while still giving Jessie her freedom to mature into a healthy adult. The DeZiels always deferred to what the coaches thought was best for Jessie and the team. They were grateful and appreciative of Jessie's experience at Nebraska, but they may not have realized that it was parents like them who helped lift the confidence of the entire team.

## 6  SPIRITUAL

I will acknowledge upfront that for some people the role of spirituality is more important than some of the other components, and for others it has no impact at all on confidence. For those who think it is an important ingredient, it usually revolves around the theme of there being a higher power that is bigger than any performance. For some, the use of prayer or inspirational Bible verses can be very calming and reassuring, leading to feeling less pressure in the moment and thereby a feeling of more confidence. For others, there is a feeling of confidence due to their belief that whatever happens is "meant to be." Many athletes get inspiration from loved ones who have passed away and the feeling that they are being looked after by those who have passed. This, too, can lead to a sense of calm and confidence for some performers.

## CONCENTRATION

When I think of **concentration**, I immediately think of focus and actually refocus, as well. I think of being in the present moment, right here, right now. I always tell people that focus is one of the tools that high performers excel at better than others. If you think about it, whether one is a CEO, surgeon, fighter pilot, teacher, firefighter, or athlete, the thing that virtually all have learned to do is focus at a high level. As Bruce Lee has said, **"The most successful warriors are average men with laser focus."**

But if I am being honest, what equally separates high performers from others is the ability to refocus. In any high-performance endeavor there are going to be many distractions. Many unplanned events can occur during surgery, leading to a loss of focus on the task at hand with the need to be able to quickly refocus. In the sporting world, a bad call, an unforced error or mistake, or a coach yelling at you can lead to a loss of focus and the mind wandering to the past or the future. Often, there are only seconds before the next play, the next shot, and so forth, and the skill of refocus is critical in that regard as well.

There are several strategies combining the use of mental skills and mindfulness that help train the skill of focus and refocus:

- A mindfulness practice, for reasons previously discussed, is the absolute top strategy for cultivating the skill of focus and refocus. The calming effects on the brain from doing even a few minutes of mindfulness meditation a day can enhance one's ability to focus and refocus while in any endeavor. As mentioned, having a focal point during meditation, such as your breathing or a mantra, actually trains your brain to focus and refocus just as if you were training your muscles. The changes in brain architecture leading to an attenuation of the fight-or-flight response, which leads to the ability to stay calm under stress, is a big factor in being able to focus and refocus when the pressure is on. Other brain changes lead directly to changes in the ability to focus.

- The use of self-talk, especially performance or instructional words as previously mentioned, is another important strategy that can be used in real time to help with focus on the immediate task at hand. Remember, using these words helps high performers stay in the present moment, which is necessary for elite performance.

- The use of visualization in the moments or seconds leading up to a specific moment, such as shooting a critical free throw, can help the brain focus directly on what's important and forms a picture in the mind of exactly how to perform, helping one stay in the present moment.

- Finally, setting specific SMART goals and then using them in the moment to reinforce what you want to accomplish in any aspect of life or sport is another strategy to help with focus and refocus.

## COMPOSURE

When I think of **composure,** I think of this phrase: "Being able to handle the mental, physical, and emotional demands of your endeavor, under pressure when it matters the most." When you think about it, many of us can stay composed when circumstances are completely going our way, if we are competing against inferior competition or doing an activity in a low-pressure situation. The best train their bodies and their minds to be able to perform in a similar and consistent way no matter the circumstance.

One example that always comes to mind is seeing those who can hit their free throws in the last two minutes of a game, in crunch time. Stephen Curry hit over fifty in a row when the pressure was on during that time period in the 2018 NBA playoffs. Most of us have noticed when the opposite has occurred—deterioration in performance from results in lower-pressure moments—especially if that person is on a team that we are rooting for. Mastering your composure is the primary factor, in my opinion, in noting these results.

During my career there have been three athletes who stand out, in my mind, at mastering their composure. Mikaela Foecke (now Richter) (University of Nebraska, 2015–2018) was a major contributor to the volleyball team's winning two national championships, and she was the MVP in both title games. She never appeared to get too high or too low. By observing her, you would have no idea if she was having the best game of her life or if she was under duress. Jessie DeZiel (I just mentioned her family) was a nine-time All-American. Gymnastics is a sport of failure, especially when you include the balance beam that is only four inches wide. Jessie was a four-year starter and usually competed in the all-around competition, meaning that she participated in all four events. During her four years she hit 206 out of 207 routines, the best I have ever seen by far. It did not matter if she was tired or sore or if she'd had a poor warm-up; when the lights came on, she always looked and acted composed—and mastered the physical, mental, and emotional demands of her sport when it mattered the most. Finally, Emily Wong (now Hilderbrand) and Jessie were teammates, although Emily was one year older. Emily was named winner of the 2014 AAI Award, given to the most outstanding gymnast in the country, and I consider her to be the most well-rounded student-athlete I've known.

In regard to Emily's composure, two specific events come to mind, both occurring her senior year in 2014. First, at the Big Ten Championships, Emily was the defending all-around champion and had won the all-around nearly every week during her senior year. However, she slipped as she approached the uneven bars, and that led to a major error, thus eliminating her from being all-around champion again. Based on what I've already said about Emily, it should not surprise you that she was able to remain fully composed (for the benefit of her team) on the very next event—the floor exercise. She only scored a perfect ten! It was one of the most joyful performances I've ever witnessed.

The following month at the NCAA National Championships, Nebraska was in position to advance to the final day of the championships called the Super Six. Going into the very last event, Nebraska was on the balance beam and needed to have their best performance of the year; even then it was going to be a long shot to beat Utah (who was number one in the country on the vault) and UCLA (one of the top teams for uneven bars in the country). Balance beam is also the event of the four that usually scores the lowest and is the most challenging. One by one the Husker gymnasts—Amanda Lauer, 9.85 (a great walk-on story in her own right!); Hollie Blanske (now Pille), 9.9; Jennie Laeng, 9.825; Jamie Schleppenbach, 9.9; and Jessie DeZiel, 9.9—completed their routines. Last up was Emily Wong in the anchor spot. She needed to hit a 9.875 for Nebraska to advance to the Super Six National Championship finals. I watched her in the couple of minutes before the judge raised her arm to let Emily know it was time to compete. Emily appeared calm, composed, focused, and excited to compete. On the most difficult apparatus there is in sport, the balance beam, and in the anchor spot with everything on the line, Emily hit a 9.9!

To this day, even having been part of several national and state championships, I have never seen a team—coaches, parents, and support staff as well—more joyful and excited than when they found out they had advanced to the Super Six. The celebration in the locker room is seared into my mind forever—in part born out of adversity with the way the prior year had ended when they fell short at the regional championships. The victory and accompanying celebration, however, would not have occurred if the entire balance beam team with Emily in the anchor spot had not been able to stay composed physically, mentally, and emotionally when it mattered the most.

Mastering the mental skill of arousal control leads to being able to use these strategies to accomplish just what I've been talking about. Can you hit that free throw, aggressively place that serve, hit that balance beam routine when it matters the most, or nail the presentation when you think a possible promotion is dependent on your performance? And remember, there are three main things that you can do to help with arousal control in the immediate moment or for a pending performance later on: (1) breathe, (2) take a power nap, and (3) do mindfulness training.

It's fun to observe athletes who you know are trying to master an elite mindset. One could tell that Isaiah Roby, a junior on the Nebraska Cornhuskers basketball team, was elevating his game in 2019 with a goal of making the NBA. There were times earlier in his career when one could observe bad body language, negative self-talk, a breakdown of confidence, and a loss of composure.

On March 21, 2019, in the *Omaha World-Herald*, head coach Tim Miles said he could see that Roby "reset" himself in recent games when he started off slow: **"You could see him take a deep breath and just, like, talk to himself in a positive manner."**

That is the use of high-performance mental skills in action that lead to the development of an elite mindset. It was awesome to see Isaiah become the first NBA draft pick in twenty years at Nebraska, sign a multimillion-dollar contract, and start to see his dreams all come true!

Hopefully, one can see how all the ingredients of an elite

mindset interface and build off each other. It is hard, for example, to feel that you've earned the right to be confident if you haven't been fully committed to the four legs of elite performance, since confidence comes from preparation—mental, physical, technical, and tactical. I will leave you with these thoughts. If one is fully confident, I believe that there can still be nervousness and anxiety with all the variety of symptoms one can experience. The caveat: with unbridled confidence, I do not believe one can be fearful. If one is confident, then fear can't and won't creep in. Virtually every coach and high performer I know wants their team and self to be able to perform in a fearless manner. Mastering commitment, confidence, composure, and concentration gives one the best chance to allow individuals and teams to be fearless. I hope you can appreciate how all four of these components build off each other while also being independently important in the genesis and development of an elite mindset.

# EXERCISES

## COMMITMENT EXERCISE

- Come up with one component where you can improve in each of the four legs (mental, physical, technical, tactical) of the elite performance stool.

- Give yourself a prescore of between one and one hundred, with one hundred being great for how you're doing with each component.

- Identify your processes that will help you improve in each of these four areas.

- Monitor yourself for a month, coming up with a weekly score of between one and one hundred for each component. Challenge yourself to improve by at least ten points for each component over the course of the month.

# 4

## THE POWER OF GRIT

GRIT IS DEFINED BY *Merriam-Webster's Dictionary of English Usage* as "firmness of mind or spirit; unyielding courage in the face of hardship or danger." When I think of grit, the following words come to mind: *tough, resilient, stamina, stubborn, doggedness, tenacious,* or *stick-to-itiveness.* A Navy SEAL comes to mind, as well. In the psychology world, Wikipedia defines grit as "a positive, noncognitive trait based on an individual's perseverance of effort combined with the passion for a particular long-term goal or end state."

Dr. Angela Duckworth, in more recent times, has studied grit as a personality trait, and her definition is very similar: "passion and perseverance for long-term goals." She was able to observe that individuals who had grit were more likely to maintain their motivation, determination, and focus even in the face of adversity, setbacks, and failure. Dr. Duckworth concluded that grit was a better predictor of success than intellectual talent or IQ. She then created a test that measured grit; those who scored highest on the grit scale were more likely to advance further in the National Spelling Bee, have a higher GPA at Ivy League schools, and not drop out at West Point Military Academy in the first year, among other things.

In 2013 Dr. Duckworth did a TED Talk outlining how grit is a significant predictor of success. She discussed how those who have a growth mindset, the belief that the ability to learn is not fixed and can change with effort, are more likely to persevere when they fail and that they don't believe failure is a permanent condition. That being said, she was very open at the end of the TED Talk in acknowledging that we didn't know much more at that time about how to train or grow grit. Of course, I wanted to scream, "Of course we know how to train grit—we do it all the time right now by teaching mental skills and developing an elite mindset!" I was partially correct in that assessment, but there was more that I couldn't immediately articulate even though I knew there were many people responsible for training grit in others.

Luckily, Dr. Duckworth continued to study and do research on the power of grit and, as a result, wrote an exceptional book in 2016 called *Grit: The Power of Passion and Perseverance.* In this book she helped to clarify what I was thinking and feeling—that you can train grit from the inside out, meaning from within yourself, and from the outside in, meaning that others (including your boss, coach, teacher, mentor, or parent) help train it in you. Dr. Duckworth described four psychological assets of grit: **interest, capacity to practice, purpose,** and **hope.**

**Interest** is about finding your passion. A Gallup poll in 2014 showed that more than two-thirds of adults were not engaged at work. We do know in simple terms that people are happier at work and perform better when they are interested. However, for those who end up being the grittiest, it usually takes several years and many explorations before they find out their true calling in life. The message to college kids is this: You don't need to know what you're going to do with the rest of your life right now! Be patient, don't panic, and don't give in to worries about what others think of you.

**Capacity to practice** is really about what we call **deliberate practice** in the high-performance world. It is an intense form of practice and usually cannot be done for more than sixty to ninety minutes at a time. There are four characteristics of deliberate practice:

- Stretch goals (a common term in high-performance training) are set by narrowing in on one specific aspect of performance, and usually on a specific weakness rather than strength.
- Full concentration and effort are required.
- Seek immediate and informative feedback, much of which is often negative, meaning what one needs to fix.
- Refine technique through repetition with introspection.

Many of you have heard about the "ten-thousand-hour rule" required for mastery. It is often said that one needs on average ten years and ten thousand hours to master any high-performance endeavor. Well, it is this many hours and years of deliberate practice that are required! The best coaches I have been around go about setting up practices that create just this environment. Go to observe one of Coach Cook's volleyball practices, and you will be exhausted just from watching. Everything is done with a purpose at a very high pace and with drills that train very specific skills—and most of these drills have a high failure rate. In his gym, grit is trained, developed, and strengthened every single hour.

**Purpose** is about interest and passion combined with the desire to help others as well. It is about finding a deeper meaning, a bigger

WHY for what you choose to do. Dr. Duckworth says that purpose means "the intention to contribute to the well-being of others." It is often the difference between a job and a calling. Having a purpose helps with motivation and the ability to stick through tasks when times get tough.

**Hope** is about the expectation that tomorrow will be a better day. As Pete Carroll, Seattle Seahawks head coach, has said, **"The world trains people to be pessimistic ... One of the most important things I must do here is make sure that my players and staff believe that tomorrow will be better than today."**

Similarly, Dr. Duckworth stated, "Grit depends on a different kind of hope. It rests on the expectation that our own efforts can improve our future." The opposite of hope is hopelessness. Dr. Seligman did some seminal research looking into hopelessness and found out that suffering doesn't lead to hopelessness; rather, it happens when one doesn't think they have any control over the suffering. Lack of control over our environment can lead to learned helplessness. Conversely, it is also important to know that hope can lead to learned optimism. Optimists, as noted before, have a competitive advantage since they look at setbacks as temporary and are always looking for solutions. The use of positive self-talk often comes in handy during these times, and certainly the notion of a growth mindset is even more powerful during challenging times. Positive self-talk contributes to hope remaining at high levels, which can lead to one being grittier.

Now, getting back to training grit from the outside in. Simply, if you want those you lead to have grit, model for them what it looks like to have grit. Leaders, whether they are coaches, bosses, mentors, teachers, or parents, can help train and grow grit by modeling its four psychological assets to others. If you show others that you have an interest/passion in what you do, those that follow you are more likely to feel the same way. Deliberate practice routines are the responsibility of those in charge, whether it be in business, sport, or the home.

In my opinion, the most important psychological asset, as described by Dr. Duckworth, is to model hope. With hope comes optimism, and with optimism one has a much better chance to overcome adversity and stay the course. So if you do nothing else well as a leader, model hope for those you lead.

Now for some examples of grit that I have either learned about or directly observed. Patrick Clare, whom I coached in flag football, is a good friend of my son, Bennett, and I've known him since he was eight years old. Patrick was a good athlete and also had a real fondness for golf. For the longest time, he played with clubs that were as tall as he was! I remember at eleven or twelve years old he had a focus that was clearly different from any of the other boys his age—especially when it came to golf. Our families lived on the same golf course, so I had the unique vantage point of seeing Patrick out there on the course. He was often alone, many times until dusk, playing in all kinds of weather and grinding away day after day. When we crossed paths, I would always tell him that he was the grittiest teenager I knew in Lincoln, Nebraska. He played for his high school team at Lincoln East. After practice and tournaments with his team, he was usually found on the practice range or the course in our neighborhood. He simply outworked everybody else his age.

He had a solid senior season in 2017. However, at the Norfolk Invitational a few days before Districts, he shot an 83. At Districts he struggled and shot an 81, but there he was on the practice range that evening, working things out. The Class A Nebraska State Championships were held again at the same course in Norfolk, Nebraska, where he had struggled just a few weeks earlier. It was also the home course of the defending state champion, Luke Kluver.

Prior to the tournament, I shared with Patrick's parents an excerpt from a newsletter called *Championship Performance*. In this excerpt was something Sergio Garcia's wife-to-be, Angela Akins, did for him prior to playing in the Masters in April that year:

Angela handed him a stack of letters. Each one was a handwritten note on green paper (symbolizing the green jacket for Masters winners). The letters came from friends and family members from Texas all the way to Spain, his home country. They addressed two key points: why they loved him, and why they thought they knew he could win. The injection of positivity added to what Garcia had already been working on to boost within himself: a self-belief that wouldn't waver, combined with an inner calm that he could endure through his worst shots. Historically, when Garcia had hit a bad shot at a crucial time, he began to sulk. So he told himself that was not an option for the Masters. In the bathroom of the home they rented for the week of the Masters, Akins covered the mirror with green sticky notes, each featuring motivational quotes from Buddha to Teddy Roosevelt. The most special was from Akins herself: "Don't forget to be awesome," it read. When Garcia made a huge mistake on hole thirteen, he could have crumbled. But not this time. He recovered from a poor tee shot to save a par. How many times have you been playing a solid round only to mess up one hole and start to think, "Oh crap, I just screwed up my entire round?" To fix this situation, focus on what is in front of you now—one shot at a time.

> Stick to your preshot routine. Turn, "Oh no" into "What now?" So adversity has hit . . . so what? Feeling bad about those rough times will not help you rebound successfully. Instead of lamenting over the past, ask yourself, "What can I do now that will get me back on track and improve my golf game?"

Several members of Patrick's family participated in a similar exercise in the week before State. The odds were stacked against Patrick. He had struggled in the weeks leading up to State, but his preparation never wavered. His years of training grit were about to pay off. As Patrick stated in the *Lincoln Journal Star* after the tournament, "I just had better preparation and gotten in a really good frame of mind. I was ready to go this week." Patrick had a great first round, shooting a three-under-par 69 for a four-shot lead, seven shots ahead of Luke, who shot a 76. Patrick told me that in the evening after his first round, he took the letters out and read them again and that they gave him the sense of calm and confidence that he needed. In the second round Luke, as expected, made a charge, shooting the low round of the day at four-under-par 68. When the round got tough, Patrick made a fourteen-foot downhill birdie on the par-four sixteenth and then followed up with a twenty-foot birdie putt from off the fringe on the par-three seventeenth. On the final hole, he had a difficult first shot followed by a nice recovery shot and made a par. Patrick secured the individual state championship and helped his team win as well!

His coach, Chad Geiger, said, "I could just see he had it together the entire time. Everything was the same. He took a deep breath before he hit every shot." At the high school level, Patrick was the most deserving champion that I've known. One of my favorite Muhammad Ali quotes, which I will repeat again, sums up why

Patrick put himself in a position to max out when it mattered the most: **"The fight is won or lost far away from witnesses—behind the lines, in the gym, and out there on the road, long before I dance under those lights."**

A favorite example of someone I don't know personally is a former Michigan State football player named Kyler Elsworth. I will start backward with the question that I often ask people: "If Kyler had never played on defense in his last game, would he still have felt very good about his role on the team and his career overall?" I believe the answer would have been a resounding yes. That being said, as a role player on special teams, he did get to make his only start as middle linebacker of his five-year career; it was in his very last game, in the 100th Rose Bowl against Stanford. He filled in for All-Big Ten linebacker Max Bullough, who was suspended for the game. The interview that he did after the game on the *Big Ten Network* is well worth watching and can be found easily on *YouTube*. If you watch it, the first thing you will see is number forty-one in green flying through the air, knocking a runner backward and stopping him on fourth and one to win the game! Kyler was also named the MVP of the Rose Bowl!

I wish that every athlete who stayed the course over many years, who embraced his or her role, and who was a great teammate could also have a fairy-tale ending. We all know that it often doesn't work that way in life and sport. In Kyler's interview on the *Big Ten Network* set, he started by saying, "It was a dream come true"—but as always, it is the details that let us know why he was successful in this situation. He talked about competing for the open spot and working together with a fellow teammate, who was also trying to win the spot, to make each other better. He was asked what went through his mind all those years in the meeting rooms while waiting for an opportunity. He said that every week he filled out a goal sheet, and he always wrote down, "Keep a positive attitude, keep a right mindset, keep working, and good things will happen." He talked about preparing every day that year, preparing in practice, and just being ready for the opportunity. He also talked about the importance of communication and replacing Max, who was a very good leader.

Is there anything harder than having to prepare like you're going to start every week in practice knowing that it is very unlikely you will ever play? The grit and mental resilience that it takes to prepare at that level and then being able to execute when it matters the most is one of the coolest things that I get to observe.

The athlete I personally have known in recent years who demonstrated the most grit is a female gymnast from the University of Nebraska named Danielle Breen. One unique characteristic of college gymnasts is that most competitors start in their sport by the age of five or six, and most end up specializing in their sport at a very young age due to the time demands of up to thirty hours per week. Danielle came to Nebraska as the underrated member of a highly touted recruiting class. Over the years, no one worked harder than Danielle. She also showed early signs of perseverance during the difficult transition to college gymnastics and through the mental, physical, and emotional demands of her sport. She became a very trusted athlete, leading off on two rotations, balance beam and uneven bars, which is rarely given to a freshman because of the importance of that role in setting the tone for the rest of the team scores.

Over time Danielle became one of the best balance beam workers on the team. Eventually, she became the anchor in that lineup, a position given to the best and most consistent athlete. However, during the early part of the 2017 season, Danielle developed a habit of balking (hesitating or even refusing to complete the skill) on her balance beam dismount in practice. It was very distressing to her coaches and certainly to her as well, especially given that she was wired for perfectionism. There were obvious concerns that it would eventually transfer to competition, which would be devastating to her and the team.

Coach Brink and I inquired as to why she felt it had not happened yet in a live meet. She told us that she was able to overpower the balking because she did not want to let the team down. Thus, we came up with a strategy in practice in which randomly a teammate would be notified that she would suffer a consequence, such as extra conditioning or having to do more assignments, if Danielle balked on her next balance beam dismount. This mimicked her desire to not let her teammates down. Only once did a teammate suffer a consequence in practice due to Danielle balking—and eventually the concern from coaches about balking in competition waned.

Fast forward to April 2017. She was last up on balance beam at the regional championships; it also just so happened that she was the very last person up in the entire competition among the six teams vying for the two spots that advance to the national championships. If she hit the routine, the team would advance to the national championships; if not, the season would be over just like that. One of the things I personally love about college gymnastics is the team aspect. Danielle summed it up best after the victory: "To me, the beam routine I did was irrelevant at that one shining moment, because I just remember hugging my coaches and my teammates and all of us celebrating together . . . I had fallen on bars in the previous event, and my team had my back, hitting routines after my fall. I guess my finish on beam was a chance to have my team's back, and that's what makes college gymnastics so special in my opinion—being able to have people to count on, and then to celebrate with."

Fast forward again a few months, and a couple of physical ailments started off her summer before her senior year in a tough way. As the setbacks mounted, she started struggling on the uneven bars and at one point struggled with skills she had mastered as a young girl. No one seemed to know how to help her, and it was starting to affect her mental state as well. One clinician was certain it was anxiety, but I had known Danielle for years and was not convinced at all that this was the cause of her issues. I came to the gym to observe, and within seconds I knew what was wrong. I could see the subtle fine-motor jerks that were barely observable to the naked eye. It made me think back to her episodes of balking in practice the prior year on the balance beam, and I knew both of these things were 100 percent related. Balking was just another form of the yips—the sudden and unexplained loss of skills (usually fine motor) in an experienced athlete.

The term *yips* was coined by Scottish golfer Tommy Armour, who said, "It was a brain spasm that affected the short game." Some say the yips are neurological in nature; some say there is a psychological component—but the yips are poorly understood, and often there is no cure. Anxiety can certainly make the yips worse, but it is not the cause. The yips have ended the careers of athletes in many sports, including golf and baseball. Some have called the yips "the monster" because of how devastating they can be to an athlete. Many athletes give up trying after a period of time, and in Danielle's case, the start of her senior season was only a month away. Besides giving her some strategies to try that were based in the science that I understood, my biggest role was to give her hope, as there was no way she was giving up as long as she had hope. One of the key strategies was to activate the right side of her brain, the creative part of the brain, which is responsible for controlling the left side of the body. Conversely, the left side of the brain is responsible for logic and analyzing situations and controls the right side of the body.

It was thought that those who are particularly left-brain dominants—who often are more analytical and prone to orderliness and perfectionism—are more likely to get the yips, especially when there are other stressors. To activate the right side of the brain, we know that one can sing out loud, for example. Ultimately, we ended up with a different strategy that she felt more comfortable with—squeezing a ball in her left hand to activate the right side of her brain. It was something that I had discovered in my research into the difficult treatment of yips. She would squeeze the ball in her hand for several seconds prior to doing any skill in practice and before her routine, thus activating the right brain. The progress was slow, with many starts and failures and, obviously, a lot of mental and emotional distress. It required all of the features that you think about when discussing grit: her passion for gymnastics, her attention to detail over many years and many hours of deliberate practice, her desire to help her team out, and her ability to find some optimism and hope even in the darkest of times.

The yips are messy. She struggled early in the season, leading to the loss of her spot in the starting lineup, the spot she had earned her entire career. But she kept battling, and there were a couple of other athletes who either were dealing with injuries or were struggling in their own right. Lo and behold, she found herself slowly improving, building her confidence and finally finding her way back in the uneven bar lineup very late in the season. At the national championships she was called upon to lead off the team on the uneven bars. As an aside, there are six competitors for each team on each apparatus, and the low score is thrown out. Thus, if the lead person counts a fall, it puts tremendous pressure on the rest of the lineup to all hit their routines. It was time to have all of her grit on display—

the passion that fueled her from a young age, the year-long perseverance required to overcome her challenges, the goal of being a competitive gymnast in college or the Olympics set years prior, the thousands of hours of deliberate practice, and the hope that through hard work and effort things would eventually change in a positive way for her in her senior year. If the yips were to hit her, it was on one of the first skills that she performed on the uneven bars. The tension was palpable, but there was Dani squeezing the ball in her left hand per her usual routine and then putting it down just prior to saluting the judges. She mounted the bars and performed her routine splendidly, under extreme pressure when it mattered the most, grit fully on display. The team built off her momentum and remained on fire throughout the entire competition, pulling off a major upset to secure a spot in the National Championship Super Six Finals the next day! Dani also went on to be named the 2017–18 Female Student-Athlete of the Year at the University of Nebraska.

I have told coaches that if sports were fair, there were two athletes in my career who would succeed in that one specific moment in time for their team. As we know, sports and life aren't always fair. The first athlete I said this about was Danielle Breen with the uneven bar routine I just told you about. There was another gymnast, Madison McConkey (now Madison Janovich), whom I wanted success for at the regional championships in 2016. Madison had the unusual journey of quitting her sport for over a year while still in high school and not competing her senior year. She then decided to make a comeback and was offered a walk-on position at the University of Nebraska. The time off made it very difficult to be able to cultivate the skills necessary to compete at the Division I level, and she chose to redshirt in 2012. When she finally gained the necessary skills to compete, her opportunities were limited due to depth on the team.

As a sophomore, she competed a few times on bars, and in her junior year she competed slightly more often but often without the results desired.

Gymnastics training is already the most challenging of any sport, in my opinion, and when failure happens, frequently the struggle is real—painful physically, mentally, and at times emotionally. Madison stuck with it when it would have been so easy to quit. Prior to her senior year, she stated, "My goal has always been to put everything on the table. I don't want to have any regrets. I want to leave a legacy and have people know that I gave a hundred percent at every practice and every competition." Through her sheer will, determination, hard work, and willingness to work on her mindset, she found herself in three lineups during the 2016 season. If someone had told me that she would lead off on the balance beam nearly every meet and hit solidly the last seventeen gymnastics routines of her career, I would not have believed it. Yet Madison hit one big routine after another, including clutch routines at regionals that helped the team get to the national championships. She then finished her career in a big way, helping the team to an eighth place at the national championships.

Coach Owen Field, current assistant coach for the University of Florida women's gymnastics team, has had a journey in his life that is all about grit. A former high school gymnast and the oldest of eight children, he has known hard work his entire life. He started helping out at the University of Nebraska in 2008, his freshman year of college, as a volunteer student-manager. He did that for another year before going to Southern Utah University for one year as a volunteer coach. Then he returned to the University of Nebraska and gave two more years as a volunteer coach before going back to being a student-manager so that he could complete his schooling. He found ways to pay for school and at times had to change roles because he couldn't afford schooling. Yet the entire time I knew him, he was upbeat, positive, and hardworking, and he invested in building relationships with everyone associated with the team. I always called him an "old soul," as he always seemed so mature for his age. He had an upbringing that required hard work and discipline given his family circumstances and dynamics, and he embraced it. I was impressed with him for a number of reasons, but his investment in learning the mental game of gymnastics and his love of learning— he was (and still is) like a sponge—allowed the two of us to form a deeper connection. I have been honored to mentor him though his journey.

Getting an assistant coaching position at the University of Florida was like hitting the coaching lottery. The difference was that while there is always a certain amount of luck and timing involved in getting any job, it was no fluke that he was seen as a highly qualified candidate, despite his age. His work ethic, character, and knowledge of the sport made it happen. He is now in charge of the uneven bars lineup at Florida, and his event and the team are routinely in the top five of the national rankings. He continues to invest heavily in building deeper relationships, building team chemistry, and helping his athletes train an elite mindset. I won't be surprised if his team puts itself in position in the near future to max out when it matters the most and becomes national champions.

Back to Kayla Banwarth, the volleyball player who went from a walk-on libero at Nebraska in 2007 to starting libero for the US Women's Volleyball national team, helping them win a gold medal in 2014 at the FIVB World Championships and a bronze medal in the 2016 Olympics. She had a tremendous senior year at Nebraska, maybe the best for a libero in Nebraska history at the time, leading them in all-time digs at that point. Yet when the postseason awards came out, she was not even named to the All-Big 12 or All-American teams, although there were many experts who thought she may be the best in the country at her position. This was just one more thing she used for fuel to continue in her growth path. She decided to continue playing volleyball beyond college and had a tryout for the US national team (USWNT) and was a member from 2011 to 2016. Most athletes who make up the national team also go on to have nice careers around the world playing professional volleyball. That being said, only two Americans are allowed on international professional teams, and those spots are usually given to setters, outside hitters, and middle blockers, as there is more scarcity of high-end talent in those positions around the world. Thus, she was not able to have a significant professional career, meaning most of her efforts were either in training with the USWNT or learning to be a coach. Finances surely were strained without the ability to play professionally, but the grind to get better in her craft always continued. She became the volunteer assistant for the Pepperdine men's volleyball program. A story on the March 2016 website of USA Volleyball demonstrated Banwarth's true grit. It was noted that Banwarth endured a challenge that had been under the radar so most people did not know about it: To accommodate her dual training schedules—her personalized training schedule in Anaheim and at Pepperdine up the coast fifty-five miles in Malibu—she got up early to avoid the troublesome Los Angeles traffic to drive to Pepperdine's morning workouts and spent nearly two and a half hours a day commuting back and forth.

"Now that I've taken on this coaching role, my spring schedule has become more jam packed," Banwarth said. "I normally wake up around four thirty a.m. and leave my house around five a.m. to drive up to Malibu. Pepperdine practices from about ten a.m. to twelve thirty or one p.m. Then I get back in the car and drive to Anaheim to get in a lift and court session. I get done at the gym around five thirty p.m. Then it's home for dinner, recovery, and an early bedtime."

Passion, perseverance, long-term goals, and dealing with setbacks and adversity were all on full display. Kayla decided to retire from the USWNT in 2016, and when an assistant coaching position at the University of Nebraska came open in 2017, she applied for it. She was the surprise pick given her limited coaching experiences. Eleven months later, in her first year as an assistant college coach at her alma mater, she embraced her coaches and team as they secured the 2017 NCAA Women's Volleyball National Championships in Kansas City, Missouri! It shouldn't surprise you that she was named head coach at the University of Mississippi in December 2019 after just three years as an assistant coach—at the ripe old age of thirty! That's grit!

Finally, the nature of the coaching profession is one of uncertainty, and it can be stressful on a coach and his or her immediate family. The path to success is filled with many barriers and twists. There is a certain amount of luck involved, as upward progression often has to do with the success of the head coach. If one is already a head coach, the success of your current team in conjunction with the timing of job openings can have a big impact on the journey. In the end, the coaching profession requires one to be passionate about the work and to have perseverance. Let's look at the career path of Nick Nurse, head coach of the Toronto Raptors, who won the NBA Championship in 2019:

# LARRY WIDMAN, M.D.

| | |
|---|---|
| **1989–1990** | ASSISTANT COACH, NORTHERN IOWA |
| **1990–1991** | HEAD COACH, DERBY RAMS—PLAYER/ COACH, BRITISH BASKETBALL LEAGUE |
| **1991–1993** | HEAD COACH, GRAND VIEW UNIVERSITY |
| **1993–1995** | ASSISTANT COACH, SOUTH DAKOTA |
| **1995–1997** | HEAD COACH, BIRMINGHAM, BRITISH BASKETBALL LEAGUE |
| **1998** | HEAD COACH, TELINDUS, ETHIAS LEAGUE |
| **1998–2000** | HEAD COACH, MANCHESTER, BRITISH BASKETBALL LEAGUE |
| **2000–2001** | HEAD COACH, LONDON, EURO LEAGUE |
| **2001, 2005** | ASSISTANT HEAD COACH, OKLAHOMA STORM, USBL |
| **2001–2006** | HEAD COACH, BRIGHTON, BRITISH BASKETBALL LEAGUE |
| **2007–2011** | HEAD COACH, IOWA ENERGY, NBA D LEAGUE |
| **2011–2013** | HEAD COACH, RIO GRANDE VALLEY, NBA D LEAGUE |
| **2013–2018** | ASSISTANT COACH, TORONTO RAPTORS |
| **2018–PRESENT** | HEAD COACH, TORONTO RAPTORS |

## THAT'S GRIT!

# EXERCISES

## GRIT EXERCISE

- Come up with an action plan to improve your overall grit.

- Can you identify one psychological asset (interest, capacity to practice, purpose, hope) that you can work on to improve your grit?

- Write down your action plan to improve in that area and be willing to ask for help from a coach or boss if necessary.

# PART II

# MAX OUT
# YOUR EMOTIONS

# 5

## THE POWER OF HAPPINESS

MANY TIMES PEOPLE TEND to overthink definitions such as the meaning of happiness. It appears that happy people make more of an effort and work harder at being happier. As you probably have figured out by now, I am a lover of meaningful quotes, and happiness can be as simple as this quote:

> *The happiest people don't have the best of everything,*
> *but they make the best of everything they have.*

It is also fitting that Emma Seppala, science director of the Center for Compassion and Altruism Research and Education at Stanford University, is the person who said that. She also wrote a book entitled *The Happiness Track: How to Apply the Science of Happiness to Accelerate Your Success*. Emma has stated that happiness "defined as a state of heightened positive emotion has a profound effect on our professional and personal lives. It increases our emotional and social intelligence, boosts our productivity, and heightens our influence over peers and colleagues." Multiple studies have shown that happiness boosts our productivity by more than 10 percent and increases resilience—the ability to bounce back, particularly under stress, more quickly.

Based on some of her empirically validated data and what I've learned over the years, it is clear that there are also many myths about happiness. The good news is that happiness can be trained like any other skill. The best news is that often just the small choices one can make on a daily basis can elevate one's happiness to a great and sustainable degree.

There are many myths about how to capture success, often driven by a culture that makes us feel like we have to constantly be on the go, always chasing something, afraid of missing out with the need to be plugged in 24/7. Many feel that they have to look out for only themselves, work to exhaustion, or only hyperfocus on their strengths. This has led to a significant increase in the number of Americans who have elevated stress, increased anxiety, and an increased reliance on mental health medications. There are also a record number of people, upward of 70 percent, who don't feel engaged or are actively disengaged in the workplace. The World Health Organization has recently classified workplace burnout as an occupational phenomenon with three main features: (1) feelings of energy depletion or exhaustion, (2) increased mental distance from one's job, and (3) reduced professional efficiency. Burnout is responsible for up to 50 percent of workplace turnover.

We've been conditioned in our society to believe that in order to be happy, we need to suffer to be successful and that only with success comes happiness. What if the opposite were true? What if happiness makes us more likely to be successful? We know that happy people are more likely to be engaged with their job, are more connected to coworkers, and create an environment of reciprocity; happy people are more productive. Happy people are more likely to make others around them be happier as well! The false notion that major life events dictate happiness (or sadness) is widespread, but in reality happiness based on events is generally fleeting. What we do know is that happiness is trained through the development of habits. Dr. Travis Bradberry, who has written extensively on the topic of happiness and emotional intelligence, discussed a study from Northwestern University that measured the happiness of regular people versus those who won large lottery prizes in the prior year. Their happiness ratings were nearly identical. There have also been several documentaries looking at the lives of lottery winners: many of them end up with complete disruptions of their family life and deterioration in both finances and happiness.

As I review with you some strategies that can help lead to happiness, you will note that many of these examples have already been discussed in prior chapters—therefore, it should be fairly obvious that happiness and high performance are often intertwined. What, then, are the key ingredients or habits that can be honed that will increase one's chances of sustained happiness?

# 1  BE PRESENT

I am sure you have heard the line, "You have to find balance in your life," but I've discovered that the secret to being happy and content is to spend less time worrying about being balanced and more time working on being present. What does *being present* mean? As discussed in prior chapters, when one is in a truly mindful state, the experience of being happy or content is more likely to occur—and it is a very productive state of mind as well. It is that state of being that is often referred to as being "in the zone," "flow," or simply being mindful. As I tell people, most high performers are not balanced in the truest sense of the word.

That being said, if you have only thirty minutes with your child this evening, be present during those thirty minutes. Take the time to savor life's little pleasures—the taste of your food, a great conversation—or even just take time to breathe. It is clear that those who engage in conversations with people at a deeper level are more likely to build emotional connections that lead to happiness. Conversely, making small talk, judging others, and gossiping are more likely to lead to distress. We have a choice in how we want to engage with ourselves and others; if happiness is one of the goals, one must develop and then train the habit of being present.

## 2   BE KIND TO YOURSELF, AND SHOW SELF-COMPASSION

One myth for success is to be hard on ourselves to get to where we want to go. However, the research shows that self-criticism weakens us (and makes us less confident) while self-compassion increases our ability to be productive, resilient, and happy.

*Being kind to ourselves makes us more likely to remember that everybody makes mistakes and has setbacks and failures. It is not failure itself but our fear of failure that leads to stress and the likelihood that we will give up when things get tough.*

Being kind to ourselves makes dwelling on negative thoughts less likely and gives us a chance to replace those thoughts with positive, motivational, or performance words.

## 3 SHOW COMPASSION TO OTHERS/HELP OTHERS

When we show compassion or help others, it actually causes a surge of brain chemicals that creates positive feelings. From an evolutionary standpoint, human beings aren't naturally selfish, although many people have learned they are supposed to look out for number one. Research shows that individuals, families, groups, and teams are better off if one nurtures supportive relationships with others. Research has shown that spending money on other people makes us much happier than if we spend it on ourselves. This is even more true when one buys or does small favors that require some effort. Compassion has tremendous health and well-being benefits by getting us outside of our own head and paying attention to others in a positive way. This also leads to less depression and anxiety. In the workplace, those who are seen as helpful are more likely to be focused and tend to receive promotions.

The good news is that compassion and helpfulness can be trained. Emma Seppala and her colleagues at Stanford University found that those who underwent a nine-session training program had lower stress, more empathy, were more likely to help others, and were more empathetic to the suffering of others.

## 4 MANAGE STRESS

We know today how easy it is to feel stressed for all the reasons previously mentioned. The mind-body stress reaction that occurs when we are constantly in overdrive can lead to burnout with both physical and mental consequences. That being said, as you know already, one can learn to manage stress and learn to be calmer. It should not surprise you by now that I am going to take you back to one of the key strategies to help with this—learning tactical breathing. Just remember there are simple breathing strategies based in science that can go a long way to helping you manage your stress levels. Paying attention to your breath is also tied to greater self-control, well-being, and resilience.

## 5 BE RESILIENT

If you remember the chapter on grit, it really was about developing resilience—or the ability to bounce back from setbacks and adversity. There are several ways to train grit, as noted, but the use of positive emotions to respond to stressful experiences also allows one to recover much more quickly to a setback, in part by not having our fight-or-flight system kick in as intensely under stress. Breathing and mindfulness meditation techniques help in this regard, as just noted.

## 6 DO NOTHING

I know this is counterintuitive to most people's notion of success or happiness, especially in our Western society. To stay afloat or get ahead, we are taught to be productive every minute. smartphones, the internet, social media, and FOMO (fear of missing out) also lead to this constant need for stimulus. We are actually more productive and creative when we are not at peak alertness. We know that turning your attention inward, which occurs in a meditative state, leads to heightened creativity as well. Our unconscious mind comes alive in this setting, and it is responsible for more than 90 percent of our thinking; thus, our problem-solving skills and creativity flourish. It is clear from the research that our well-being and happiness also increase in an environment where we build low-intensity activities and quiet time into our day.

In the high-performance arena, the happiest leaders, coaches, and athletes I have observed or been around have also generally been very successful. They tend to be the most optimistic, caring, resilient, and compassionate people. The names that come to mind are some already mentioned: Coach Kirsten Bernthal Booth, Coach Dan Kendig, Coach Terri Neujahr, Coach Renee Saunders, and Coach Owen Field. All are happy and optimistic coaches who have had success in their craft and in growing people. Kenny Bell and Emily Wong are the two happiest and most optimistic student-athletes that I have crossed paths with over the years, and no doubt they will make a huge impact on society in the years ahead.

# EXERCISES

## HAPPINESS EXERCISE

- There are six strategies identified in this chapter to help one improve his or her happiness.

- Can you identify one strategy and an action plan to help you improve your overall happiness?

# 6

## THE POWER OF APPRECIATION AND GRATITUDE

YOU HAVE PROBABLY FIGURED out that there is a clear overlap among the various powers discussed in this book. Simply put, the purpose of this chapter is to demonstrate that the act of being thankful, expressing gratitude, or being appreciative can increase your chances of attaining lasting happiness. I will use the words *gratitude*, *thankfulness*, and *appreciation* interchangeably, because cultivating gratitude costs nothing and takes little or no time to perfect. Research clearly shows there are numerous benefits to one's life and with performance when one makes a commitment to being grateful. Repeated studies show that an "attitude of gratitude" has tremendous power in business, sport, and life. Some of my favorite team projects in both business and sport revolve around the notion of being grateful or appreciative—either for what we have or, in particular, for the relationships that we have in our lives.

Let's look at some of the scientifically proven benefits of gratitude with the mindset of thinking about how being grateful can lead to improvement in individual performance as well as team performance. In general, we will see improvements in happiness, relationships, and the impact we have on others.

## 1 OPPORTUNITIES FOR MORE RELATIONSHIPS

Being grateful and showing appreciation can open up our world to meeting new friends. A 2014 study published in *Emotion* found that just thanking a new acquaintance for something he or she did, such as holding the door open for you, made it more likely to seek an ongoing relationship. It can be as simple as sending a thank-you note to a coworker who helped you out with a project or telling a new teammate that you appreciate the advice they offered. Showing gratitude to others makes them see you as a better person and more likable, thereby contributing to the likelihood of building a deeper relationship.

## 2 IMPROVED PHYSICAL HEALTH

The science of gratitude reveals that those who practice gratitude often have an improved immune system, decreased blood pressure, healthier eating habits, and improved sleep and overall well-being. Grateful people are also more likely to exercise and follow through with regular checkups with their physicians.

## 3  IMPROVED PSYCHOLOGICAL HEALTH

In addition to the two points above, there is significant research into gratitude that shows a clear link with psychological well-being. There is evidence of overall decreased rates of depression, stress, anger, hatred, and negative emotions. There is an increase in self-esteem, love, and empathy. We have also found that mental strength is improved, leading to increased resilience and improvement in willpower and making better long-term decisions. Counting one's blessings on a daily basis is a simple and effective way to begin your journey to well-being.

All three of these benefits markedly increase the chances of optimizing the performance of individuals, groups, and teams. It has been clearly shown, for example, that self-esteem is essential in maximizing performance. When you are grateful, you're less likely to be resentful toward others (coworkers or teammates) who may have received the promotion or have the role you wanted on the team. This leads to an improved ability to appreciate and be happy for others' accomplishments, which is essential when we start to look at the ingredients of high-performing teams.

Practicing gratitude can be easily done. Simply close your eyes and think of a couple of people you're grateful for and who have had a positive impact on your life. You can start a gratitude journal and identify a few things each day that cause you to be grateful. Some people like to take a daily walk while focusing on gratitude. Just find some time every day to cultivate the feelings of gratitude, and the benefits will flow.

One of the books that illuminated for me the importance of appreciation was written by Mike Robbins and is called *Focus on the Good Stuff: The Power of Appreciation*. He identified five principles of appreciation that are worth noting:

- Be grateful
- Choose positive thoughts and feelings
- Use positive words
- Acknowledge others
- Appreciate yourself

We have already discussed the power of positive thoughts, feelings, and words as they relate to the development of an elite mindset that includes confidence. In some ways, learning to master your self-talk is about appreciating yourself—and if you can't learn to appreciate yourself, it becomes very difficult to have a positive view of the world and others. In fact, it is even hard for most people to accept a compliment with ease. It is harder than most realize to not feel uncomfortable when somebody is giving us praise. It takes practice and an awareness of the necessity to take a deep breath, be present, and learn to accept praise and believe it.

The power of acknowledging others is best illustrated in a story that I want to put in here in its entirety. It is the story of Mark Eklund as told by Sister Helen Mrosla:

> He was in the first third-grade class I taught at Saint Mary's School in Morris, Minnesota. All thirty-four of my students were dear to me, but Mark Eklund was one in a million. Very neat in appearance, but had that happy-to-be-alive attitude that made even his occasional mischievousness delightful.
>
> Mark talked incessantly. I had to remind him again and again that talking without permission was not acceptable. What impressed me so much, though, was his sincere response every time I had to correct him for

misbehaving: *"Thank you for correcting me, Sister!" I didn't know what to make of it at first, but before long I became accustomed to hearing it many times a day.*

*One morning my patience was growing thin when Mark talked once too often, and then I made a novice teacher's mistake. I looked at Mark and said, "If you say one more word, I am going to tape your mouth shut!" It wasn't ten seconds later when Chuck blurted out, "Mark is talking again." I hadn't asked any of the students to help me watch Mark, but since I had stated the punishment in front of the class, I had to act on it. I remember the scene as if it had occurred this morning. I walked to my desk, very deliberately opened my drawer, and took out a roll of masking tape. Without saying a word, I proceeded to Mark's desk, tore off two pieces of tape, and made a big X with them over his mouth. I then returned to the front of the room. As I glanced at Mark to see how he was doing, he winked at me. That did it! I started laughing. The class cheered as I walked back to Mark's desk, removed the tape, and shrugged my shoulders. His first words were, "Thank you for correcting me, Sister."*

*At the end of the year, I was asked to teach junior high math. The years flew by, and before I knew it Mark was in my classroom again. He was more handsome than ever and just as polite. Since he had to listen carefully to my instruction in the "new math," he did not talk as much in ninth grade as he had in third. One Friday, things just didn't feel right. We had worked hard on a new concept all week, and I sensed that the students were frowning, frustrated with themselves, and edgy with one another. I had* to stop this crankiness before it got out of hand. So I asked them to list the names of the other students in the room on two sheets of paper, leaving a space between each name. Then I told them to think of the nicest thing they could say about each of their classmates and write it down. It took the remainder of the class period to finish their assignment, and as the students left the room, each one handed me the papers. Charlie smiled. Mark said, "Thank you for teaching me, Sister. Have a good weekend." That Saturday, I wrote down the name of each student on a separate sheet of paper, and I listed what everyone else had said about that individual.

On Monday I gave each student his or her list. Before long, the entire class was smiling. "Really?" I heard whispered. "I never knew that meant anything to anyone!" "I didn't know others liked me so much." No one ever mentioned those papers in class again. I never knew if they discussed them after class or with their parents, but it didn't matter. The exercise had accomplished its purpose. The students were happy with themselves and one another again.

That group of students moved on. Several years later, after I returned from vacation, my parents met me at the airport. As we were driving home, Mother asked me the usual questions about the trip, the weather, and my experiences in general. There was a lull in the conversation. Mother gave Dad a sideways glance and simply said, "Dad?" My father cleared his throat as he usually did before something important. "The Eklunds called last night," he began. "Really?" I said. "I haven't heard from them in years. I wonder how Mark is." Dad responded quietly. "Mark was killed in Vietnam," he said. "The funeral is tomorrow, and his parents would like it if you could attend." To this day I can still point to the exact spot on I-494 where Dad told me about Mark.

I had never seen a serviceman in a military coffin before. Mark looked so handsome, so mature. All I could think at that moment was, "Mark, I would give all the masking tape in the world if only you would talk to me." The church was packed with Mark's friends. Chuck's sister sang "The Battle Hymn of the Republic." Why did it have to rain on the day of the funeral? It was difficult enough at the graveside. The pastor said the usual prayers, and the bugler played taps. One by one, those who loved Mark took a last walk by the coffin and sprinkled it with holy water. I was the last one to bless the coffin. As I stood there, one of the soldiers who acted as pallbearer came up to me. "Were you Mark's math teacher?" he asked. I nodded as I continued to stare at the coffin. "Mark talked about you a lot," he said.

After the funeral, most of Mark's former classmates headed to Chuck's farmhouse for lunch. Mark's mother and father were there, obviously waiting for me. "We want to show you something," his father said, taking a wallet out of his pocket. "They found this on Mark when he was killed. We thought you might recognize it." Opening the billfold, he carefully removed two worn pieces of notebook paper that had obviously been taped, folded, and refolded many times. I knew without looking that the papers were the ones on which I had listed all *the good things each of Mark's classmates had said about him. "Thank you so much for doing that," Mark's mother said. "As you can see, Mark treasured it." Mark's classmates started to gather around us. Charlie smiled rather sheepishly and said, "I still have my list. I keep it in the top drawer of my desk at home." Chuck's wife said, "Chuck asked me to put his in our wedding album." "I have mine, too," Marilyn said. "It's in my diary." Then Vicki, another classmate, reached into her pocketbook, took out her wallet, and showed her worn and frazzled list to the group. "I carry this with me at all times," Vicki said without batting an eyelash. "I think we all saved our lists." That's when I finally sat down and cried. I cried for Mark and for all his friends who would never see him again.*

This story was so powerful to me that I came up with a couple of team projects I truly love to help everybody associated with the team to be more appreciative, thankful, and grateful for those who have had an impact in their lives. These team projects also serve to start work on learning to be more vulnerable with each other, which I delve into in the next chapter. The two project names are "The Power of Appreciation" and "Let It Shine."

The first project—the Power of Appreciation—can take many forms and, depending on the size of the team (a gymnastics team versus a football team), may require a different approach. My favorite format has been to have each member of the team, including the coaching staff and often key support staff, write at least one sentence or paragraph outlining areas of appreciation they have for each teammate. It is critical to involve the coaches, since those who are in unequal relationships with people that lead them sometimes forget that their coaches or bosses are people with real emotions and lives that also may be filled with challenges. Similar to the story above, I then compile all the comments about each teammate into a document that he or she can read. One of the coolest things about this project is that every person learns about the impact they have had on others—and often common themes about that person emerge. This can be very powerful for those who weren't aware of how others felt about them, especially if they felt like they played an insignificant role on the team. Reading something like this about oneself often leads to deeper or new feelings of gratitude and love for the other members of the team. I believe that this also leads to increased empathy for one another.

I love doing this project with high-performing teams in between the season and postseason, when worries about the outcome become a bigger issue—that's just the nature of the one-and-done time of year. It's good to have the team members get outside of their own heads and focus on what they learned from the comments about themselves. This translates into less worry about the next game and a greater focus on the process. If the team is under duress at any point in the postseason, the feelings generated by a project like this will lead to improved resilience as well.

In April 2015, just prior to the national championship tournament, I had the University of Nebraska women's bowling team do the Power of Appreciation exercise with the additional caveat that they all write to their parent or parent figure as well. For some, it was the first time that any of them had ever given their parent a handwritten letter letting them know how much they were appreciated. As you can imagine, many of the parents were moved to tears and told me that they had never received anything like this before. What the team didn't know was that I also asked the parents to write them back with a similar message. Why is this relevant? Fast forward to February 1, 2018. I received a text out of the blue from Melanie Crawford (Epperson), the bowling athlete I told you about who helped the 2015 team win the national championship. She asked me if I still had my Power of Appreciation file from that 2015 project and informed me that her father had recently become ill and had taken a turn for the worse. She needed to leave immediately for Texas to be with him, and she couldn't find the booklet I had given her. You see, her father had written to her as part of the project, and like most parents, it was the only time he had ever shared his feelings in writing to her. She wanted to have it in Texas, as she knew his time was short.

Words can be powerful. Words matter. Written words are permanent and can be powerful and a source of comfort like in this situation. It may sound cliché, but it is never too late to let important persons in your life know how much they are loved and appreciated. I have had several persons who participated in this exercise let me know years later—like the Mark Eklund story—that they have gone back and read what others wrote to them!

The second project—Let It Shine—is something I came up with in 2017, but it was born out of a real tragedy that happened in September 2013. Earlier I shared a story about one of Emily Wong's performances in March 2014 (her senior year) with the University of Nebraska women's gymnastics team. This will significantly add to her story and give it another powerful example. Her father was a quiet, calm, and wise man as well as a steady presence with his loud, booming voice at all of Emily's meets. John had a stroke that he succumbed to shortly thereafter, and it rocked Emily's world to the point that she even briefly thought of quitting the sport. However, in part due to her faith, she was able to regain her zest for life and gymnastics, but there was still an obvious void without her father's presence. It was noticeable more than ever at her first meet of the season. Her boyfriend (now husband) had texted her the night before, "Let your light shine for him," and it was able to provide her with some comfort. As the year progressed, Emily said, "I think just with each performance, I do it to glorify God and my dad. I just feel like I'm trying to show His presence through myself, and I feel as though when I perform, that's what I'm doing." *The Daily Nebraskan* did a story on April 16, 2014, about Emily's loss and her journey that season with her team.

The night before they competed at the national championships, I had the team go around the room and talk about who they could "let it shine" for the next day—keeping the spirit of John in mind—to take pressure off the outcome by thinking about whom they appreciated and who had made a positive impact on them. When teams experience an adversity like this, they often find themselves on a deeper mission. I think it was true of this team, as it brought them closer while finding ways to support Emily and her family. The next day, as you may remember, they rocked it, pulled the upset, and advanced to the Super Six Finals at the National Championships.

Move forward to March 2017. The women's gymnastics team was feeling some additional pressure since they were the host site of the regional tournament with the top two teams advancing to the national championships. Some gymnasts were focusing more on the outcome and acknowledged that their performances often defined how they felt about themselves as well. The team was given the assignment to identify one or more persons in their life they were going to dedicate or "let it shine" for at regionals no matter their role. The next step was for each person to write a letter to the person(s) they chose, telling them why they were picked to let it shine for and letting them know how much they were appreciated.

The last part of the exercise was that each member of the team went around the room the night before regionals and shared whom they picked and why. It's a powerful way to practice being vulnerable and to learn about each other at a deeper level. That night I also had Emily Wong come speak to the team to share some thoughts and to tell them about her journey. It was an emotional and memorable night. The next day they advanced to the National Championships, and the team maxed out when it mattered the most, getting the highest score in NCAA history for a team not making it to the Super Six championships. But make no mistake—they left it all out there, and there wasn't anything else they could have done, and that's all you can ask of a team.

A very interesting thing happened in the fall of 2018 when getting ready to do this exercise with the Creighton women's volleyball team. Jaali Winters expressed some apprehension about dedicating the season, in this case to a grandparent. She was concerned that if she played poorly at any point, she would be letting her grandfather down—perfectionists tend to feel this way. I was so glad that she was open about her feelings (and you know that others have felt the same as she did) since it gave us a chance to really talk as a team about what it meant to let it shine. The first thing I thought would best illustrate my perspective was my favorite quote by the head coach in the *Friday Night Lights* movie, from his locker-room speech at the state championship.

> *Being perfect is not about that scoreboard out there. It's not about winning. It's about you and your relationship with yourself, your family, and your friends. Being perfect is about being able to look your friends in the eye and know that you didn't let them down because you told*

*them the truth. And that truth is you did everything you could. There wasn't one more thing you could've done. Can you live in that moment as best you can, with clear eyes and love in your heart, with joy in your heart? If you can do that, ladies—you're perfect!*

I wanted them to know that "letting it shine" for others is about doing everything in your power to prepare to put yourself and your team in a position to max out when it matters the most. It doesn't mean that you'll play well all the time. In fact, you may play poorly, and that's just reality sometimes in sport. It means that you do what you said you were going to do so that you can look your coaches and team-mates in the eye. It's about having a *commitment* mindset—being all in with all four legs of the high-performance stool: physical, mental, technical, and tactical. With that assurance, as you would expect, the team knocked it out of the park with this exercise.

The twist to the 2018 exercise, for both the Creighton volleyball team and the Nebraska gymnastics team, was to write to someone in a supportive role within the Athletic Department as well as to the others they had chosen. In the Creighton case, about a quarter of the ladies wrote to the custodian who was responsible for keeping their gym so clean. What a great lesson—that everybody has a role, and when you do it well, it is so cool when it is acknowledged. The letters to him were very powerful and impacted him in a profound way. Similarly, several of the gymnasts wrote to Ruth, known as "the sand-wich lady to the Huskers," who was famous for knowing the names of all six hundred–plus student-athletes. Also, for those who ordered sandwiches, she knew what they liked from memory. She was so moved by the letters that she insisted on giving each student-athlete a handwritten letter in return. I loved that the ladies chose people who are not in the spotlight and rarely get recognition for the work they do and took the opportunity to tell them how much they were appreciated.

# EXERCISES

## APPRECIATION/ GRATITUDE EXERCISE

Choose from one of three exercises to do for yourself or with your team:

- Do the Power of Appreciation exercise.

- Do the Let It Shine exercise.

- Identify one person you are grateful for, and write a letter telling that person why you feel this way about him or her.

# 7

# THE POWER OF VULNERABILITY

VULNERABILITY IS THE PATHWAY to meaningful connections and powerful teamwork.

Learning about the importance of being vulnerable and then getting good at being vulnerable is something I may spend more energy on than anything else when working with high-performing individuals and teams. You see, vulnerability is the only way to truly build deeper relationships—and if a team or organization wants to advance to what I call **"ultimate trust,"** building these relationships is a must. Brené Brown, an expert on vulnerability, did a TED Talk in 2011 called "The Power of Vulnerability" and followed that up with a book entitled *Daring Greatly*. She fundamentally changed my view on what it means to be vulnerable and why it is so important for overall well-being. I feel so strongly about her work in this arena that she will be quoted several times.

*Vulnerability* is defined as "uncertainty, risk, and emotional exposure," and it's about allowing oneself to truly be seen by others. We are often taught in Western society to hide our emotions or even run from them—to numb them with all types of things such as alcohol, pills, or food, to name a few. As Brené Brown pointed out, when humans numb their feelings, they also numb feelings such as joy, gratitude, and happiness. Brown also said, **"Vulnerability is the birthplace of connection and the path to the feeling of worthiness. Vulnerability is the birthplace of love, belonging, joy, courage, empathy, and creativity."**

And yes, it takes courage to allow yourself to be vulnerable to others, as you may worry that you won't be liked or accepted after some inner thoughts or fears are revealed—but by doing so, you can get in touch with your authentic self, giving you the best chance to live a fulfilling and happy life. The goal is to get to the place where you believe "what makes you vulnerable makes you beautiful."

The most common example that most can relate to is the emotional risk that one takes when getting into a relationship. Do you know for certain that they will love you back? That they will never leave you? As Brené Brown says, **"To love is to be vulnerable, to give someone your heart and say, 'I know this could hurt so bad, but I'm willing to do it; I'm willing to be vulnerable and love you.'"**

Practicing vulnerability with another person, group, or team does sometimes require a leap of faith. How much time a group or team has already spent together and how much trust has already been built determines where to start. For many teams—since they form anew each year with people leaving or graduating and others coming on board—I like to start with an exercise called the "The Story of Me" that is a relatively safe way to begin opening up a bit to one's group or team. It is broken up into two parts: "Journey" and

"Insight." It is designed to start learning surface information in the journey portion and then to go just a bit deeper in the insight portion. Everybody on the team fills out the questionnaire like the one that follows. I will usually put a booklet together for everyone on the team to read, and the team will also share face to face with each other in a team meeting. We have even played Jeopardy-type games where this information is used for all the questions.

While the journey information is important to know, it is the insight questions that get others in your group or team to start to understand how everyone thinks and ticks. Some of the best vulnerability exercises I use with teams take a deeper dive into areas, like the song picked in the insight portion.

# QUESTIONNAIRE

## JOURNEY

- Name?

- Where did you grow up?

- Parents? Where did they go to school? Parents' occupations?

- Brothers and/or sisters? Ages? Where they currently go or went to school?

- Is there anyone else in your life that you would like to tell us about who could be attending some matches this year?

- What made you get into volleyball?

- Where did you play club volleyball?

- Why did you pick Creighton University?

- What have you learned since you've come to school, and how are you different from when you first arrived at Creighton? (Freshmen— answer the best you can!)

# INSIGHT

- Tell us one thing you wish your team knew about you.

- Tell us about one person in your life whom you are grateful for and why.

- What is the one quote that would help us understand you better?

- What is your WHY (your reason and motivation for what you do)?

- Identify and tell us about a song meaningful to you that meets the following criteria:

  ⇒ Lyrics that have a special meaning to you
  ⇒ A song that you believe will still be meaningful to you in five to ten years
  ⇒ A song that will help the rest of the team understand you just a little bit better

- Name and describe a movie scene of your choice that describes or gives us better insight into you. Please provide a link, if possible, to this scene.

**Note:** Be prepared to elaborate on your quote, song, and movie clip later during the season.

While one may think that practicing vulnerability and building deeper relationships are important in one's personal life and with athletic teams, they are just as important in the workplace. It isn't critical just for coaches to show vulnerability; managers and bosses need to do so, as well—really, anybody in a leadership position. With positional authority comes the risk that those you lead don't see you as human but rather just as the person who has control over their life. Leaders often hold back, showing toughness with a lack of emotion and missing out on the genuine connection that vulnerability creates to avoid being seen as weak. On the contrary, being able to reveal your true self is actually an act of courage that allows for connections to be made with those you lead, fostering trust. Being vulnerable as a leader can be as simple as being aware of your emotions and acknowledging that they don't all need to be buried in the work setting. It can be about letting others know that you also have insecurities, as this allows a leader to be seen as human. It can be admitting you don't have all the answers. As Coach Cook says, "The longer I coach, the less I know."

Leaders can show vulnerability by being compassionate. This can be done by helping somebody out who may have an unfortunate situation in his or her personal life or simply by showing gratitude for the extra work someone has put in for you. Vulnerability allows a group at work to develop into a caring and engaged team, but it has to start at the top. For when we delve into psychological safety, the term I identified earlier that allows for an environment in which members of a team feel safe to be their own true self, it is the leader who permits this to happen. Innovation and creativity will only happen in this type of environment. As Brené Brown says, "No vulnerability, no creativity. No tolerance for failure, no innovation. If you're not willing to fail, you can't innovate. If you're not willing to build a vulnerable culture, you can't create." This is the genesis of how great teams are formed and made.

In order to get individuals on a team to buy into these vulnerability exercises, give their best effort, and feel safe to share, the "why" behind doing these things and the ground rules are laid out. For example, whatever is discussed in the room stays in the room, and people only have to share what they feel comfortable sharing. Some will naturally go deeper than others; some will be more guarded and not open up as much. They just need to know that the outcome goal is to understand each other a bit better after completing the exercise together. To quote Brené Brown again:

> *Vulnerability is based on mutuality and requires boundaries and trust. It's not oversharing, it's not purging, it's not indiscriminate disclosure, and it's not celebrity-style social media information dumps. Vulnerability is about sharing our feelings and our experiences with people who have earned the right to hear them. Being vulnerable and open is mutual and an integral part of the trust-building process.*

One of my favorite exercises with teams is in the insight portion of the "The Story of Me," and that is to select a song that has lyrics special to each of them. I ask them to think about a song that is not a fad song, but one that is most likely to still be meaningful for years to come. There is something about a song that can bring out deep emotions in humans. Songs activate the right side of our brains, and it is in part why certain songs take us right back to situations in our lives that are attached to certain intense emotions—first love, break-ups, the birth of a child, and so on. Similarly, it is why most of us know where we were on 9/11 when the airplanes hit the towers in New York but have no idea what we did on any other day around that same time. So whenever one can engage the brain in this way, in this case through song, there is a better likelihood of sharing thoughts, feelings, and emotions attached to that song—leading to a better chance to practice being vulnerable.

It is human nature to think that a group of high-achieving student-athletes—sometimes on full scholarship—have relatively few life problems, that life has always come so easy for them. I have learned to have a great appreciation for the struggles that so many have, no matter how "perfect" they may look to the outside world. It is made even clearer after the completion of this exercise with teams—and I mean every single time. Most of you have heard some version of this quote: "You never know what people are going through, and sometimes the people with the biggest smiles are struggling the most, so be kind." This quote takes me directly back to the time that this exercise was the most powerful from my observation. As you will see, it is somewhat emotional, as it involved Emily Wong and her 2014 gymnastics team that advanced to the Super Six National Championships. One thing that I will never forget is Emily's smile—and her infectious laugh. In fact, in my mind I can still hear her laughing as she sat with her teammates at dinners the night before meets. She was very well liked by her teammates, but I do think there was a feeling at times, because of her personality, her constant smile, and her overall performance as a student-athlete, that life must be and always had been easy for her.

I usually like to introduce these exercises shortly after the team forms to start the process of building deeper relationships and trust, so this exercise occurred in early September 2013, a few months before the team started actually competing in January 2014. You never know how deep each person on the team is willing to go, and that was certainly true for Emily, who generally kept things on the surface like many persons her age. For the song exercises, we would go around the room one at a time, play the song for everybody to hear (often people would sing along), and then that person would tell us why she picked that song. Remember that the goal was to understand that person just a bit better, at a deeper level. While I don't remember the song, Emily shared with everyone a struggle that had affected her in a very deep way. I won't share the contents, but it was intense and emotional, and by the end, the perfect bubble some had imagined she lived in was popped. Emily showed her vulnerability, and everyone was better off for it. She was understood in a different and important way. Deeper connections were made—and if it was possible, she was respected even more. Emily set the tone that day for what I remember to be the most vulnerable a group has ever been in this setting. It was shortly thereafter that Emily's father passed away. I believe that her willingness to allow herself to be seen in a different way just a few weeks earlier brought her team closer together, allowing them to help her through what was about to be the most difficult time of her life.

Besides the song exercise, the one I like the best and have done the most often is some version of "Hero, Highlight, and Hardship."

I first read about it, I believe, from a UCLA women's coach. In this exercise, the goal is to share with everybody else a hero they have, one life highlight, and one hardship that they've been through. Similar to the song exercise, it can be highly emotional and revealing. There are three opportunities in this case, as with the other exercises, to get to know each other a bit better. Depending on the person, it may be easier to be more vulnerable when discussing a hero than a hardship. I can say from experience that this can be an emotionally draining exercise by the time everyone has told their stories. And remember, I always ask the coaches and sometimes key support staff to participate.

The best example of this exercise being done was the 2016 Creighton women's volleyball team, who was coming off their first Sweet 16 appearance in school history. There was excitement and pressure, as a new team was being formed after the loss of several great seniors—Ashley Jansen, Kate Elman, Melanie Jereb, and Lizzy Stivers—and the entrance of some exciting new additions, including Brittany Witt, who went on to be a four-year starter at libero and third-team All-American! On that day we focused just on hardships, and similar to most teams, some were very good at sharing and taking the risk to be vulnerable, while others were less willing to go deep. What sticks out to me that day was the beginning of real growth for Jaali Winters and many others as it related to expressing their vulnerability.

Jaali's teammate Samantha Bohnet was an incoming sophomore who was about to play a bigger role on the team. Samantha was one of the first to speak and share her thoughts—not particularly revealing, but she appeared to accomplish her task in a comfortable manner. At the end of the exercise, I asked if anybody had any other thoughts. Samantha spoke up, saying that she had more to share with the team after listening to so many others take the risk to be more vulnerable. This time it was something deeper and much more important to her at that moment in time: Samantha had recently been the victim of a sexual abuse experience. It was powerful for all parties, and it explained the behaviors of being more distant, distracted, and sad that the team and coaches had been noticing for several days. I asked Samantha during the writing of this book to reflect back on that day. Here is what she told me:

> Once I opened up to the team and coaching staff that day, I decided to tell my family. If I never would have decided to speak up again after already sharing that day, I never would have received the help from internal and external resources that Creighton and specifically Coach Booth and our trainer Casey Northcraft [now Casey Grams] had worked really hard for me to get! The amount of patience and grace they showed me in a time of healing and wavering mental health was incredible. I never truly understood how much mental health matters when competing at that level, so them investing into that once I decided to be vulnerable probably kept me in the sport, to be completely honest. Without that support I would have crashed and burned that year. They kept my head above water.

The stories that Emily and Samantha shared were the most powerful that I've heard in all my years of doing exercises like this. Fast forward: the season was a memorable one on and off the court. Creighton made a run to the Elite Eight in the NCAA tournament, a feat thought impossible just years earlier. Yet you always wonder if the lessons you hoped to impart were internalized. How much growth is actually occurring in their lives both in and out of sport? And then you see the social media post on Instagram on December 11, 2016, right after the completion of the season by Jaali! I will let her words do the talking, but I think you can appreciate the deep satisfaction someone lucky enough to be in my role must feel after reading this:

> Anyone who knows me knows that I am absolutely awful at being vulnerable (but that I'm working on it). And I now realize that playing at the highest level of Division I volleyball, I put myself in the ultimate position to be at my most vulnerable every time I step out on the court. Being able to experience the extreme highs of this sport is incredible, but it comes with no shortage of devastating lows. It's just part of the game. Find a way to deal with it, and keep moving forward. I'm not yet the player that I want to be, but I am a few steps closer. I had two really big goals for the season: (1) to put my teammates first at all times and forget about myself, and (2) to allow myself to be human. Both goals were very hard for me for different reasons. The first goal was hard because I have always worried about my own growth as a player more than my teammates'. I understood the "we before me" mentality, but I had never fully given into this idea until this year. It wasn't that I was selfish or mean; I was just too focused on self-growth and hadn't realized the power that I have to make those around me better. By default, putting everyone else before me has made me grow as a player more than ever before. I highly rec-

ommend this strategy. As for the second goal, allowing myself to be human, it really just means that I allow myself to make mistakes. Over the years, I have gotten into an awful habit of thinking I am some superhuman who has to be perfect all the time; I knew I would come up disappointed each and every time if I continued with this mindset. I was expecting the impossible from myself ... I am human, and I will never be perfect—and that is okay! Make a mistake; move on; do better next time. Being vulnerable sucks, and most of the time I hate it (even just posting something as raw as this makes me cringe), but vulnerability is necessary for growth ...

There was power in Jaali's words, and she committed to practicing the vulnerability necessary to share that openly. You can decide what role her growth played in her team performing as never before. Vulnerability is the key ingredient, in my opinion, for the development of deeper relationships, which in turn are necessary for growth and trust to develop—whether it is a connection with one other person, a group, or a team. You now have a chance to max out when it matters the most.

# EXERCISES

## VULNERABILITY EXERCISE

- Watch the TED Talk called "The Power of Vulnerability" by Brené Brown. If you are a member of a team, have a discussion about what you've learned.

- Select a vulnerability exercise to do as a team:

  ⇒ Hero, Highlight, and Hardship
  ⇒ Meaningful Song
  ⇒ Meaningful Movie Scene
  ⇒ Let It Shine
  ⇒ Defining Moment in Your Life
  ⇒ Adversity in Your Life

The goal of the exercise is to practice vulnerability and know each other at a deeper level than before.

# PART III

# MAX OUT
# YOUR TEAM

# 8

## THE POWER OF POSITIVE TEAMS

ANYTIME TWO OR MORE people come together to collaborate on something more than just themselves, it is considered a team. While stating the obvious, there are plenty of underperforming, average, and outstanding teams in business, sport, the military, and life. Of course, there is a lot of interest in trying to understand the magic ingredients that lead to making a great team. Many who have been on a team that has maxed out try to recreate the feelings they had during that experience for the rest of their lives. I simply ask teams to put themselves in a position to max out when it matters the most. No regrets. It doesn't mean they always get the final outcome desired, but that team knows they left no stone unturned. It means that they can look each other in the eye and that each team member knows there was nothing else they could have done. I want to share with you what I've learned from research and observations that will help your group or team max out when it matters the most.

Let's start off with some recent studies done by Google, MIT, and EcSell Institute. In 2012 Google embarked on an initiative to help their organization understand the secrets to team effectiveness—in other words, what makes teams great. Google gathered several of their best and brightest statisticians, organizational psychologists, sociologists, and engineers to help the cause. Interestingly, before the study, they also had a hypothesis that you could build the best teams just by compiling the best people—the perfect team, if you will. Julia Rozovsky, Google's people analytics manager, summed it up succinctly: "We were dead wrong." I had observed this same thing retrospectively in both the business and sport worlds.

In 1994 a group of "superstars" formed a company called Long-Term Capital Management. These superstars included the former head of bond trading at Salomon Brothers, a Nobel prize–winning economist, and the vice-chairman of the Federal Reserve, to name a few. A can't-miss "perfect team." In 1998 they initially had remarkable returns, but due to arrogance and taking outsized risks, they lost $4.6 billion in less than four months, in part due to the financial crises in Asia and Russia. Their master hedge fund, Long-Term Capital Portfolio, collapsed in the late 1990s and had to be bailed out by the US government because our government feared a worldwide financial crisis as a result of the collapse. If interested, the book *When Genius Failed* is worth the read.

In 2014 Penn State was just coming off winning its sixth national championship in eight years in the sport of volleyball. It was said that their incoming 2014 class was the best in NCAA history. They had three of the top ten and five of the top fifteen players in the class. It was loaded with Under Armour high school All-Americans and Gatorade Players of the Year. While I am not privy to the factors that led to their underperformance, I do know that class went 0–7 against the University of Nebraska from 2015–2017 and did not win a championship.

Google proceeded to study 180 teams over a two-year period and analyzed the data after conducting more than two hundred interviews and examining more than 250 team attributes. There were still no definitive answers as to what made a team successful—until Google started studying the intangibles. A *New York Times* article revealed that "they kept coming back to what was referred to as 'group norms'—the 'traditions, behavioral standards, and unwritten rules that govern how teams function when they gather . . . Norms can be unspoken or openly acknowledged, but their influence is often profound.'" Google determined it was these group norms that helped magnify the collective intelligence of the group, which are the abilities that emerge out of collaboration. In simpler terms, "The whole can be greater than the sum of its parts."

Here is what Google learned about what ingredients are crucial to create the best teams:

## DEPENDABILITY

Simply, team members get things done on time, and they meet expectations. In other words, they just do their job.

## STRUCTURE AND CLARITY

Team members have clear, well-defined roles within the group as well as clear goals.

## MEANING

The work has personal significance for each team member.

## IMPACT

Team members think their work matters, which positively impacts the greater good.

## PSYCHOLOGICAL SAFETY

Team members feel safe to take risks and be vulnerable in front of each other.

***Google learned that psychological safety was the one ingredient that stood out from the rest—by a far margin!***

Most of us have been in situations when we worried about feeling incompetent or where either the leader or somebody else in the group would react to our commentary. We may have held back from asking a question or sharing an idea. In fact, most people never forget if they were humiliated or embarrassed in front of other people by an insensitive boss or team member. Similarly, those who have ever been in an environment where they felt safe to voice opinions and ask judgment-free questions (a culture where everyone felt safe to let down their guard), experienced psychological safety. It is the responsibility of the coach/ boss and key team members/captains to create these safe zones. In these environments, the building of trust—even ultimate trust, which is another of level of trust between all parties—can take place.

Another way of looking at this is to understand what happens when opposite feelings exist: those of psychological danger. In these settings there is often a fear of admitting mistakes. Group members tend to blame one another. There is less likelihood of sharing differing views. Conversely, when one feels psychologically safe, there is a comfort in admitting mistakes—and a key feature is willingness to learn from failure. All of these things lead to better innovation and decision-making.

In 2010 MIT studied the performances of groups, looking for the common ingredients that make up the best teams. In the research setting they put together teams to complete all types of hard problems, and one of their conclusions was very similar to Google's: "Having a bunch of smart people in a group doesn't necessarily make the group smart," says Thomas Malone, one of the authors of the study.

In 2015 entrepreneur and author Margaret Heffernan did a TED Talk called "Why It's Time to Forget the Pecking Order at Work." She called attention to a study by Purdue biologist William Muir, who was studying the productivity of chickens, with two groups central to the experiment. He chose a flock of chickens, average in their productivity (measured by egg count) and left the group to itself for six generations. He compared this average group to a group of "super chickens"—the highest-producing chickens were put together into a flock for six generations as well, with their superstars leading the breeding. The super chickens certainly had to be the more productive of the two groups? Not so fast! The end study found the average-chicken group was plump, healthy, and had an increased level of output versus the first generation. Among the super-chicken group, only three were left alive. *All of the others had been pecked to death.* It turned out that the superstar chickens reached such status by suppressing the other chickens. So what did the MIT study find that separated out the best teams from the rest? There were three things:

## 1  EVIDENCED A HIGH DEGREE OF SOCIAL SENSITIVITY TO EACH OTHER

What we are talking about here is a higher degree of emotional intelligence. Emotional intelligence has to do with such things as a person's ability to recognize, understand, and manage his or her own emotions and the emotions of others and to be able to handle interpersonal relationships empathetically. Do you pay attention to others, and can you tell if something is bothering them? Individuals in the highest-performing groups were more tuned in to one another and to the subtle shifts in others' moods and demeanor. They scored more highly on a test called "Reading the Mind in the Eyes," which is broadly considered a test for empathy. These groups were socially alert to one another's needs.

## 2  GAVE ROUGHLY EQUAL TIME TO EACH OTHER

MIT found that in the best groups, there were no superstars and no slackers. In a given task, a person who had expertise in that area may take the lead. Overall, however, the group all fully participated in helping the team solve the problems and complete the various tasks. Equal participation requires that each member of the group feels psychologically safe.

## 3  HAD MORE WOMEN IN THE GROUP

It appears that this has to do with a doubling-down effect of the first point, meaning women are more likely to have a higher degree of social sensitivity than men. In the end, the groups with more women had elevated levels of collective intelligence, which is a shared or group intelligence that emerges from the collaboration, collective efforts, and competition of many individuals and appears in consensus decision-making.

There were two themes that really stood out also: social capital and helpfulness. I like Margaret's definitions for both of them. Think about the interconnection between psychological safety and both of these themes.

- **Social Capital is the trust, knowledge, reciprocity, and shared norms that create quality of life and make a group resilient.** In any company you can have a brilliant bunch of individuals—but what prompts them to share ideas and concerns, contribute to one another's thinking, and warn the group early on about potential risks is their connection to one another? Social capital lies at the heart of just cultures; it is what they depend on—and it is what they generate. Building social capital makes organizations more productive and creative, because high levels of trust create a climate of safety and honesty. That makes companies more efficient and profitable too. How? By making it easier to ask for help.

- **Helpfulness** may sound like a rather anemic quality, but studies of teams across industries as varied as paper mills, banks, pharmaceuticals, and retail all demonstrate that the helpfulness of a group has a direct impact on profits, costs, productivity, and efficiency. Helpful teams of people accelerate the sharing of knowledge and expertise; they don't let one another stay stuck or confused; they try to prevent problems before they arise, and they won't let colleagues become isolated or cut off. Social capital compounds even as we spend it. The longer groups work together, the more social capital they accrue and the more these benefits grow. Trust, helpfulness, practice, and courage become the simple renewables that power our working lives.

These two themes, along with psychological safely, are completely intertwined, which leads to one of my favorite phrases that have come out of this research: **it's the mortar, not the bricks.**

It's the mortar, not just the bricks, that makes a building robust. The mortar in this context is social capital: mutual reliance, an underlying sense of connectedness that builds trust. I was at a What Drives Winning conference in St. Louis a few years ago. The conference was put on by a phenomenal person, Brett Ledbetter, who works in the high-performance arena. He was talking with the Florida Gators softball coach, Tim Walton, who is one of the top coaches in his sport. He told us about an exercise he did with his team that I have since used in a similar fashion. Each lady was given a brick to put motivational words on and decorate. He had his team build a wall made out of all of the bricks. The coaches then came into the room and took a look at the project, then proceeded to push the wall over—much to the chagrin of the group! You see, the coach didn't give them any mortar, and without the mortar the wall was not stable and could be easily broken. They then were given the mortar (or I believe they actually learned how to make their own) and proceeded to build a wall that was sturdy and would hold up under stress. This new wall was a representation of what the team stood for and who they wanted to become. What a cool team exercise!

Now I want to tell you about a wonderful company, EcSell Institute, and specifically Bill Eckstrom, the CEO and founder who had given a TED Talk that went viral: "Why Comfort Will Ruin Your Life."

Bill also coauthored the book *The Coaching Effect* with Sarah Wirth, who is the president of EcSell. Their vision is "a world where everyone knows what great coaching feels like." Their mission is "to help leaders elevate their coaching effectiveness in order to drive more performance from their team." Performance Mountain has also partnered with them with something we call EcSell Sports to provide an assessment tool and feedback to coaches as well as learning opportunities with the goal of improving the student-athlete experience.

One of the things EcSell has done really well is to document, study, and provide the research on more than a hundred thousand coaching interactions and then use this information to educate, train, and provide systems to help organizations build world-class coaching teams. We just discussed the role that social sensitivity plays in growing great teams, and there are a couple of questions that fascinated me (but didn't surprise me). The questions were answered differently by those being led when compared to the top 20 percent of sales manager performers (coaches) versus the bottom 80 percent of sales manager performers (coaches):

## DOES YOUR MANAGER KNOW WHEN SOMETHING IS BOTHERING YOU?

A full 93 percent of the top sales managers knew when something was bothering someone they led versus only 52 percent of the rest of the managers.

# DOES YOUR MANAGER CARE MORE ABOUT THE NUMBERS THAN THE PEOPLE ON THE TEAM?

Only 7 percent of the top sales managers cared more about numbers than their people versus 36 percent of the rest of the managers.

These questions have nothing to do with the technical or tactical aspects of your craft. The best managers simply had better social sensitivity and cared more about those they lead. According to Gallup, more than 70 percent of bosses do not have the talent to maximize the performance of their team; when looking specifically at sales bosses, EcSell Institute research shows the bottom 80 percent deliver an average of $4.1 million less per team when compared to the top 20 percent of bosses. Wow! Just like in sport, relationship building is absolutely critical and may be the most important variable in building successful business teams.

In the end, the bottom line is that **"they don't care how much you know until they know how much you care."**

From experience, observation, and research, I have identified several common ingredients of championship teams. You may notice that there is tremendous overlap with what Jeff Janssen has found as well in his years of working with high-performing teams. Here is my take:

## 1 COMMUNICATION

The best teams learn the value of communication, both verbal and nonverbal, on and off the playing field. It is important to recognize that women and men handle communication from others a bit differently. Women tend to value *how* it is said rather than *what* is said, meaning if the tone is loud or angry, they may tune out what you're actually trying to get across. I've learned in working with men over the years that they care about this more than most people realize. I have worked with many tough, strong men who have been broken down psychologically by the way their coaches communicate with them. Coach John Cook called me years ago about an athlete who had broken down emotionally after set two, after he had gotten on the team in the locker room and specifically called her out with regard to her performance. He told me that it took him by surprise how hard she took what he said. Others who were there said, "Coach was just getting our attention and holding us accountable." He wasn't being abusive at all, but he did raise his voice, which he rarely did, and this athlete took his *how* differently from the rest of the team. Why was that? He didn't know it at the time, but through my exploration I found out that she had a male parent figure in her life who had a history of being verbally abusive, and when Coach raised his voice, she heard the voice of her abuser. This was very important information for Coach to know, and he committed to communicating differently with her forever going forward.

It was also a good reminder that *how* we communicate is critical if we want to get our point across. There are so many different ways to communicate today that can get in the way of being effective. I am old school, so I always prefer face-to-face communication (the next best thing is hearing each other's voice on the phone or FaceTime versus all of the other formats), especially when resolving conflict. Jack Riggins teaches P2P (person-to-person) communication strategies, and like many things that seem so simple, it is harder to do today than ever before.

## 2 RESOLVING CONFLICT

Handling conflict is the number one issue among women's teams, meaning it is the top barrier to maxing out if the team doesn't do this well. Talking behind one's back is often what causes a conflict to escalate with women. For men's teams, what often gets them in trouble in resolving conflict is that they are more prone to having their fight-or-flight system activate. When this occurs, men often lose that "space" to decide how to best handle the conflict and are likely to get into a verbal or physical altercation. It's one of many reasons that a strategy to diminish the fight-or-flight response when under stress is critical to high performance with individuals or teams. On the positive, men are much more likely to fight it out and then forgive and forget. Women are more likely to hold a grudge and stew about issues.

Recommendations are fairly simple in regard to how resolve conflict:

- When resolving conflict, if at all possible, do it face-to-face with the person(s) involved. At all costs, avoid texting, email, or forms of social media, as one misses out on the emotional content of the communication. This often leads to misreading intent, and escalation of a conflict is a possible outcome.
- Do not go to other people on the team to tell your version of the dispute. This can often lead to gossip and worsening of the conflict.
- There may need to be a "cooling-off" period and time to think about how one wants to respond to a conflict, especially if someone has done something particularly hurtful. That being said, it is a good idea to resolve the conflict within twenty-four hours or, even better, before going to bed at night.

An example that comes to mind involved issues with communication and conflict resolution in equal parts. It was in 2010 between Coach Ron Brown, at the time tight ends coach at the University of Nebraska, and tight end Kyler Reed. There were a couple of unique solutions that I would like to share.

Kyler was dealing with a nagging knee injury and didn't feel like he was living up to his nickname, "Speed," at that time. Since he got his confidence from his speed, his mindset and practice performance were suffering. Coach Brown thought that Kyler seemed to "shut down" at times during challenging interactions or conflict. They were not always on the same page about solutions. After some exploration, it was clear that both sides needed to own their part in the communication breakdowns and that individual wiring and prior life experiences played a role in how they communicated with each other. For a period of time, they spent a few minutes after every practice for an "airing-out session" to make sure they were on the same page and that nothing was left unsaid.

When I told Coach about the notion that Kyler thought he was known only for his speed, Coach was astonished, telling me that Kyler was one of the more powerful players in the room. We came up with a plan for Coach and others on the team to start calling him "Power" to help change his mindset and to have Kyler start believing this as well. Coach changed the way he communicated with Kyler, especially in stressful situations. Kyler worked hard to get stronger and improve his blocking technique. He saw himself as more powerful and quicker, the latter especially as his injury healed. His performances and confidence soared. He became a mismatch problem for any defense. I credit both Coach Brown and Kyler for working on communication and resolving conflict in a positive manner. In the end, they developed a healthy relationship that allowed Kyler to feel like he could share anything on his mind with Coach Brown and vice versa.

## 3  SHARING COMMON GOALS

Goal setting for teams can take on a number of forms, anywhere from setting the big end-outcome-type goals to the goals that focus on the many aspects of being a student-athlete, including team GPA or life-skills participation activities. One of the advantages teams have when they share common goals is that they can handle conflict better by taking it back to the agreed-upon team goals. For example, if the team commits to getting eight hours of sleep per night during the season and a team member identifies that somebody is on social media at two in the morning and has eight o'clock practice, it is much easier to confront that person with a reminder of what the team agreed upon regarding sleep.

When a team has a focused mission, the motivation to train hard in the off-season and fight through any adversity can be stronger than in other years, often because of a disappointing end to the prior season or a life setback involving the team or a team member. Team goals can take the form of team values, or what the team wants to be known for. I like to do a team exercise in which we identify all of the possible team values and then narrow them down to their top four if possible.

During the eight years I worked with Creighton Volleyball, the 2019 season was the first time they didn't set outcome goals, such as winning the Big East Championship or advancing in the NCAA tournament. On their own they identified a few values, what they wanted to stand for:

- They wanted to be known as a great practice team every single day.
- They didn't want any comparisons to past teams. Focus only on this team's strengths and getting better each day.
- They wanted to have a feeling of equality among all the teammates. No superstars, no upperclassmen/underclassmen divide.
- They wanted a culture of team helpfulness—meaning if you've already won the starting spot or are competing for that spot, you will be equally helpful to those in your position group by helping them get better.

I call this a second scoreboard: something that you can measure as a team on how well you're doing, separate from the win/loss record at that moment in time. I ask teams to choose values—or what they stand for—that are meaningful to them and that, if done well, will put the team in a position to max out when it matters the most. The team eventually came up with one more mantra during the season, as they recognized that they needed to do two other things well in every match: **"fun and focused"** was their cue that they performed at their best when they did both of these well in practice, pregame, and during the match itself. If you have ever watched a Creighton volleyball team play over the years, you have witnessed the fun and joy that most of their teams play with—and the love that they have for each other!

The Golden State Warriors have done the best job of any professional team by coming up with clear team values—in this case they call them **the Golden State of Mind.** Coach Steve Kerr has set the tone for his team, and it is reflected in their values. Keep in mind that this is a group of macho, tough men. The four values that they choose to embrace are as follows:

- Joy
- Compassion
- Competition
- Mindfulness

What I loved most about the Warriors over the past five years—and it isn't the three NBA Championships—was that the team lived these values on and off the court. In interviews, right after games, individuals would talk about how these values impacted their performances. In the end, the team fully believed that if they lived these four values well, the outcome of the game would take care of itself.

The New England Patriots team—arguably the most successful franchise in professional sports—also has four values. And I know they live by them, because when Danny Woodhead, former NFL player who played a few years for the Patriots, joined Performance Mountain in the fall of 2019, one of the first things he told me was that New England's culture was different because of their adherence to core values. Danny said that at New England, the number one thing you had to do was your job. Here are their four values:

- Do your job.
- Be attentive.
- Speak for yourself.
- Put the team first.

Some of the best team values come from the high school teams that I work with, and I always ask them this question: *If I am a newcomer to your gym or watching you play for the first time, how will I know if you're living your values?* A high school volleyball team in 2019 came up with the following: *relentless, united, strategic, and positive energy.*

So if positive energy is a top value, what will that look like to me as an observer? What will the bench players appear to be doing, and so on? It is important to define what each value means to the teams and review them periodically to make sure they continue to be key ingredients that, if done well, will put the team in a position to max out when it matters the most.

I will also challenge individual athletes and those in life to come up with their own core values. A CEO I work with who struggled with staying calm and composed in certain meetings and who also struggled with staying focused, came up with the following values: calm, present, trust. By focusing on these three values and using self-talk to remind himself of what is important to him, he will then be able to demonstrate the values to his team—then the outcome he wants will take care of itself.

And one of my favorite examples is from Carsen Edwards, an NBA rookie who had written this on his wristband: "Help Mama out, thank God, have fun, kill everything."

Having focused values helps the team align with their mission, as well. The example that gives me my best sports fan memory was the 1994 Nebraska football team. The year before, as big underdogs, the Huskers lost on the last play of the game to Florida State in the national championship game. That crushing last play (a missed field goal) fueled them in the off-season, giving birth to their new mission statement: *Unfinished Business.* They put 1:16 on the scoreboard every day at practice to remind them of how close they were to winning it all—one minute and sixteen seconds. During the 1990s the Nebraska team ran option football, a punishing type of football that required those on the team to value toughness and value being the strongest team in the fourth quarter. Sometimes it took time in the game to wear down the other defense and turn three-yard gains into six-yard gains. It required discipline and dedication to values even if results weren't immediately going well, trusting that there would be a payoff as the game wore on. Nebraska had a chance on January 1, 1995, to vanquish all the demons of the past several years (losing to teams from Florida) when it mattered the most.

Long story short, Nebraska dominated the fourth quarter on both sides of the ball and left the Miami Hurricane superstars Warren Sapp and Ray Lewis, and the rest of the defense, exhausted and defenseless. Living those values every day in practice and in the weight room, committing to their top value of being the strongest and most physical team, especially in the fourth quarter, combined with their mission statement, Unfinished Business, brought on by the prior year's close call, allowed them to max out when it mattered the most. If you ever get a chance, I encourage you to find a copy of the video *Finished Business* and watch the halftime talk that Coach Osborne gave the team to see just how prophetic he was in everything he said. It is cool for anybody studying high performance, but if you're a Husker fan, it will bring out some powerful emotions.

Finally—I've mentioned this team before—the 2014 Nebraska women's gymnastics team. The previous year was one of their best regular seasons in history, followed by a dominating victory at the Big Ten Championships. However, this year they got upset at regionals despite making a valiant comeback on the last event, the vault, scoring one of the top vault scores in school history. The team was devastated in not making it to the nationals. It was one of the toughest post-competition scenes that I've ever witnessed. That being said, there is no question it set the tone for the following year, when they pulled off a major upset to advance to the Super Six National Championships and achieved miraculous scores on the beam. This led to one of the happiest post-competition scenes I've ever been a part of.

Adversity, if used correctly, can be a powerful motivator, contributing to a team's coming together in ways they may never have before.

## 4  COMMITMENT

The interesting point I want to make about commitment is that it is also one of the ingredients of an individual's elite mindset. Thus, it has been discussed extensively in the chapter on mindset. First, one has to decide to be committed as an individual, and then the team has to collectively decide to commit as well. It can be as simple as making sure one is focused on the four legs of high performance. In the team setting, the challenge can be that if the team is in a slump or at risk for not reaching their goals, can the collective team still do what they said they were going to do, what they committed to doing as a team? As Willie Mays, a famous Major League Baseball player, once said, "It isn't hard to be good in sports. What is tough is being good every day." Can you be good every day when circumstances aren't going the team's way? Can you be good every day when a few members of the team didn't earn the role they wanted, which happens on virtually every team? Can the collective team continue working on getting better every practice, doing the right things on and off the court? Simply, can a team collectively commit to all four legs of elite performance—physical, mental, technical, and tactical?

## 5  EMBRACING YOUR ROLE

Honestly, this may be the most important ingredient of all: accepting your role and learning how to complement each other. Nick Saban, one of the most successful coaches in college football history, said with regard to his success, "I tell them it's so simple that you're not even going to write it down, and you're going to think I'm hiding something from you. It's this: everybody has a defined role and expectation, and you're held accountable to that. That's what it is to the nth degree. Your role is defined. You're going to have a very high expectation, and you will be held accountable." Bill Belichick, the most successful coach in NFL history, says it even more succinctly: "Do your job."

I had already seen many examples that supported this belief, but the team exercise I came up with for the 2015 University of Nebraska women's volleyball team validated it even more. One day, while observing spring practice that year, I asked Lindsay Peterson (a former player, winner of the 2000 National Championship and current director of operations), "How did your team do it? How did they win it all?" Her team had the same head coach, same pressures/ expectations, and the same demands of being student-athletes. She gave me her thoughts as to why her team was successful and found a way to max out in ways nobody imagined that year. I will elaborate more on this subject later in the book, but Coach Cook's teams had not made the Final Four since 2008, and one of my roles was to identify and help teams break down barriers that could prevent them from reaching their goals. I thought about his teams that had completely maxed out and about the 2000 and 2006 teams that had won it all. And I thought about the 2008 team that advanced to the Final Four in Omaha and took Penn State to five sets in a season in which Penn State had not lost a set all year! What I remember about the 2008 team was that most of them did not take off their jerseys that night—that's how much they didn't want that season to end! The exercise, the one I am most proud of, was the following:

- We had each athlete on the 2015 team interview two athletes from the 2000/2006/2008 teams on the phone or in person.

- The ladies were given a series of questions to ask in addition to anything they wanted to ask on their own.
- The goal of the exercise was to learn about all the factors that allowed those three teams to max out from the perspective of ladies who shared similar roles as current team members. For at least one of the interviews, we tried to match up a current player who was injured or redshirting, for example, with somebody who had a similar role on one of the prior teams. I remember the excitement of one of the freshmen who got assigned to call Jordan Larson, who was considered to be one of the best, if not *the* best, player in the world at the time!

After all of the interviews were completed, we got together, and each of the ladies shared who they talked to and what they learned about why those teams were able to max out. We also learned information we didn't anticipate that was just as helpful—why teams in the years around them failed to max out. For example, why did the 2001 team, who may have had more talent, fail to max out? Why did the 2007 team, who arguably was Coach Cook's most talented team on paper, fail to reach their goals? As an aside, it is interesting that Coach Tom Osborne had noted in prior interviews that, with the exception of the 1995 team, his most talented teams were not the teams that won the national championships, and vice versa. So what were the findings from the interviews with more than thirty-five former players? There were only two findings that stood out.

- The teams in 2000/2006/2008 completely embraced their roles. If players didn't get the role they wanted, they didn't sulk or complain. They were 100 percent committed to the roles they were given and did them to the best of their ability every day. That didn't mean that everybody was content with their role—certainly not the competitors. However, they learned what they needed to do better to get the role they wanted and continued to compete for that position. Interestingly, we learned that the teams in the years around them may not have always done this nearly as well.

- The teams in 2000/2006/2008 spent a lot of time building deeper relationships and learned to love one another. Some of the other teams around these years didn't invest in relationships to the same degree.

That's it! Learn to embrace your role, spend energy building deeper relationships, and love your team. Easy to say; hard to do!

One by one, over and over, we heard about the importance of role acceptance and loving your team. Most high performers will tell you that they are willing to do what's necessary to help the team—including embracing the role given to them—until they are given a role that they don't want. Ironically, just prior to and during the first month of the 2015 season, Coach Cook made a couple of major changes to the lineup. He moved Kadie Rolfzen from left-side hitter to the right side and Amber Rolfzen from right side to middle. For those who know volleyball, the move Kadie had to make was a big one from a mindset and emotional standpoint. The lessons learned from the exercise, done just a month earlier, contributed to the acceptance of changes in these roles by both of these ladies.

My favorite individual example of an athlete accepting her role was Jess Bird with the Creighton University volleyball team in 2016. She was a senior that year, had been a three-year starter as outside hitter, and had already won numerous conference awards during her career. She didn't do anything wrong; she just got beat out by a future

All-American, Taryn Kloth. It happens all the time in competitive endeavors, but that doesn't make it easy, especially for a senior. The way Jess handled the role change had everything to do with how the team did that year. She was respected so much by her teammates that she could have caused a rift within the team if she sulked or complained. I know she was a competitor, so it had to be very difficult on her emotionally, but you know what she did? She came to practice every day with the mindset to get better and make the team better. She was "team first" in every interview. She prepared and was ready to go when called upon, which happened several times that year. She helped others on the team have the same mindset about embracing their role.

In the first round of the NCAA tournament, Creighton was in a battle with Northern Iowa. They were in game five, up 13–12. Off the bench cold, with a stat line of zeroes across the board, Amanda Foje, a senior walk-on serving specialist from Omaha, Nebraska, came into the game. It is in these moments that you hope the preparation in practice was done at a high level while not knowing if she would ever get to play. Did she get her mind right to be able to handle pressure at a moment's notice? Did she put herself in a position to help the team max out when it mattered the most? If she put her first serve into the net or long, or played it safe and it became 13–13, the odds to win the match would change dramatically. Amanda proceeded to have a service ace to make it 14–12 and then had a brilliant serve that led to an overpass kill—and Creighton won 15–12!

Creighton went on to upset number one seed Kansas Jayhawks on the Jayhawks home court—and what I remember most about that match was Kenzie Crawford, another athlete who had a few role changes during her career, standing on the service line during an extended referee delay, just smiling and keeping the team relaxed, bringing that positive energy the team needed in that moment—something she did all year for the team. Creighton then beat Michigan to make their first Elite Eight—something thought to be impossible just years earlier. Ten years from now, twenty years from now, their people will be able to look at the record books and see that Creighton's first Elite Eight was in 2016. What I will always remember are the role players and the impact they had on that team!

I'll also remember how cohesive that team was, how much they loved each other. When Lydia Dimke, the awesome setter on that team, was interviewed and asked about what the team said to each other when they came together in the huddle between points, she stated, "Most of the time, we just told each other that we loved each other." To this day, that is the best response I've heard for what to say in the brief seconds between points in the huddle.

## 6 TEAM BONDING

Teams that put themselves in a position to max out in business or sport have to learn to respect each other and learn to care for each other. One doesn't have to be equal friends with everybody on the team. One does have to commit to getting to know teammates at a deeper level, just like we learned in the team exercise with the 2015 Nebraska volleyball team. As mentioned before, there is no way players can do this without committing to learn the backstory of their teammates, as this is the genesis of building the respect and trust across the workforce on the team. One of the mental skills that isn't traditionally talked about is having fun. This is something I ask every team to commit to working on, since having fun is a choice and it does not come naturally for every team, especially if the core of the team is wired to be more serious.

One of the athletic teams that I worked with naturally had more fun, and another had to "orchestrate" it. I would like to share the following: First, there were several University of Nebraska women's gymnastics teams that made a commitment to having fun, but the ones that stood out were the 2013 and 2014 teams. Several ladies contributed to this, but Desi Stephens was the ringleader. While waiting to warm up at meets, they were always juggling balls, playing hacky sack, singing, and dancing. I remember sitting in the front of the bus with Coach Kendig as we headed to the Big Ten Championships, and as if it were possible, the team was being louder and having more fun than ever. Desi had hijacked the bus microphone and intercom, and the gymnasts were taking turns singing songs or singing in unison. For a brief moment, Coach Kendig considered having them tone it down (and they were very loud!), but I reminded Coach that they had competed their best all year long when they were having fun and were relaxed. They were also a team that knew when to turn on the focus. I remember thinking that if the team fell short, he would hold me to the fire for telling him I was fully confident that how they were acting on the bus was an excellent sign, especially since the pressure at conference championship competitions can become too much for some teams. This is the same team I talked about earlier in the book that had done the candle exercise, a mindfulness activity that Coach Brink used with the team. And it was this same team that went out and crushed the competition with one of the highest scores in Nebraska history, to capture at the time their second consecutive Big Ten Championship!

Next was the 2013 University of Nebraska women's bowling team. Coach Straub had already won a couple of national championships but hadn't made the championship finals in a few years. I had secretly always wanted to help the bowling team, because it was the only sport where I personally had Division I talent myself, winning the 1980 Nebraska State singles and team championship that year. As mentioned in the introduction, I engaged with Coach Straub in a chance meeting to congratulate him on his recent tournament victory, and that is when he let me know the team needed help. After I interviewed the team and coaching staff, one of the barriers I identified was that the team struggled to have fun, but they also recognized that they performed at their best when they found ways to have fun on and off the lanes, with opportunities on the bus/plane, in the hotel, and on breaks at the lanes. When things got tight or they felt pressure, they had been able to look back on those outcomes and pair their lack of having fun as a team to a deterioration in overall performance, often with a decrease of positive energy during competition.

Randy York, a wonderful journalist, had a column at the time called N-Sider that he wrote for the University of Nebraska Athletic Department. After the season he wrote a piece called "Orchestrated Fun" that spelled out how the team made a commitment to having fun, including having certain persons be in charge of the fun. Since the collective team's wiring didn't make it as easy or natural to spontaneously have fun, they had to "orchestrate" it, and Coach Straub coined the phrase *orchestrated fun*. Their goal was to take their "fun meter" score to an eight or nine out of ten rather than the seven out of ten that it had been in times of stress. My favorite part was that Coach Straub contributed to having fun by the outfit he chose to wear (an outrageous red-and-white short-sleeved shirt with a bright white tie) in the national championship match. It was very rewarding to see the team very loose and relaxed during the entire three-day event. Tournament officials commented that they hadn't seen a Nebraska team this "loose and lighthearted" before. Did committing to having fun mean they were going to win it all? We all wish it were that simple. What I do know is that it was one of the strategies, including their work on mindset that Randy wrote about, that put the team in a position to max out when it mattered the most. And as Coach Straub concluded about the strategy, "Our performance was in direct correlation to the way Larry helped us prepare for the biggest pressure points. The goal all along was orchestrated fun, and I have to say, it worked. It really worked." And yes, they became national champions!

# 7  CONFIDENCE IN LEADERSHIP—COACHES AND TEAM LEADERS

Confidence in leadership includes the coaching staff as well as team captain and leaders. In the end it always starts at the top with the CEO, the boss, the manager, the teacher, or the head coach. There are several keys I've identified in observing and working closely with leaders that they must do well if they want to be elite:

- Having self-awareness and the willingness to answer this question when there is any issue: "What's my contribution to the problem?" If the team is struggling with communication, the leader must ask, "What's my role in the team's struggling?" Many leaders are quick to blame any issue on everyone below them without looking in the mirror, having self-reflection, and taking ownership for their role with the issue. Only when they take ownership can a leader get into true solution mode.
- Modeling the behaviors that you want from those you lead. I love the short video called *Calm Is Contagious*, done by a Navy SEAL. He tells the audience it is the number one lesson he learned, and he elaborated that anything is contagious— positive energy, kindness, and fear, just to name a few.
- Consistency. One of the biggest ways to break trust or prevent

trust from being built is for those you lead not to know what to expect from you on any given day. This may be purely how you present yourself emotionally each day or how quickly your emotions change. It could be as simple as having a conse- quence for someone that breaks an important value, like being on time, but then not following through on the consequence if that person is a top earner on your team or one of the top players on your team. Human beings actually crave structure and like to know what to expect physically, mentally, and emo- tionally from their leaders.

- Alignment of time/effort to what you value. There are many leaders who preach what they believe to be important but then don't put any effort into showing that on a daily basis. For example, if building deeper relationships with team members is an important value to the leader, yet that leader makes no effort himself nor makes time for it to happen within the team, then there is a misalignment.

- Open-door policy. The best leaders not only have this policy, but those they lead feel comfortable coming to visit their leader about almost anything. I often ask leaders who state, "My door is always open" how often people come in of their own accord. The answer is usually, "Not very often." It all starts with the leader making an effort outside of the office with those they lead. It's about finding time to meet for coffee or for a meal just to learn more about each other's lives and making an effort in relationship building.

- Healthy mixture of love and accountability. The best leaders find this balance. This is true for business, sport, and life. Think about the role of a parent. My favorite quote from an athlete leader comes from one of the best to ever play the game—Tom

Brady, former QB of the New England Patriots. He stated, "My connection with my teammates is through joy and love. It's not through fear or insults. That's not how I lead. When you have a group of people who hold each other accountable every day, those are the teammates that you're looking for." Danny Woodhead, one of my partners in Performance Mountain, can attest to this statement on how Tom Brady led his team during the three years Danny played with him.

I have seen this one go very badly with coaches in team sports. While I won't spend much time on knocking anybody specifically, persons that observed the Nebraska football program under Mike Riley (2015–2017) knew that there may have been some love, but there was also almost no accountability. One could choose not to attend classes or find himself having some legal issues, yet there were no consequences given.

- Willingness and ability to evolve and adapt. I have yet to be around a great coach/leader/teacher who was not willing to evolve and adapt, whether in learning to relate differently to younger people or in exhibiting a willingness to learn new technical and tactical skills in the ever-changing world of business or sport. Coach Bobby Knight, of Indiana basketball fame, had his career peak in 1986 followed by a relatively downward path over the next twenty years as he failed to adapt his coaching style to a different generation of athletes. Conversely, Coach Tom Osborne changed offensive styles in the early 1980s to option-based attack and then in the 1990s changed his defensive philosophy completely. He also focused much more on relationship building as his career went on. Without these changes, there is no way his teams would have won three national championships in his final four years.

While Bobby Knight's career went backward, Coach Osborne retired at the peak of his career. Apple, the company, was on the brink of bankruptcy in 1997 when Steve Jobs returned. He helped Apple evolve into one of the most successful companies in the world. Conversely, companies like Kodak (which at one time must have seemed invincible) didn't anticipate the disruption from digital photography and never recovered.

- Building trust. The best leaders find a way do this better than others. It is really about doing the above well, as these are all the building blocks of trust.

The company EcSell, mentioned earlier, also identified three ingredients that are critical to team performance. Each of these is the responsibility of the manager/coach to implement:

- Order: Creating processes, tools, and systems that enable people to operate efficiently and drive consistent outputs. This is about having structure, having well-defined goals, and having all persons know their individual roles. The top leaders (managers) are identified as doing this 81 percent of the time versus 71 percent for the rest of the managers.
- Complexity: Creating or embracing an environment that promotes discomfort. Just as we discussed in the chapter on grit, it is the job of leaders within their structure to create a deliberate practice structure—to allow those they lead to identify and have stretch goals, and to fail on occasion. This requires that they feel psychologically safe. Top managers are identified as creating this type of environment 90 percent of the time versus 71 percent for the rest of the managers.

- Relationship: Establishing trust connections with those on your team. This is important. It should be no surprise by now that the best leaders/teams spend a lot of time building relationships, which leads to connections, which then leads to trust. If all this goes well, one can get to a place of ultimate trust. The best managers build trust with those they lead and create an environment that allows the rest of the team to build trust. The top managers do this 85 percent of the time versus 71 percent for the rest of the managers.

To wrap things up, a number of top organizations have studied how the best teams get formed, and I've spent thousands of hours observing and working with businesses and teams at all levels. The best news is that leaders who choose to study and follow some very common themes can either create the environment for the team or be part of the team that has a chance to maximize its talents, leading to creativity and, at times, profits. In the sporting world, it gives a team the chance to max out when it matters the most. I will leave you with two of my favorite quotes about teams:

> There are plenty of teams in every sport that have great players and never win titles. Most of the time, those players aren't willing to sacrifice for the greater good of the team. The funny thing is, in the end, their unwillingness to sacrifice only makes individual goals more difficult to achieve. One thing I believe to the fullest is that if you think and achieve as a team, the individual accolades will take care of themselves. Talent wins games, but teamwork and intelligence win championships.
>
> —Michael Jordan

Here is another quote/story from a former famous New York Yankees baseball player and captain about the power of the team. Maybe every one of you can find something in this that you can relate to individually as well:

> Team sports are usually difficult things. Sometimes your team wins because of you, sometimes in spite of you, and sometimes it's like you are not even there. That's the reality of the team game. Then at one point in my career, something wonderful happened. I don't know why or how, but I came to understand what a "team" meant. It meant that although I didn't get a hit or make a great defensive play, I could impact the team in an incredible and consistent way. I could impact my team by caring first and foremost about the team's success and not my own. I don't mean rooting for us like a typical fan—fans are fickle. I mean care, really care, about the team . . . about "us." I became less selfish, less lazy, less sensitive to negative comments. When I gave up me, I became more. I became a captain, a leader, a better person, and I came to understand that life is a team game . . . And you know what? I've found that most people aren't team players. They don't realize that life is the only game in town. Someone should tell them. It has made all the difference in the world to me.
>
> —Don Mattingly

# EXERCISES

## BARRIERS EXERCISE

• Have your team identify in a whiteboard exercise all the possible barriers that can get in the way of *any* team reaching its goals.

• Narrow them down to the possible barriers that can get in the way of *your* team reaching its goals.

• Identify strategies to address each barrier identified for your team.

• Periodically review these barriers. Find out if there are any new barriers that have developed on your team, and remain proactive in addressing them as a team.

# COMMUNICATION EXERCISE

- Have the team members go around the room, one at a time, and tell the others how they get when they feel stressed in competition and what they need from their coaches or teammates to help them feel less stressed.

- Be prepared for a variety of answers and needs, but the key is to understand what each person needs—and this only happens with good communication during this exercise.

# 9

## THE POWER OF POSITIVE COACHES

THE FOCUS OF THIS chapter is on a number of exceptional coaches I have either worked with or observed over the years. I will share the common characteristics of top-level coaching professionals and leaders who are first and foremost great teachers. Elite coaches and leaders invest in relationships; they coach through a positive psychology framework, which includes coaching out of love. Mike Krzyzewski, the Duke University men's basketball team coach, has said, **"Almost everything in leadership comes back to relationships. The only way you can possibly lead people is to understand people."**

There have been so many other great coaches over the years—too many to name—but those who have had impact on my growth include Pat Summitt, John Wooden, Geno Auriemma, Bill Belichick, Sue Enquist, Rhonda Revelle, Nick Saban, Jill Ellis, Urban Meyer, and

Mark Manning. There were different reasons for all of them, but in the end they all found ways to evolve, focus on the process, build connections and trust with their players, and, of course, put their teams in a position to max out when it mattered the most. These ten coaches have won over sixty national championships combined and more than one hundred conference championships!

Although I have discussed this man earlier, I want to add just a few more comments about Coach Tom Osborne. He was part of two national championships as an assistant coach (and play caller) at the University of Nebraska under Coach Bob Devaney. He then became head coach from 1973 to 1998. He retired with a career record of 255–49–3 (.836), thirteen conference titles, and three national championships. He coached fifty-three All-American athletes, including 1983 Heisman Trophy winner Mike Rozier. Osborne's 1995 National Championship team is considered by many to be the best in college football history. As noted earlier, his last five teams had a combined record of 60–3—amazing accomplishments!

In 1991 Tom and his wife, Nancy, founded the TeamMates Mentoring program. Here are some words from the TeamMates website:

> *Coach Osborne felt that the athletes in his program could make an impact on the middle school students, and twenty-two football players began meeting with middle school students in the Lincoln Public Schools. Of the twenty-two original mentees, twenty-one went on to graduate from high school while one left school early to pursue a successful motocross career. Eighteen of the original mentees also obtained some form of postsecondary education.*
>
> *The program has changed quite a bit since then. We now*

*serve thousands of boys and girls across the Midwest, and our mentors come from all walks of life. One thing, however, remains the same—our mentors just have to be there. It's that simple.*

Of course, Coach Osborne is considered one of the best college football coaches of all time, and I know he is proud of what his teams accomplished. He was the first coach to influence me on the importance of "the process" and "the journey" and of the relationships made along the way. He adjusted and evolved. He was an early adopter of nutritional support, academic tutoring and support, and giving the players a voice. In conjunction with Jack Stark, performance psychologist, the Unity Council was started in the early 1990s. Team leaders had an important voice in the program, and it led to more player-driven accountability as well. For a long time people said he couldn't beat Oklahoma. Then that he couldn't win the big game. Then that he couldn't beat the Florida teams when they played in Florida. It took twenty-two years before one of his teams won a national championship, defeating the University of Miami in the 1995 Orange Bowl played in Miami. Bob Costas announced for this game and gave a postgame monologue that most Huskers fans will never forget:

Because it has finally happened for Nebraska, in another marvelous and memorable contest at the Orange Bowl, they've finally done it. Three times now Nebraska coach Tom Osborne has brought an unbeaten, untied number one ranked team to this game. Again, his reputation for losing here ringing in his ears—now he's trying to get the water out of his ears. He has borne all of it through the years with a dignified, self-effacing manner, and now his great coaching resumé is complete. While those of us in network television aren't supposed to root, I think we can allow ourselves a chance to smile and some words of appreciation for a man who has studiously avoided self-aggrandizement in an age all too devoted to style over substance. As we leave you now, try to imagine what it must be like right now in Nebraska, where there are no major professional sports teams and no other major university within its borders. And in Lincoln now and all across the Nebraska plains, this first national title in a generation is a wonderful way to start this new year, and a wonderful and crowing moment in the career of Tom Osborne. Nebraska national champs 24–17.

I still tear up when I listen to Bob's commentary. He used words and phrases that many of us can't come up with, but he captured the essence of Coach Osborne so well in those couple of minutes.

Coach Osborne has written several books, some during his coaching career and some after. You can tell a lot about what is important to Coach just by reading these titles:

*MORE THAN WINNING*
*ON SOLID GROUND*
*FAITH IN THE GAME*
*BEYOND THE FINAL SCORE*
*MENTORING MATTERS*

Coach Osborne evolved over the years, and he has discussed how earlier in his career he was a coach who focused more on the mistakes that players made. He changed his philosophy on how he went about trying to change a behavior, and this is the expanded version of a quote I shared earlier:

> *Probably the best way to change behavior is to catch somebody doing something right and reinforce it or praise it. That doesn't mean you don't correct. But you can do it in a way that is not demeaning or attacking the person's character.*

I will leave you with this about Coach Osborne. I've said it before, but he is a mentor of mine, and he was a mentor for at least twenty years before I met him at my age of forty-four in 2007. He is a servant leader—the best kind of leader. For many of us, if there were just one person in this world who considered us a mentor, that would be an honor. Coach Osborne has dozens of people, from every race, religion, and socioeconomic status, who consider him a key mentor in their life.

The first head coach who embraced my role within a team setting was Dan Kendig, the University of Nebraska women's gymnastics coach who was at the helm from 1993 to 2018. Before I share more about him, I need to set the foundation for how we met. When I first came to consult within the Athletic Department at the University of Nebraska in the fall of 2007, my role was primarily to take care of the mental health needs of the student-athletes. Many athletes shared with me that they didn't feel they were getting their mental performance needs met by others on staff, and after a period of time, Dr. Albers and Coach Osborne (who was now the athletic director) authorized me to start working on mental performance issues as well. Given my familiarity with certain sports such as football and basketball during my formative years, I naturally felt more at ease with the athletes in those sports. In fact, I saw myself as somebody who would probably end up working with mostly male athletes—but that ended up being the furthest thing from the truth!

I frequently worked there in the evenings to accommodate the schedules of the athletes, and generally the appointment process flowed through Dr. Albers. However, one evening in the spring there was a knock on my open door. It was a female athlete, short in stature, and she asked if she could visit with me. She proceeded to tell me that she needed help staying on the balance beam. I had seen a couple of gymnasts for their mental health needs in the past, but this was the first who asked for help with performance. I told her I would be happy to visit and that she needed to get approval from Dr. Albers.

I also asked her time frame as to when she needed the help. She stated that they were leaving the following day for the Big 12 Championships! We ended up visiting that evening—and I was not able to confess to her that I knew absolutely nothing about her sport other than as a spectator of some Olympic competitions over the years! She informed me that she had only hit about 50 percent of her routines that year and needed to get that corrected as they were headed into the postseason.

We talked through some basic mental performance strategies, and luckily at the meet she hit her routine. (She was fifty-fifty to hit it anyway given her recent history, but she wanted to credit me for her success!) The hitting of that routine changed the course of my professional life. Shortly thereafter, this athlete showed up with one of her teammates and asked if I could help her as well. At that point, I decided to learn everything I could about the sport of women's gymnastics so that I actually could make an impact. As a result, Danna Durante, balance beam coach, heard from her athletes that

I was making an impact and asked if I would start working with the team. I was granted permission by Dr. Albers in 2010 to work with the gymnastics team leading up to the 2011 season. Coach Kendig was very open to the process of adding a sport psych component. He offered "a seat at the table," and our collaboration from 2011 to 2018 was one of the most rewarding of my life. In fact, most team exercises and assignments that I've done with teams over the years were done first with his teams.

The 2011 team will always be special to me, because they got better every week, and they embraced the process of building team unity. They entered the Big 12 Championships ranked number ten in the country and proceeded to upset number four Oklahoma using some strategies the team leaders agreed to impart to the team. When Oklahoma had come to Nebraska earlier in the year, they won the energy battle to the point that it rattled the Huskers. I was at that meet and made mental notes, because it also took me by surprise just how loud and connected Oklahoma was at that time. The Husker women committed to doing things differently at Big 12s, and after the victory Maddie Steinauer (now Byers) stated, "Oklahoma beat us every meet last year and beat us at home this year. The most frustrating part of this year's loss was Oklahoma showed more outward emotional support for their teammates than we showed for ours in our own facility. I think Saturday in Columbia was the loudest I've ever heard our team pull for each other. It was real love for our teammates, but it came with a strategy. Our seniors talked about it [with me]. Dr. Widman showed us how we can reinforce each other like we never had before and do it without being obnoxious. We cheered each other on and helped each other perform at Missouri. We wanted to step it up in terms of loudness, and I think it worked. The idea wasn't so much to intimidate the opponent, but I think we had so much fun they could see it, and it might have gotten a little bit intimidating."

This won't be the last time that you hear about the importance of winning the energy battle. The 2011 team's mantra was "Don't count the days; make the days count." They used the time between Big 12s and regional tournaments to continue to get even better. The four seniors (Brittnee Habbib, Erin Davis, Maddie Steinauer, Maria Scaffidi) led the team collaboratively, and they advanced from regionals to the National Championships. This was amazing, since despite their ongoing improvement during the season, they were given little chance to make it to the Super Six. I wasn't able to go to Cleveland, so I sent them a note that closed with this: "Be confident in yourselves, because you have earned it through all of your hard work. Believe in yourselves and trust your training, and remember how good you really are. Have fun together, and focus on just your team. Enjoy the process, and enjoy all the moments ahead this week . . . and may all your dreams come true. I am so proud of all of you."

The first night of nationals, the meet was going along smoothly with a great team vault performance. When the team moved to uneven bars, Maria Scaffidi nailed a 9.9 routine and stuck her landing but suffered a season-ending knee injury in the process. This is where the story gets really cool! The team moved right to balance beam, but Maria was unable to compete. With little warning and no preparation that day, Janelle Giblin (now Kingston) was asked to compete on the toughest apparatus in sport, on the big stage, under pressure. In my observation and in talking with athletes, there is nothing more gratifying than knowing you've prepared the right way in practice—never knowing if you will get an opportunity—and then delivering when called upon for your team! Janelle did a great job, along with the rest of the beam lineup, and kept the team's hopes alive to advance to the Super Six. The final event was the floor exercise. Brittnee Habbib had been a multiyear starter on the floor before losing her spot during her senior year. She initially did not handle the demotion very well but eventually focused on what she could control and prepared very hard during practice each week. She was called upon to replace Maria and proceeded to have a beautiful routine, helping her team pull off the big upset to advance to the Super Six! Two wonderful examples of athletes who prepared hard behind the scenes and put themselves in a position to help their team max out when it mattered the most.

I booked a plane ticket and surprised the team in Cleveland the following day. There is one final story that reflected how this team fought hard for each other. The team probably would not have advanced that far in 2011 without the steady, consistent performances from Maddie Steinauer. At Super Six, the team started on balance beam, and Maddie as the leadoff person fell. That meant the other five needed to hit their routines, which is often difficult to do, as everyone feels extra pressure when there is an early fall. After weeks of having everyone else's backs, the team repaid her by hitting all five routines. It set the stage that allowed the team to finish number four in the country! The 2011 season was the start of a wonderful journey with Coach Kendig and his teams.

As I learned about Coach Kendig and what made him tick, it was clear that he may to this day be the most optimistic coach I've been around. He always believed tomorrow would be a better day. He always believed that the team was never out of a competition, and it translated into a never-give-up attitude that permeated throughout his teams. He gave his athletes hope—and as you may remember, hope is one of the key psychological assets of grit. His main mantra, **"Team above self,"** guided every decision he made about his teams. Coach Kendig also was a big believer in the mantra **"Success breeds success,"** and it was one of many reasons that the smallest details mattered in practice. The foundation of success started with deliberate practice, day in and day out. He also supported his teams setting big goals outside of competition, such as with team GPA or winning the Life Skills competition, in which teams earned points for doing community services, or supporting other teams at Nebraska. Many of his athletes were named the Female Student-Athlete of the Year or received postgraduate scholarships.

Coach Kendig did his best to evolve, and I saw a real willingness to find new ways to motivate his athletes, to be more open to such things as piercings and tattoos, to model staying calm, and getting even a better balance between love and accountability. One example that is relevant played out in the week before the Big Ten Championship in 2015. I had the team read an article called "One Mission" from *The Players' Tribune*, written by Russell Wilson, the quarterback of the Seattle Seahawks. In his words, "A lot of people have been asking me the same questions this week. They want to know how we were able to come back against Green Bay. They want to know how we were able to right the ship this season and get back to the Super Bowl. It starts with a little red button. When we were down against Green Bay in the fourth quarter in the NFC championship game, it seemed like everything that could go wrong had gone wrong. Personally, I was having one of my worst games of my career. But after every single throw—whether it was a tipped ball or an incompletion or a touchdown—I'd turn back toward the huddle, close my eyes, and think of a table in an empty room. On that table was a big, red RESET button, just like in the movies. I'd imagine pressing the button. *Boom.* On to the next one. What's the situation now? How can I make a play? It might sound silly, but I've been working on that visualization for years now ... It's like my very own mind trick. No matter what the situation, no matter how bad the circumstances are, I can close my eyes, hit the red button, and focus on the moment at hand."

At gymnastics championship meets, there is a practice day to get a feel for the equipment and venue and to have a light workout. The night before in our team meeting, we discussed the concept of being able to hit the reset button to help move on to the next moment and stay present. Coach reminded the team about the purpose of the practice and that it was only for the purposes mentioned. That being said, practice on the uneven bars in particular did not go well. Jennie Laeng, a sophomore at the time, was our best performer, but she struggled as well at practice and at that time of her career had a tendency to show her emotions. Jennie went on to have a wonderful career, improving her mental game, becoming a great leader, and helping her teams to qualify all four times for the national championships. She also was the recipient of many performance and academic awards. I loved her growth as a person and performer!

Now back to what happened after practice. That evening before the team meeting, Coach Kendig told me *he* was very upset and was going to let the team know just how he felt about their practice. I asked him if they accomplished what he asked them to do the night before—to get a feel for the equipment and the venue and to get in a light workout. When he answered yes, I asked how the assignment the night before could apply to him, and he knew exactly what I meant. He went to the team meeting that evening and was his usual positive and optimistic self. He told them they accomplished what they needed for the day and that tomorrow, competition day, was going to be a great day. If he hadn't hit the reset button, it may have hurt the confidence and trust of the team, as there is always more stress at championship meets. As a result, the team competed hard and pulled out a late second-place finish, which also helped them with their seeding at regionals. Fittingly, it was the excelling of the uneven bar lineup that allowed the team to move from fourth to second in the last rotation—and Jennie Laeng won the Big Ten Championship on the uneven bars!

Another story that sticks out to me about this team and Coach Kendig is that on April 19, 2014, he had to pay up on a bet he had made. Remember, the 2014 season followed a very disappointing time when one of his best teams of the decade was defeated at regionals in 2013, so this was a bet he was happy to pay up on to the team! He agreed to have his fingernails painted if the team made it to the Super Six National Championships that year—and when they pulled the upset, he made good on his bet! These types of situations all play into the building of team cohesion and having fun—both of which give a team a competitive advantage.

Coach Heather Brink, the current gymnastics head coach of Nebraska, may understand Coach Kendig better than anyone else, given that she was a student-athlete during his tenure and became a two-time NCAA champion. She has said, "He definitely has a heart of gold. He genuinely wants what's best for his athletes. He had a lot of patience with me. Instead of leading the way for me, he stood by my side and let me make mistakes, learn from my mistakes, but really never put me down because of those mistakes. I came to college after having done the elite program for a good five years. I really came with some emotional and maturity issues. I had done gymnastics at that point more as a job. Having come to Nebraska, Coach Kendig taught me how to love the sport again." Coach Brink, in part because of what she has learned under Coach Kendig and in part due to her unique skill sets, is going to be a great coach who will certainly put future teams in a position to max out when it matters the most.

My favorite memory of Coach Kendig was in the spring of 2014 when I put together a scavenger hunt for the team before the postseason. The coaches were all on one team, and the rest of the team was put in groups of five, as well. One of their tasks was to figure out the title of a song based on a series of clues—and then they had to sing the song and make a video for the rest of the team to see. The song was "Bohemian Rhapsody." The coaches' team was made up of Coach Kendig, Dan Miller, Heather Brink, Owen Field, and Alina Weinstein. They shot their video while driving their car à la *Wayne's World*—everybody saw another side of Coach that day! Not only was it hysterical, but it was a chance to see all the coaches in another light, particularly Coach Kendig. You can still find it on *YouTube*, so check it out! It was just one of many factors in helping that team connect in ways that few teams ever do.

Finally, Coach Kendig proved to be the best head coach that I've been around when it came to participating in vulnerability activities with his team. His actions with the team supported this quote: "Everyone has a story to tell, something that they've been through, and we need to show empathy toward our fellow human beings and listen to their stories, just like we want people to hear our stories. Everyone in this world is important; we need to remember this." And you know what? Everybody was important to Coach Kendig. The best part of these exercises was that he would always tell me beforehand that he wasn't going to cry this time. Yet within seconds of sharing a life adversity or describing his hero, he would get so choked up he often had to pause! He did a great job modeling vulnerability, and there is no question in my mind that's why he was able to connect with his athletes.

I intentionally left out his record of success to focus on the processes that put his teams in a position to be successful. It should not surprise you that he was a national championship coach at Indiana University of Pennsylvania prior to coming to Nebraska. From 1993 to 2018 during his time at Nebraska, he won fourteen conference championships, two Coach of the Year honors, and twenty NCAA appearances, including twelve Super Six team competitions. During this time period his teams finished, on average, as the number seven team in the country. Finally, one measure of success is how your assistant coaches have fared, and his coaching tree is lined with many who have gone on to highly successful head coaching careers. I am grateful for the relationship I have with Coach Kendig.

I have already mentioned my 2013–2015 collaboration with Coach Bill Straub, who retired after the 2018 season after a career that included five NCAA championships. In 2017 a reporter from *The New York Times* did a wonderful story called "With Rigor and Mystique, Nebraska Builds a Bowling Dynasty." *Real Sports* followed up in 2018 and did a very cool segment, as well. The notion that Nebraska's bowling program would be a national story would have been unheard of to most people. For Coach Straub it all started with preparation. He cared about his student-athletes and pushed them hard technically and tactically. His practices were intense, and the drills were meant to be very challenging. He expected his teams to be the most prepared physically and emotionally. As he stated, "It's all about being able to handle the physical and emotional demands at crunch time. It you can't do it when it counts the most, what is the point?" Now you know one of the many reasons Coach and I were in complete alignment!

Coach was old school and wasn't afraid to have a challenging conversation with an athlete right on the lanes. I remember at the 2015 national championships that Coach and Liz Kuhlkin, who had been named NTCA Bowler of the Year, had a very animated conversation front and center on the lanes. The content of that conversation remains elusive, but it always reminded me of a statement by Jill

Ellis, former head coach of the US Women's National Soccer team: "Connecting with players is a part of who I am as a coach. Building relationships so there is trust there . . . so you can have challenging conversations." He built up collateral and trust based on his mastery of the game and his connections with his players. It was why I had such a great feeling about the 2015 outcome at the national championships. He said, "Over the last two weeks, the team has been more interested in hard work and preparation than maybe any team we have ever had. It does not mean things are going to go well in St. Louis, but the preparation and effort have never been better."

The week I spent with the team in St. Louis was memorable for several reasons:

- It was a team that fell short the prior year in the championship finals, and they had spent the year trying to cope with a medical illness that almost took Coach Straub's life and prevented him from coaching most of the season. The assistant coach (and now current head coach), Paul Klempa, did a remarkable job with the 2014 team, helping them deal with the adversity of Coach Straub's issues and the pressure of trying to repeat as national champions.
- It was memorable because of the Power of Appreciation exercise the team did that was very meaningful to all of them.
- It was memorable because of the Nebraska crowd (mostly family members) in the preliminary matches—how much fun they were having and the encouragement and confidence it seemed to give the ladies.
- It was memorable because Gazmine "GG" Mason led the charge on the lanes for having fun, even having a couple of trademark moves, including "the dab" and a robot-and-gun

173

move that GG did not have a name for when I asked her about it recently! GG said, "No matter what you do, you should always enjoy doing it. Having fun should be at the top of the list, main priority." Isn't it interesting that the 2013 and 2015 teams both made fun a priority? GG, who earlier in her career had won a gold medal and several silver medals in the Pan American Bowling Confederation Youth Championships, then became a gold medalist in the World Bowling Youth Championships in 2016.

- It was memorable because it was a deep team with future stars Briana Zabierek, Beth Hedley, and Kelly Belzeski, who didn't make the starting lineup but pushed the team to be better.
- It was memorable because every lady who bowled contributed to the success of the week, including transfer bowler Melanie Crawford, whose story I already referenced in regard to her learning to maintain composure and beat her former team.
- It was memorable because Julia Bond, a freshman, bowled fearlessly and was recognized as the most outstanding bowler in the tournament. Here is some insight into the mind of a perfectionist, high-performing athlete. I remember congratulating her on the bus after the team won the national championship, and she was still thinking about the perfect ball she threw but that resulted in what is referred to as "leaving the solid nine pin"—meaning that the way the ball/pins collided resulted in an outcome that would only occur once in a hundred times. The cost of being elite, at times, is a laser focus on the minute details of the event that just transpired. It should not surprise you that Julia has gone on to be a member of Junior Team USA and won a PWBA professional event in her rookie season in 2019.

- It was memorable due to Liz Kuhlkin's steady presence as she delivered in the powerful anchor position.
- It was memorable because Coach Straub continued to show why he was an elite coach even though he was still not fully recovered from his illness of the previous year.

Due to decisions made within the Athletic Department, outside consultants were starting to be eliminated from helping teams at the University of Nebraska, so the 2015 team was the last one that I was able to work with. It was a very fun three-year run, with the bowling team playing in all three national title games and winning two of them!

I will always be grateful for the trust Coach Straub put in me, as he wasn't a coach that let many come into his team. His wit, his willingness to adapt, and his recognition of what his teams needed to put them in a position to max out when it mattered the most are things that will always stick with me. Here are some of Coach Straub's records: three NTCA Coach of the Year awards, five NCAA team championships, five IBC women's national championships, two IBC men's national championships, and nine ITCA Collegiate Bowlers of the Year!

My initial thoughts concerning Coach Pete Carroll were not positive ones, as he seemed a bit arrogant to me—but I made the judgment without knowing a thing about him and having never met him. I then read his book *Win Forever*, the updated version that came out in 2011 after he had spent one year as head coach of the Seattle Seahawks following a very successful stint as head coach of the USC Trojans. Here is a succinct review of his book from the *Books-A-Million* website:

Pete Carroll is one of the most successful coaches in football today. As the head coach at USC, he brought the Trojans back to national prominence, amassing a 97–19 record over nine seasons. In this book he shares the championship-winning philosophy that led USC to seven straight Pac-10 titles and is now shaping his program with the Seattle Seahawks of the NFL.

Carroll developed his unique coaching style by trial and error over his career. He reveals how his recruiting strategies, training routines, and game-day rituals preserve a team's culture year after year, during championship seasons and disappointing seasons alike.

*Win Forever* is about more than winning football games; it's about maximizing your potential in every aspect of your life. Carroll has taught business leaders facing tough challenges. He has helped troubled kids on the streets of Los Angeles through his foundation, A Better LA. His words are true in any situation: "If you want to win forever, always compete."

After I read the book, my view of Coach Carroll completely changed. I admired the fact that he took some time after being fired as a head coach in the NFL at the age of forty-eight to revamp himself and embark on a process of discovery about who he was as a coach and a person. He realized that he didn't even have a philosophy to live by. Two words that resonated with him were *always compete,* and they ended up being his guide for how to set up his program when he was hired at USC. His master's thesis was on Abraham Maslow and his theories of self-actualization. "He finally figured out over the years that by giving others the tools to discover their purpose—

and understanding and fulfilling their potential—he could become a better leader and coach." He studied John Wooden and recognized that it took Coach Wooden sixteen years to win his first title—and it wasn't until he had developed his own philosophy in a complete and systematic way.

Coach Carroll decided to center his vision on having everyone associated with his team do things better than they ever had before—even the janitor. He concluded it was his job at USC to make sure that "my next team would be built around the goal of maximizing everyone's potential." He came up with his three rules:

NO WHINING, NO COMPLAINING.
BE EARLY.
ALWAYS PROTECT THE TEAM.

Coach Carroll made it clear that coaches are teachers and challenged his assistants to do a better job of being positive coaches. Here is a great example of how Coach Carroll wanted his assistant coaches to manage their "space" and choose their responses in a positive manner:

> Every year, before the start of spring and fall practice, I would remind our staff that players will make mistakes and that in the window of a few seconds after a particular mistake, we make the choice between yelling at the player or helping them to learn from their missed assignment. It is in those few seconds that coaches can have the most impact. Resisting the impulse to respond in a negative way is one of the biggest challenges coaches face.

He challenged people to come up with their own philosophy in twenty-five words or less. I organized a book club in the winter of 2015 with the University of Nebraska volleyball coaching staff, and we all did this assignment. It was a powerful outcome for me, and I believe it helped those coaches think about what they stand for personally and what they stand for as individual coaches. My initial philosophy (which I have since modified) was the following:

*Helping high performers through a positive psychology framework by teaching them critical mental skills to help them max out in sport and life.*

Coach Carroll connected with Dr. Michael Gervais, a high-performance psychologist who I believe is the very best at his craft. They talked about building a masterpiece together. There has been great synergy between the two of them, and it is one of the many factors that have helped them create a winning culture in Seattle. Coach Carroll said his work with Gervais has given him "clarity of purpose. The more clarity you have in being who you are, I think, the easier it is to find your way back to that and the more consistent you can become. I have found that, and it's been really helpful." His vision in 2010, which he stated at his introductory press conference, was to build a team "better than it's ever been done before." He brought with him "a relentless energy, an infectious optimism, and one audacious experiment," per an article in *The Seattle Times* by Adam Jude in January 2020. Cynics said the approach he used at USC wouldn't work in the NFL. In the same article, Carroll stated, "People wonder all the time, 'How do you have as much fun as you do?' Well, wait a minute. It's football. That's what you're supposed to do . . . but we've been able to create a way and an environment where we ask for people to give us everything they have and enjoy the heck out of it while they're going, and feel connected to the whole approach."

Coach Cook, who I will be elaborating on quite a bit shortly, talked about Carroll in a recent podcast on *The Dark Side of Elite* (hosted by Jack Riggins). In discussing advice for younger coaches, he suggested that they watch other coaches and also watch themselves on video while coaching. He asked this question: "Who do you want to look like when you're coaching?" He asked if they wanted to look like a coach who was angry and yelling at their players or somebody like Pete Carroll. Coach Cook says that before his own matches he uses positive self-talk and says "I'm going to be Pete Carroll tonight" in regard to his positive coaching style and his energy. What a compliment from one elite coach to another!

Steve Kerr is a former NBA player and has been coach of the Golden State Warriors since May 2014. In a league that is supposed to have parity, Kerr's teams have managed to win three NBA championships. At the very beginning of his journey with the Warriors, he met with shooting coach Bruce Fraser nearly every day to discuss the culture they wanted to create with their team. In the summer of 2014, interestingly, Kerr spent a few days in Seattle with Pete Carroll and learned about many of the points discussed above, including the need for a philosophy that reflects your own identity and the development of core values. Then, at a retreat in Napa, the Warriors coaches came up with a list of four values that has served as their guide for what they have become:

MINDFULNESS
COMPASSION
JOY
COMPETITION

Kerr encourages others to come up with a list of their ten top values and narrow it down to their top four just like the Golden State Warriors did. In an article entitled "The Golden State Warriors, the happiest team in sports" dated June 8, 2016, Luke Walton, their assistant coach at the time, stated this: "And when we hit all four of those things, we are not only tough to beat, but we are very fun to watch—and very fun to coach and to be around."

In the article, written by Les Carpenter, he described a scene at Cleveland's practice arena, where Golden State was practicing while trailing 2–1 in the championship series: "Music boomed from mini-speakers the team brings on all road trips as players kicked balls around like they were on a soccer field. Several of them lined up half-court shots. They were laughing. Anyone who walked into the arena that day would have gazed at the spectacle, more open gym at the Y than NBA workout, and decided the Warriors didn't care. But Bob Myers, Warriors GM, said, 'Sitting in the stands I had this epiphany . . . I get it.' What he meant by that was that basketball was supposed to be fun. Myers went on to note that Kerr was different from every other coach he had known. Kerr didn't scream or push, but 'his brilliance came from not how hard he coached, but how content he made his players.' Myers said, 'Steve had kept those guys relaxed all year round. Ask anybody if they can perform better at their job if they have a level of joy around their job. They will say yes. And if you can create joy while working with people you like, then you can do an even better job.'"

Coach Kerr didn't use the typical motivational tactics of having an enemy or using bulletin board quotes to get them angry. Kerr's motivation was not the fear of losing, but rather the joy of winning together. Whenever I watched Golden State, they played with a joyful spirit about them. During player interviews after the game, they often used words like *joy* or *mindful* when describing the team or game situations. The team lived their values!

Kerr has done a great job of studying other elite coaches as well as implementing concepts from coaches he has played with or coached, such as Lute Olson, Gregg Popovich, and, of course, Phil Jackson—who coached him for five seasons when he played for the Chicago Bulls. From Jackson, for example, he encouraged his players to try mindfulness or yoga, or canceled practice to take them bowling on days when he determined they were worn out and tired.

Steve Kerr has learned to trust what his players see on the court and recognizes that it may be different from what he is seeing on the sidelines. He learned about this firsthand when he played in San Antonio and observed an argument between Popovich and player Avery Johnson about what to do in a specific game scenario. Johnson got upset, sallied his fist on the table, and shouted, **"You don't see what we see out there!"** This leads to his players using words like *freedom* and *trust* and saying, "He lets us be ourselves." Kerr also has great empathy for the role players on the team, given that he was a role player most of his career. He has been able to get buy-in from more of these players—and as you may remember, the number one ingredient for success on a team is the willingness to embrace your role.

Kerr spends time building relationships with his players. This allows him to understand how to motivate each of them differently. Case in point: Draymond Green. Kerr has intentionally yelled at Green at times because he knows that Green will get fired up and yell at the others on the team to do their job. Kerr and Green can have challenging conversations because they trust each other. Green stated, "We're as close as anybody on the team. I mean, I can talk to Steve about anything. We can go at each other and know it's never personal." In fact, Kerr talks about the concept he got from Lute Olson and Popovich: create a balance between a really good relationship with the players where they know you care about them, and every once in a while snapping to "remind them how much you're asking of them and you're in charge." The right balance of love and accountability!

It is clear that one of Kerr's strengths is a high degree of emotional intelligence. He is great in picking up nonverbal cues, knows how to check up on players and ask the right questions, and uses body language to evoke calm and compassion rather than appearing to be in a position of authority. Dacher Keltner, a social scientist who runs a lab at UC Berkeley, said that Kerr has a combination of the following personality traits, not expected to be found in an NBA coach: intellectual curiosity, empathy, and humility. Kerr's slogan for the team is "Strength in Numbers," signaling the importance of everybody's role on the team without the usual hierarchy seen in some organizations.

Coach Kerr was shown a study completed by a couple of guys who were studying leadership, Jim Kouzes and Barry Posner. They identified five practices that great leaders share:

MODEL THE WAY.
INSPIRE A SHARED VISION.
CHALLENGE THE PROCESS.
ENABLE OTHERS TO ACT.
ENCOURAGE THE HEART.

When Kerr had this study read to him, he said, "Yeah. Right, right. Interesting. I'd never thought of that before, but when you read that, it all made sense. That's basically who we are."

In a 2017 *Sports Illustrated* story called "Steve Kerr's Absence: The True Test of a Leader" (due to a back injury), there was commentary about what one has to do to lead like Kerr:

> *It's easy. Just be humble and grateful, curious, self-aware. Communicate, value family, and empower others. When bad things happen, keep a broader perspective. Most of all create something bigger than yourself, as the real test of a leader is what happens once they leave.*

Coach Kerr is a really special coach in my book.

There are three high school coaches I have spent a couple of years or more with that I need to mention. First is Brett Froendt, Omaha Westside High School head football coach. I met Coach Froendt in 2017 after he learned about Jack Riggins's work. Westside is also my alma mater—and there is something to be said about having an opportunity to give back to a place that gave you so much. He wanted his team to have more exposure to training the mental game for both sport and life. Coach already had established a great culture and had periods of really high performance. His staff fully bought into the process, and they have done a wonderful job of carrying our message day after day, modeling the mental skills and mindset necessary to max out, and thus the team bought in as well.

The 2017 and 2018 seasons made it easy to see the growth by the team and coaching staff. They made the playoffs both years and won their first-round games before losing in the second round. They worked hard in the off-season, physically and mentally, to get better. During the 2019 season they got punched in the mouth by a couple of teams but learned from these failures. The team was able to identify that they had played their best when they had communicated in a positive manner and played with great energy. They suffered a late-season loss that dropped them to the number seven seed in the sixteen-team Class A playoffs. After beating their main rival, Creighton Prep, for a second time, they had the opportunity to play Lincoln Southeast again, who had dominated them in the fourth quarter in their first meeting, where they lost 22–17. They crushed Lincoln Southeast 35–0! They then got a rematch with number two seeded Millard South, who had defeated them easily on Westside's home field 41–26 just a couple of weeks earlier in the last game of the regular season. The men practiced well, committed to the values of energy, communication, and having the proper run fits. In warm-ups, the team was calm, composed and focused. Westside had a dominating performance, winning easily 31–14.

They played for a state championship on a snowy and icy field against Bellevue West, who came into the game undefeated, and then showed everyone why they were the best team this season. In the end, other than winning it all, it was a team that did everything you would hope to see—exhibiting unity of purpose, a desire to get better, and growth through discomfort, and then playing about ten quarters of the best football a team could play in the first three rounds of the playoffs, giving them a chance to play for it all. It was an honor to play a small role in the team's 2019 journey.

Coach Terri Neujahr, head volleyball coach for Waverly High School, and I crossed paths in 2018 when she was working on a project that led her to visit with Coach John Cook. Coach Cook suggested that we talk about her project, which resulted in a conversation about working with her team. It was clear that she had also established a culture of love and accountability. However, her teams had lost in the district finals the past few years, keeping them out of the Class B state championships, and she was open to exploring—or as I would say, *leaving no stone unturned.* What transpired since then in the past two years has been, for me, very rewarding. The ladies on the team invested in working on mindset, communication, and vulnerability. In 2018 they had a very bad loss to an inferior team in late August, but like many great teams I've been around, they learned from that failure, and they got better and better—including beating a great Class A team, Omaha Marian. When they reached the district finals against Beatrice, there was a confidence in the team that put them in a great position to max out. They rushed the court after winning to advance to the state tournament, and I was never happier for a team in that moment, including all of the national championships of which I've been a part.

This group of high school ladies and coaches did everything they said they would do. I wish that guaranteed the right number of wins; we all know it doesn't, but it's great when one is rewarded for hard work and doing things the right way. They advanced to the state semifinals in 2018 and did so again in 2019. Coach Neujahr sets the standard on how to foster a culture of love, a culture of inclusion, and having high expectations about how to act on and off the court.

Coach Renee Saunders is the head volleyball coach for Skutt Catholic High School. She and I crossed paths in 2018 due to her long-standing relationship with Jack Riggins, as Jack's wife Kate and Coach Saunders were volleyball teammates under Coach Pettit at the University of Nebraska. (Coach also played basketball at the University of Nebraska.) She started her head coaching career at Omaha South High School, and according to her statements on Coach Pettit's podcast, she honed her craft there while losing the vast majority of games with often-undermanned teams. I had falsely assumed that she had one of those fairy-tale careers where her first head coaching job landed her directly at Skutt Catholic. I will say that

I was perplexed, as her team was just coming off their third straight state championship, yet she still needed some help with her team's mental game. It didn't take long to realize that she was a lifelong learner who wanted to take it to another level with her team. There is also the weight of expectations that go along with trying to repeat, and as most of us know, it's very difficult to repeat at any level of competition. Her team was very interested in the mental game and was always engaged during our visits. Their gym was as lively and as loud as any practice gym I have ever been around. Coach takes her teams to compete against the best teams in the country, giving them a chance to learn from those challenges. I like to say that Skutt Catholic will play anybody, anytime, anywhere. Teams like hers have the challenge of learning to accept and embrace their roles.

Her team was going along as expected in 2018 until the week before the state tournament. They lost to the two top contenders, Elkhorn South and Omaha Duchesne. Everyone was feeling the weight of pressure and expectations, and a little joy was being lost in the process. Two things happened to set the stage for what was about to happen: (1) the team was able to identify the key controllable that allowed them to play their best, and (2) Coach Saunders made some changes to her lineup that some of the best coaches in the country told me they wouldn't have had the courage to do at that moment in time. She moved her outside hitter to libero, moved her libero to defensive specialist, inserted a new middle blocker to middle/right side attacker, and moved right side to outside hitter. Wow! The funny part was that I came to the end of practice, since we were meeting right afterward, and she came up to me and said, "This is the lineup that is going to win State!" She was completely confident in her decision, and because of the trust built up over time, the team completely bought in. They crushed both of the teams that had defeated them just a couple of weeks prior, capturing their fourth straight state championship. And the 2019 season saw a young but still seasoned group of ladies play another incredible schedule. Their practices continued to be deliberate in nature, and their collective mindset was strong. They played with a joy that was consistent with their off-the-court cohesiveness. The team captains took control and identified the key ingredients necessary to put themselves in a position to max out.

Both the 2018 and 2019 teams met the challenge given to them by us to have everybody on the bench stand up and cheer for every single point for the entire tournament! It was a relatively smooth ride at the end of the season and in the state tournament, leading to a fifth straight state championship! In the end, it all starts at the top with Coach Saunders setting the tone and modeling the behaviors necessary to put her team in a position to max out when it matters the most.

# EXERCISES

## VALUES EXERCISE FOR COACHES

- Identify the values that you want your team to be known for, similar to the Golden State Warriors.

- Define each value for your team.

- Use these values as a second scorecard to measure how well the team is living up to these values, no matter the win-loss record.

- Have the team score themselves, at least monthly, on how they are doing on each value with an identified action plan on how to improve each score if necessary

# VALUES EXERCISE FOR TEAM

- You can choose to do this same exercise, but this time have the team identify the values that they want to be known for. You can layer these upon the coach-set values; it becomes even more powerful when the team takes ownership for their own values.

# PHILOSOPHY EXERCISE FOR COACHES

- Each coach on the staff should come up with a philosophy in twenty-five words or less, similar to Pete Carroll.

- Go around the coaching room and share with each other your philosophy, then discuss.

# 10

## THE POWER OF POSITIVE LEADERSHIP

### COACH KIRSTEN BERNTHAL BOOTH

I AM JUST GOING to start off and say it: Coach Kirsten Bernthal Booth, head coach of the Creighton University women's volleyball
team, is the most well-rounded coach I have ever been around. One of
her WHYs is in complete alignment with one of mine: to help empower
young women and to do our part in helping them become the best
versions of themselves as they transition into adulthood. Nobody does
it better than Coach Booth! She has been the head coach since 2003
when she was still in her twenties, and I met her in January of 2012
after she inquired about getting some help for her team. The past eight
years collaborating with Coach Booth and with her staff and team have
been some of the most joyful experiences of my life.

The best way for me to describe who she is, what she stands

for, and how she empowers others is to first go back in time and see how she got the job just five years removed from college. How did a coach whose first love was tennis end up coaching volleyball? Why would she even want the job at a school that had only three winning seasons from 1994 to 2003, was playing their home games at Omaha South High School, and just finished the season 3–23?

I would not be writing this chapter if she had been offered a college tennis scholarship at the University of Nebraska; Coach Booth was only given the opportunity to walk on there. Instead, she accepted a volleyball scholarship at Truman State in Missouri, and her life would never be the same.

Her plan was to become a college administrator, such as a dean, after college. While in grad school at the University of Iowa, she volunteered as a volleyball coach for the women's team at the university. When the season ended, the entire staff was fired, and after a delayed search she was asked to be the interim coach between seasons, to which she agreed. Booth decided to pursue coaching and accepted the head coaching position at Kirkwood Community College in Iowa for the 2000–2002 seasons and amassed a 112–41 record there, building on an already successful program.

When the Creighton job opened up, Coach Terry Pettit, who had previously been the head coach at the University of Nebraska, suggested that she be a candidate. (Coach Pettit was doing consulting work after he retired, and one of his clients was Creighton.) Coach Booth had indirectly crossed paths with Coach Pettit years earlier when she was still in high school, as she played on the same volleyball team as his daughter Katherine for one year. Later on, Coach Booth worked at a couple of his summer volleyball camps, and she must have made an impression on him during these past encounters. When she applied for the Creighton job, a search committee and the Jays volleyball team interviewed all the candidates. Both the search committee and the team recommended a different candidate! It was Bruce Rasmussen, Creighton's athletic director, who vetoed their decisions and hired Kirsten Booth anyway. According to Rasmussen, the team initially threatened to walk out, feeling that Coach Booth was too young.

One of Coach Booth's first hires was Angie Oxley Behrens, a former standout volleyball player at the University of Nebraska who played under Coach Pettit. It is hard to articulate just how important it is—and the competitive advantage it gives your team—to have staff continuity. Angie has remained with Coach Booth the entire tenure at Creighton and is such a driving force in the rise of this program that she was recognized in 2019 as the AVCA Assistant Coach of the Year!

Coach Pettit continued to stay involved by taking on a mentoring role. One of the first pieces of advice he gave to Coach Booth was, "You can never be held hostage by a player." What I think he meant was that if you have a great player who is not buying into the team culture, that player is holding you back from going forward. That advice became very important as we got to the 2011 season. From 2003 to 2009 Booth built the team from the bottom up and instilled the culture that is still the foundation of her program today. Her teams continually improved, and in 2010 Creighton made the NCAA tournament for the first time in school history. They even beat Iowa State in the first round of the tournament, and Coach Booth was named National Coach of the Year! The team and Coach had high expectations entering the 2011 season, but now the team had a target on them as well. I am not certain of everything that occurred that season, but it ended on a disappointing note, and they backtracked for the first time, ending the season with a 17–14 record.

Cultures have to be jealously guarded, because cracks in the system can sneak up on you and go unnoticed or overlooked for a period of time. When I received the call to help out, Coach Booth was not feeling good about a number of things—including what role she played in the turmoil. She wasn't certain exactly how she contributed to the problem. What I do know is that she parted ways with one of the top players on the team. I got a sense that it had to do with what Coach Pettit had told her about not letting a player hold her hostage. There are always heightened emotions when somebody is let go, because some teammates won't be happy with that decision; there may even be disgruntled fans. Issues like this can lead to some splitting on the team as well. What I didn't know at the time was that Coach also felt like she had lost her team at the end of that year. She spoke about it on Coach Pettit's podcast in 2019, and you could tell—even eight years later—that the feeling of losing her team was very traumatic for her. I am cautious about going into too many of the details of what I learned from the team. What I can tell you was that they were in a tough place—some of them individually for very different reasons—but communication, conflict resolution, and trust building were all things the team needed to work on together. I also sensed that Coach Booth was questioning her future role as a coach as well, but I didn't know her well enough at the time to inquire more deeply.

A team-building survey filled out anonymously, which I gave them the first week, confirmed that communication and constructive conflict were the two main skills they needed to learn how to do better if they wanted to improve team chemistry. I will never forget the first Sunday evening we met in January of 2012. I could tell that none of them really wanted to be there, and I didn't blame them, since they didn't know my colleague and me at all. We asked the team members to raise their hands if they wanted to be there. Maybe two did so—and we weren't sure they were being truthful!

The team had had an experience with some other "team builder" the year before that involved the use of a horse, and they just wanted to make sure that a horse wasn't going to be used again!

That was a good icebreaker for all of us! It took time to build trust with the team, but what helped the team was knowing that the coaches were also going to work on themselves and be committed to listen intently to whatever came out of our meetings regarding issues the coaches needed to address. Coach Booth, in part due to her high emotional intelligence, knew that a coach always bears some responsibility for whatever is going on with the team members—so if they were struggling with healthy communication, conflict resolution, or trust issues, the coaches needed to understand what their contributions to the problems were as well. As you may remember from before, the best leaders I have been around take the following question very seriously: **What's your contribution to the problem?**

We met weekly (just with the team and no coaches) for a few months, and slowly the team came to trust us and know that we had their best interests in mind. They worked hard on improving team chemistry and also started to open up about what they thought the coaches needed to do better. The coaching staff was open to the feedback, and they addressed every issue and followed every recommendation that was made to them. The only team concern that I want to share about Coach would fall under the category of the open door policy. As I have already told you, the best leaders create an environment in which those they lead want to come into the office and visit on their own. In January 2012, the team did not feel that way at all. The individuals on the team unanimously felt that the only time Coach called them into her office was to tell them what they had done wrong. This was the team's perception, but what I always say is that to *some* degree perception is reality. It turns out there wasn't enough time spent by Coach devoted to meeting with individual players *outside* of the office, getting to know each other and building deeper relationships. We have to remember that Coach was still very young by coaching standards, and she was not perfect by any means. There were still lessons to learn to become the best version of herself as a leader. The team left the spring ball season in a much better place.

Then the art of forming a new team began as incoming freshmen joined in the summer. What happened next was nothing short of amazing. The 2012 team included a good combination of upperclassmen leadership (Brooke Boggs, Heather Thorson, Megan Bober, Natalie Hackbarth) and unselfish play. It also demonstrated excellent team chemistry born out of discomfort. They went from 17–14 the prior year to finishing the year 29–4 and getting to the NCAA tournament for the second time in school history! They won their first-round game and had Minnesota on the ropes in Minnesota before losing to them in four games. The 2012 season was validation that if a team works hard on team chemistry, and if there is enough talent on the team, there is no telling what the final ceiling can be. This 2012 team set the foundation for all future Creighton teams and gave us the blueprint of what we needed to focus on in the years ahead if we wanted to be in a position to max out when it mattered the most. I believe that Coach Booth found joy again in coaching with an excitement for the future!

Now that the team was on solid ground again, it was time to really understand the values that Coach Booth stood for. It became clear that she is a relationship builder, and even though she veered a bit in 2011, her pattern of open engagement with the ladies is one of her strengths. In a 2017 interview in *VolleyballMag.com*, the article highlighted what is important to Coach Booth, especially after being named National Coach of the Year. When asked what it meant to be named coach of the year, she responded, "Obviously, it's the same way you talk to your players. Honors are nice, but we play a team sport. Any honor that I get is a reflection on the team. If you're around our team at all, you know that our staff is very collaborative. So any award that has my name behind it is something that's definitely shared. I think, more than that hour, it's reflecting on a really great season with fifteen amazing young women."

When asked about her excitement for the upcoming season, her answer gives us great insight into Coach and her values:

> I think the biggest thing that makes me excited is I like these players, these young women. That's what drives me to coach. I like their relationships. I like, hopefully, helping them grow into strong, independent women. I like them all as people, so that makes me excited. We're very process driven, so we want to do things the right way. We want to work hard. We want to take care of things off the court, in the classroom, and in the community. Hopefully winning will be a byproduct of doing those things right. If not, hopefully we can look back and be proud of the process that we took.

Note that she didn't mention winning until the very end of this quote. When Coach talks about being process driven, she lives that every day.

Now, don't underestimate her focus on relationships and doing things right as a lack of competitiveness, because she does not like to lose! Her focus on the process serves the team so well because she sets a competition schedule in the month of September that is often one of the toughest for any team in the country. The positives of this schedule are that the team learns quickly what they need to improve upon—if they can win some of the games, it helps their national ranking, and it is simply fun to play great competition. The downside is that if you take too many lumps, confidence can take a hit, especially if the focus is only on the win-loss record. Coach Booth had a simple philosophy, though: "It doesn't matter where we are at the beginning of the season. It matters where we are at the end." To get there, her teams must stay process focused. We knew that the 2015 preseason schedule was going to be very tough and that there were some talented incoming freshmen who were going to be playing right away, so we had an exercise that we scheduled after they played matches for two weeks. At the time they completed the exercise, their record was 2–4. The team and coaches had to answer several process-focused questions:

- What did the team do well?
- What are a couple of areas in which the team could improve?
- Did the team improve during the two weeks?
- Would the team feel like they had improved had they not defeated a ranked Kentucky team?
- What did the win against Kentucky do for the team?
- What is one thing that each player and coach can identify that they can do better in the next two weeks to help the team improve regardless of outcome?

The revelation that came out of this exercise was that their answers to most of the questions reflected what Coach modeled for them. It demonstrated that they were focused on the process of getting better and that their confidence had not waned, as they were able to identify areas that the team did well. It identified clear team strengths as well as areas that needed work.

From this exercise, Coach Booth was able to identify that when she was calm, the team was calmer, and vice versa. For the record, they finished the tough preseason 6–7, but the challenging schedule and their willingness to stay process focused set the stage for what was about to happen.

The team proceeded to go 17–1 in conference play, winning the Big East regular season title as well as the Big East Conference tournament. I thought this would be a perfect team to do the Power of Appreciation team exercise before the postseason to help them get outside of their own heads and focus on positive attributes of each other. With teams that are already close, I have found that it takes them to a higher level of cohesiveness. As mentioned earlier, I believe that exercises like this help teams care about each other more off the court, which then helps when the stress elevates on the court, like it always does in the postseason. The team surprised the coaching staff as well, as each team member wrote to each of their coaches and key support staff to say what they appreciated about them.

The team had to go on the road in the NCAA tournament, and after winning the first-round game, they defeated North Carolina on North Carolina's home court to secure their first Sweet 16 berth in school history! It was the only time in my career that I had tears streaming down my cheeks as I watched the game on the computer and saw the final point that secured the win. I was so proud of this team and coaching staff for growing during the season, learning from failure, and sticking with processes put in place by the coaching staff. The team learned through our process-focused exercise in September that team leadership was doing a great job, cohesiveness was strong, and work ethic was excellent. These ingredients made it easier to trust the process even while suffering some defeats. Similarly, they learned that working on strategies for self-talk, composure, and concentration were necessary, and they improved in all of these areas.

One can't underestimate the Kentucky win proving that past successes can help with overall confidence—and that win also gave them the road map of how to beat great teams. The 2015 season had one last lesson to teach: the rewards from the culmination of a four-year process of focusing on team chemistry and culture. The seniors on this team—Ashley Jansen, Melanie Jereb, Kate Elman, Lizzy Stivers (redshirted 2011), Maggie Baumert (transferred in)—and Lauren Smith (redshirt junior) were freshmen in that first year we were together in 2012. Assistant coaches Angie Behrens and Tom Mendoza had been with Coach Booth for a while, and that certainly helped her confidence level. Despite some really tense moments in the postseason, Coach was able to take it to another level with regard to maintaining a level of calm and composure that helped the ladies be in the best position to max out when it mattered the most.

Coach Booth is wonderful in the off-season, finding a balance between letting the ladies do their thing while still asking a lot from them to continue to get better during that time period. Coach Booth is very proactive in looking ahead to the next season before the team separates for summer break. One issue that was identified by the team in our end-of-spring meeting in 2016 was a potential barrier to maxing out: the acceptance of new roles on the team because of the level of talent that was already there and with the new players coming in the summer. The wonderful thing about identifying potential issues in advance is that we can have open communication and come up with strategies to make sure the team works through those issues.

We repeated the same team survey that the ladies took in 2012, and this time, instead of average team chemistry, they scored in the good/great range. The team was very cohesive, which is something that Coach values and continually works on with the team. They scored the lowest on role acceptance, as it mirrored what they had already acknowledged. We talked that year about everybody "doing things just a little bit better than they ever had before" (à la Pete Carroll) in the eight areas they identified as important to the team to get to great team chemistry:

- Developing relationships off the court
- Selflessness
- Role acceptance
- Incorporating the freshmen
- Conflict resolution
- Accountability
- Communication
- Positive communication

Keep in mind that they were already practicing these areas very well, but the challenge when you're living on the edges of elite is to find just one more inch, one more degree, one percentage point more.

In August, during two-a-days, we did the vulnerability exercise on discussing a hardship covered in an earlier chapter. It was powerful and even more important, as the setter, Lydia Dimke, had transferred from Purdue—it was important to hyperdrive building deeper relationships since that is such a key position on the court. This team had great senior leadership from Lauren Smith, Amanda Foje, and Jess Bird. You may remember that Jess was in the tough position of losing her spot after being a three-year starter. Midway through the season, when it became clear that her starting days were generally over, she made a conscious effort to find other ways to contribute by connecting with every person on the team. Jess figured out that she could still be a vocal leader and be the person others would come to for advice. She said, "It made me appreciate things and people and what every person does on the team—what impact everybody makes, no matter if they are starting or on the bench. We are young women, too, and we're developing our whole self. When I was able to do that and be impactful, I was finally okay with everything." Coach Booth's values and beliefs were all over Jess's comments. Coach Booth agonizes over circumstances like these, and she feels true emotional pain for what her players are going through. It is one of Coach Booth's best qualities—her ability to empathize and try to find ways to give perspective and to keep people like Jess engaged with the team.

The 2016 schedule was very challenging again, but Coach was better than ever at helping the team navigate it. The two losses in the preseason to Kansas and Nebraska gave the team the confidence that they could soar to new heights. They lost game four to Kansas 28–26 and game five 15–13, so the team already knew how close they were to being great. The last game of the preseason was against Nebraska. Creighton won game one and had a chance to take control of the match in game three but lost late 27–25, eventually losing the match in four. However, Nebraska coach John Cook told the media that Creighton was the best team they had faced that season, including highly ranked Florida. Creighton finished the preseason 6–6, and I truly believe that they entered conference season with a level of confidence that belied a team that was 12–0. Yes, they had to work on finishing games, but that was a fixable issue. The team went 18–0 in conference play and won the Big East tournament as well.

It was a tough-minded team with players like Megan Ballenger (one of the most mentally resilient athletes I've known), Lauren Smith, and Marysa Wilkinson fitting that bill and taking control of the front middle and right side. It was a team made up of role players like Jess Bird and Kenzie Crawford, who had changed positions but played defensive specialist. The two serving specialists were Samantha Bohnet and Amanda Foje (and you may remember the big serves Foje had against Northern Iowa in the first round of the NCAA tournament). Brittany Witt had the tough task of replacing a four-year starter at libero, Kate Elman, and played at an incredibly high level as a freshman. Lydia Dimke made a smooth transition and became a great setter and quarterback of the team. The bench energy spearheaded by Kelsey O'Connell, Jaclyn Taylor, and Mac Conlon gave the team a competitive advantage. Finally, it was the true coming-out party for Jaali Winters and Taryn Kloth, as they were now both left-sided outside hitters and gave the team one of the most explosive offensive attacks in the country. Watching Taryn emerge this year was rewarding, as she started her career injured and then played out of position before finally showing the nation why she was one of the best left-sided hitters around. The coaching staff had the usual cohesiveness and expertise and added Ryan Meek, who challenged the team to take it to another level at the service line.

As the team entered the postseason, there was a sense of calm and confidence that I hadn't seen in a Creighton team before. Coach Booth had pushed all the right buttons that year, and yet the margin between winning and losing was still razor thin in the postseason. And if I am being honest, the draw that Creighton got was unfair—not only to Creighton but to the top seed Kansas. That being said, Coach Booth never once complained about the draw and focused simply on the factors the team could control.

Lauren Smith, who was named the Big East Female Student Athlete of the Year, was one of the players who led with confidence and explained this team's competitive advantage: "I'm really appreciating every moment on the court with these girls. It's been really special. This group and this team dynamic we have here is something I can't even explain." Remember, this is the team that came into the huddles between points, and as Lydia Dimke said, "If you only knew how many times we came into the huddle and just simply said 'I love you' to each other and moved on to the next point." Wow! As I have stated many times before, it all starts at the top—and in this case with Coach Booth!

Earlier I told you about the first-round match against Northern Iowa that Creighton won in a five-set thriller. The reward was getting to play Kansas—ranked number four in the country and one of the number one seeds in the NCAA tournament—and they had to play them on Kansas's home court. It was a battle for the ages, with Creighton finding a way to win 20–18 in game five! The video of Coach Booth entering the locker room made the hair stand up on my neck. Love was the common denominator of the team and staff. Asked why this team was so resilient, Dimke said, "We just love each other so much, and it's genuine." And to sum up how the team feels about Coach Booth, Jaali Winters said, "Coach recruits winners. She empowers us as women and tells us that we can do anything we want in this world." Wow!

Back to the Sweet 16. The next opponent was a Big Ten school—Michigan. I had watched them play Nebraska earlier in the year and noticed that the team broke apart under stress and almost stopped coming together in the huddle between points when things weren't going well. In contrast, one of Creighton's strengths was their ability to get on to the next point or the next play while remaining very connected, even when under stress. Coach modeled this behavior during matches, especially during time-outs. It became very hard to know if Creighton was winning or losing that year if you observed Coach

Booth's body language and demeanor. Michigan took early control of the match and was up 2-1 going into game four. Sure enough, as the stress hit Michigan, you could see them become less cohesive, and huddles became loose. You could really see it in game five as Creighton pulled away under the serving of Winters and Bohnet. The stat sheet showed so many contributors, again from a cohesive team in which the whole was greater than the sum of the parts—and the parts were already pretty special. They got beat in the Elite Eight by Texas but went down with a fight. In a span of fourteen years, Creighton went from a 3-23 team to an Elite Eight finish. I have said it before: what Coach Booth has done is very similar to the turnaround that Bill Snyder did for Kansas State football a generation ago.

The 2017-2019 campaigns showcased that Creighton is now a contender nationally every year.

The 2017 team felt the weight of expectations of the past two seasons. They beat two top ten teams in Washington and Kansas in the preseason. They won their fourth straight regular season conference championship and tournament championship. They were ranked number nine at the end of the season but faced another very tough draw and had to face number twelve Michigan State in the second round of the NCAA. (If seedings were based on rankings, Creighton should have faced the number twenty-three ranked team in the second round.) A senior-laden and very physical Michigan State team defeated Creighton, ending their quest for a third straight appearance in the Sweet 16. I don't know if this Creighton team fell short or not, given how talented Michigan State was that year. I do know that despite the team having full awareness of the pressure and expectations they were feeling (as the media constantly asked them if the next step was the Final Four), it was still a struggle, and I think a little of the joy was missing from the team because of the pressure they felt.

The 2018 team still had very high expectations with a veteran team, and they knew how to win. They were going on a summer trip to Europe to play, which meant they had to form a team earlier than usual. The team added a new assistant coach, Craig Dyer, and merged two transfer setters, Megan Sharkey and Madelyn Cole, into the team. Grace Nelson, a defensive specialist, transferred in as well. There were also four freshmen, of which one, Keeley Davis, made the decision to redshirt—and that is always a difficult time for an athlete. Coach was very proactive in starting to work on building relationships and working on mindset; thus, we met in June instead of August. When we do vulnerability exercises—in this case Hero, Highlight, and Hardship—I always challenge the coaches to put the same effort into it as the players do. Coach Booth and her staff have never disappointed in that regard, allowing the team to see the coaches as human beings with the same types of challenges in life. The team and coaching staff did a wonderful job, helping to hyperdrive getting to know each other and building that trust.

The team ran off twenty straight victories after having a successful preseason campaign again (although they lost a heartbreaker to Nebraska in five sets), winning the Big East regular season championship and the Big East tournament as well. They finished the season ranked number nine in the country. The team lost in the second round of the NCAA tournament against a very good Washington team. I do believe this team thought they were going to make a deep run in the tournament, but I honestly don't know what they could have done differently. What I have observed with programs that are relatively new to the national scene is that there is extra pressure, especially in the postseason, that a team puts on itself. I believe that Coach Booth felt the pressure as well. In the 2016 run to the Elite Eight, every match went five sets, confirming the fine line between winning and losing at this level. I just think Washington was the better team on that day, but based on what the team decided to focus on for 2019, it does seem to suggest that certain outcome goals, even subconsciously, can create pressure and expectations that can be a barrier to maxing out.

The 2019 team had to replace the most decorated senior class in Creighton history. It was the first team I had been around that set no outcome goals. (Of course, they wanted to win the conference again and advance to the NCAA tournament.) Instead, they decided to identify a few values that they wanted to be known for, as stated below:

- A team that never had a bad practice
- No comparisons to past teams
- A feeling of equality on the team
- Helpfulness within the team

They went on to define what each value meant and how they would go about measuring each one. The team felt that if they took these four steps, the results would take care of themselves. Coach used the book *Chop Wood Carry Water* with the team, as the messages were about the processes it takes to become great. Several ladies emerged into wonderful players or took it to another level, including Erica Kostelac (before her season ended due to injury), Naomi Hickman, Jaela Zimmerman, Keeley Davis, Grace Nelson, and Annika Welty. Seniors Brittany Witt, Madelyn Cole, and Megan Ballenger were great leaders and played at the highest of levels. Brittany Witt ended up being the first All-American libero in Creighton history! This team beat USC for the first time ever and then beat number ten Marquette on Marquette's home court to take control of the conference race.

As you may remember, the team realized that they tended to play their best when they also had a great balance of fun and staying focused. Thus, **"fun and focused"** became the team mantra, and when combined with the four values they identified before the season, it became a great second scorecard. The team got better despite season-ending injuries to Erica Kostelac (their starting outside hitter), Annika Welty (who missed much of the year), and Megan Sharkey (who was not able to finish the year due to a concussion). They found a way to win their sixth straight Big East regular season championship but lost in the conference tournament. This team had all the right ingredients to play with confidence and put themselves in a position to max out. They won their first-round match against Iowa State and then had to face a great Minnesota team on Minnesota's home court. Creighton played fearlessly, and after getting down 1–0 in games, the team took control of the match and actually had a couple of set points to try pulling off the upset. The goal from Coach was to play fearlessly and attack—and that's what they did. They were close to victory, as one set point attempt was wide by no more than an inch. I did find it ironic that one of the chapters in *Chop Wood Carry Water* was called "How Important Is an Inch?"

The loss to Minnesota, who made their own run to the Final Four, should have left the 2019 team with no regrets. This year, more than any other, demonstrated the strength of the culture that Coach Booth has built—to overcome the personnel losses and injuries and still play at the highest level of your sport. Maybe it's because of comments like this from some of the best players to ever come to Creighton: Jaali Winters said she felt so comfortable with Coach that she committed to her without ever seeing the team play, as she just expected that Creighton would continue to be successful. I will repeat what Jaali has said: **"She empowers us as women and tells**

**us that we can do anything we want in this world."**

Taryn Kloth said, "I guess I just had faith in the program. I saw something. This was the perfect fit for me. And when I have a gut feeling, I just have to go with it. I knew that Kirsten wanted to build a program, and I was ready and willing—I wanted to help. The people that came before us did all the tough work. We're just trying to keep building up. It keeps getting bigger and bigger." Taryn recognized that all the prior teams, even those before 2012, contributed to where Creighton is today.

John Dunning, retired Stanford volleyball coach who consulted with Creighton, identified two necessary components for success: resources and people. He said, "CU has talented coaches and players who are supported by a committed administration. That's the foundation you need." And you'll never find an administration, led by Bruce Rasmussen, that does a better job of supporting their coaches with emotional support and the resources necessary to succeed. Who wouldn't want to support or play for a coach who thinks this way:

> What we tell recruits is that if you want to be great in this program, we will give you the opportunity and resources, but we aren't going to hold your hand every step of the way. We will provide support, but if you don't want to go to class, I'm not going to walk you to class. We'll give you lots of information on making good nutrition choices, but I'm not going to be coming to look in your refrigerator. I want players that want to be great, and developing women is making them take ownership in developing their greatness.
>
> We always say you can develop by fear—and I think there are a lot of people that have success on fear-based

programs—or you can develop by love. We want players that love the process and are so bought into being the best version of themselves that they want to do the right things. Now, do they sometimes not get a great night's sleep and sometimes not eat perfectly? Of course. I want them to be real people, but it is about finding the right balance and being committed to, and hopefully loving, the journey.

This quote from Coach Kirsten Bernthal Booth highlights why she is the best leader and most well-rounded coach that I know. It is also because of the following ingredients that I previously identified in the best leaders:

# 1  WHAT'S YOUR CONTRIBUTION TO THE PROBLEM?

Coach has a high level of emotional intelligence, which helps her be aware of what her role is with any particular team issue. She also spends a lot of time getting into solution mode with any problem that arises, including considering what she needs to do better. She has grown so much in this area over the years.

# 2  MODELING BEHAVIORS

Nobody does a better job showing others how to think, act, love, parent, coach, and lead. She is competitive yet process focused. She shows people how to care, how to invest in each other, how to communicate in a positive manner, and how to maintain composure. Coach spends time in the off-season with the leaders or emerging leaders, often using leadership books to facilitate growth. With regard to modeling emotions and mindset, Bruce Rasmussen, her AD, quoted, "If a leader is calm, then everyone is calm. If a leader is frustrated, then everyone is frustrated. If a leader is confident, then everyone is confident."

## 3 CONSISTENCY

This is an underrated feature of great coaches. Coach is great at being virtually the same person every single day. No, she's not perfect and certainly has her moments in a world where there can be many stressors when you're a wife, coach, mother, daughter, colleague, and friend. That being said, her staff and her players know that they are going to see a stable, emotionally-in-control person day after day. They know what she expects of them on a daily basis as well. When a coach models behaviors well and shows consistency on a daily basis, long stretches of high performance can occur. Coach Osborne also modeled behaviors and was known for his consistent nature. One way it manifested was by being process focused and never underestimating an opponent, even when there was a talent differential. Over twenty-five years, only a couple of his teams were ever beaten by a lesser opponent. Similarly, Coach Booth's teams in Big East Conference play (where there is a talent differential at times) from 2014 to 2019 have gone 100–6, and two of those teams went undefeated in conference play! Records like this don't happen by accident, and much of the credit is due to a process-focused approach. As Coach John Madden said, "Winning is a great deodorant. It covers up what stinks about your team. Great teams have positive discontent. Even when they are experiencing successes, they still look for ways they can improve and always strive to get better." This is exactly what happens with Creighton Volleyball, and it starts at the top. It leads to consistency of approach, and when the leader is consistent on a daily basis, there is a much better chance to see consistency in those you lead.

## 4 ALIGNMENT OF TIME AND EFFORT WITH WHAT YOU VALUE

Coach spends a significant amount of time communicating and building relationships with everyone on the team and asks them to do the same. She invests in others who can help hyperdrive and maximize an already great culture. Because of past experiences, Coach knows the importance of giving energy to maintaining a culture, because it can deteriorate otherwise. She wants all members of her team to grow into healthy women who believe they can take on the world, and she puts time and effort into not only modeling how to do so, but talking about it with them.

## 5 OPEN DOOR POLICY

This means your door is always open AND people *want* to come in your door. Coach learned from the 2011 season challenges and has worked very hard to make sure that anyone on her staff or team feels comfortable at any time to come in and talk about anything. It is one of her strengths at a time when it can be very hard for some coaches who are ten or more years into their careers to relate to those they coach. It all starts with empathy and caring. When something doesn't work out for her athletes due to issues either on or off the court, Coach internalizes their struggle and feels their pain, but there is an authenticity about her that resonates with everybody that she touches.

## 6  HEALTHY MIXTURE OF LOVE AND ACCOUNTABILITY

For a Coach who loves her players and staff so much, one would think it would be a challenge to find the right mixture when it comes to accountability. It is a gift that she has, but she also knows when to ask for advice, either from her boss, her assistants, her team leaders, or somebody like me. She takes the accountability part very seriously, yet she does it in a very loving and caring way. And as I mentioned, when something goes amiss to the point where somebody leaves the program, it is very hard on her.

## 7  WILLINGNESS AND ABILITY TO EVOLVE AND ADAPT

Coach Booth learned some important lessons from the 2011 season and worked very hard to improve in the areas that were necessary for her maturity and the team's growth. She was open to the process, and she initiated the "ask for help" stance. Considerably more time has been spent on maintaining her culture and investing in relationships. Coach still provided reminders to the team about the importance of not overlooking an opponent, and she would even discuss the ramifications of a bad loss or a good win on RPI, the computer-based ranking system that was one of the factors in determining seedings in the postseason. As she gained coaching experience, however, Coach spent more time focusing on the key ingredients in a match that would give the team the best chance to be successful and less time discussing how important it was to win that particular day.

## 8 BUILDING TRUST

There are many ways to say this, but here is one way: Transparency drives trust. Trust drives relationships. Relationships drive culture. Culture drives results. When a coach learns about their lives, holds them accountable, is honest with them, shows empathy, believes in them, teaches them life lessons, listens to them, and appreciates the uniqueness of each member of the team, it is hard to not build trust.

Her process-focused approach has translated into high-level performances year after year. Her record in the eight years I've known her is 213–50, with eight straight NCAA appearances, two in Sweet 16, and one Elite Eight appearance. Her teams have won six straight Big East Conference championships, and five of the past six Big East tournament championships. She is a better person than coach. I will leave you with this quote from Maya Angelou that gets at the heart of what makes Coach so special: **People will forget what you said, people will forget what you did, but people will never forget how you made them feel.**

# EXERCISES

## MODEL BEHAVIORS

- Identify three behaviors that are most important to you for your team.

- Give yourself an honest self-assessment about how well you model these behaviors. For example, if you want your team to be calm under pressure, how calm are you under pressure? Give yourself a score between one and one hundred for each behavior, and then identify what you need to do to improve your own score for each behavior you want to model.

# 11

## THE POWER OF EVOLUTION

### COACH JOHN COOK

EVOLVING MEANS FOCUSING ON a path of self-growth and lifelong learning. The best way for me to demonstrate how necessary and powerful this course of action is will be to relate my observations and interactions with Coach John Cook, head coach of the University of Nebraska volleyball team.

In 2018 I attended a talk by Coach Cook in which he made a statement that, in my opinion, is the best starting point to tell his story. He said, and I quote: **I wish I had learned to coach out of love instead of anger earlier in my career.**

But the story really begins in 2007 when I began consulting with the university's Athletic Department. I had been living out of state and had made the decision for me and my family to move to Lincoln a year earlier. It is important to share with you my role and what I observed over the years, and in the end, this chapter is about the evolution of Coach John Cook.

If I am being honest, I hadn't paid much attention to Nebraska Volleyball before 2006. I was certainly aware of their success but took notice when they won the NCAA National Championship that year, the third championship for the program and the second of Coach Cook's career.

With all their past success, the 2007 season fell short. Although working part time with the Athletic Department, I had not yet crossed paths with Coach or any of his athletes. I did vaguely remember the controversy after the 2007 season when one of his star players left the team and another said some hurtful things about the team in the school newspaper. The sense I got was that those two events were important factors in building a tight-knit team in 2008.

I first spoke to Coach John Cook in the fall of 2008 to coordinate a plan for one of his athletes. I was nervous to speak with him because others told me he was intimidating, and to this day I remember exactly where I was when he returned my call—outside of one of the mental health units at the Bryan Hospital where I worked at the time. And I also remember how engaging he was on the phone, his eagerness to understand the situation, and his curiosity about who I was and my role within the Athletic Department. There was an intensity about Coach, yet I could tell that he was very thoughtful in the questions he asked and in his openness to the plan I shared with him. We stayed in touch that season, as I ended up working with a couple of his key players, but I had no role with the team itself.

I remember watching the regional final matchup against Washington, played in Washington. Nebraska was down 0–2 in games and then in game five was down 9–3 before making the amazing comeback to win and advance to the Final Four in Omaha! Penn State was the opponent in the Final Four, and they had not lost a set that year! Penn State dominated and won the first two games before Nebraska made another incredible comeback, winning games three and four. Nebraska was on the verge of pulling off the upset, leading 10–8 in game five before losing 15–11. The postgame press conference was emotional, and the following day the ladies said they had slept in their jerseys since they didn't want to take them off. There was that much love for the team and of their not wanting the season to be over. It left a big impression on me, and it was that feeling I wanted all teams to crave once I started working in that capacity.

The 2009 season started off by being swept in the opening match against Michigan in a tournament in Omaha, Nebraska. Frustration continued, and in a match a few days later with Creighton University, it was marked by Coach Cook slamming his hand into his notebook, which echoed throughout the NU Coliseum.

A couple of weeks later, they had a deflating loss to UCLA at the Bob Devaney Center (not their true home court) with Lauren Cook (Coach Cook's daughter) as the setter on the UCLA team. The following Wednesday, an article in the newspaper noted, "Cook is someone that doesn't normally lose his cool from the bench, but after a point in the first set against Texas Tech, he slammed his clipboard on the seat next to him, jumped out of his chair, and yelled at his players."

After the team had its nineteen-game home win streak broken at the coliseum on September 23 against Texas A&M, Coach had seen enough. In a November 23, 2009, *Daily Nebraskan* article, Coach Cook made a comment that reflected how he was feeling after that loss to Texas A&M. The article stated that Cook had found himself asking a troubling question six weeks earlier: "Is this going to be the worst team at Nebraska in the last ten years? There was just a lot of doubt and fear and anxiety."

It was clear that Coach was under stress. And when a coach is feeling stress and anxiety, those who are being led tend to feel the same way. To compound circumstances, there was a void in senior leadership, with only Kori Cooper (already a graduate student) fulfilling that role, as compared to the leadership roles of the 2008 team. Coach Cook reached out to me and confided that the team was having a hard time playing with trust; the team needed help, as it was feeling lots of pressure to live up to past teams; and he needed help with his leadership group.

He identified four leaders he wanted me to meet with as a group. When I walked into the room, they looked stressed. It was clear that they weren't experiencing the joy of playing volleyball. They were open about how they were feeling, and it didn't take long to identify what each of them could do as a leader to be genuine. I told them that the first meeting was per Coach, but we would only meet going forward if it was something they wanted to do. They asked to meet every one to two weeks during the season to talk about leadership, communication, and building relationships. We identified four words that summarized their concerns: **fun, respect, genuine,** and **trust.**

Eventually, the ladies were able to express their feelings to Coach. I had not built up enough trust with him yet to challenge him, but I did support the ladies' concerns. However, these issues resurfaced over the years, and eventually we made a commitment to tackle them head-on. I do remember talking with Coach right before they left for Oklahoma on September 29, and when I told him that the team played best when they had fun, he asked, "How do you have fun?" I found that to be a very interesting question and simply told him, "Fun is a choice." In the first several years that I worked with him, he struggled with the concept of having fun.

The four leaders that Coach identified began to grow into their roles, feeling connected with each other and becoming more pro-active in solving issues. As a result, they started to invest more of themselves into the team. On October 12, in *The Daily Nebraskan*, setter Sydney Anderson noted that she not only had to help the team on the court but also off the court vocally and emotionally as well. She took responsibility for keeping the team on track: "We need to have focus before every match. We need to know that we can never take a day off. As Nebraska Volleyball players, we have a target on our back—people are out for us. For us, the pressure is a privilege—a privilege that people want to come out and compete against us."

There was only one more unexpected setback in the 2009 season—on October 22 in a loss to Iowa State—and they had one other loss to Texas on October 30. Other than that, Nebraska had ten straight victories via a sweep. Nebraska then went on the road and played Iowa State on November 7, sweeping the number eight team in the country on their home court.

Confidence that had taken a hit earlier in the year was now a strength, both individually and collectively, and this mindset continued into the postseason. In a November 11 article in *The Daily Nebraskan*, Kori Cooper said, "After four years here, I've come to realize it's all about the relationships that you build along the way . . . I think embracing that has helped me be who I am." In the same article Coach said this about Kori Cooper, Sydney Anderson, Kayla Banwarth, and Tara Mueller: "Those four are one leader. They're the package deal." Cooper noted her leadership was about the relation-ships. Banwarth stated that she wanted to be the rock that shows the team how it needs to be in practice and matches. Mueller leads the way in the weight room and sets the tone there. Anderson is the quarterback who has consistency and direction and runs the team. Coach also showed a side of himself, with regard to the up-and-down season, that is typical of great leaders: "I think nothing has given me more wisdom as a coach. I've made a lot of mistakes this year; I wish I could go back and redo things."

The week before the postseason, I asked each of the ladies to review the four words from our first meeting. Their answers indicated that there was clear improvement with all of them.

Nebraska won their first two matches in the NCAA tournament. The Sweet 16 matchup happened to be back in Omaha against Iowa State. Coach remarked, "Their trust level is going to be tested more than it ever has before ... We're going to find out just how deep that is." Coach noted camaraderie and communication had grown, and he credited the four leaders for the unity and togetherness that this team created. Tara Mueller said, with regard to the high level of team chemistry: "That comes from great communication, from asking everybody what it is they need. That's something we've worked on, and now I know what each person needs and what I need from them. That's how you make a great team." Kayla Banwarth said, "At the beginning of the season, we questioned whether we could do it, whether we could be here. Now we know. We stuck with it. We stuck with him as a coach, and we trusted in him even though we didn't know what was going to happen. His faith in us is motivation."

In the Elite Eight matchup, they took set one versus Texas and played a great match but could not overcome the play of Texas's superstar, Destinee Hooker. In the end, the 2009 team improved significantly as the year progressed, and there was growth in the leaders on the team. They won thirty-one straight sets from November 4 to December 11 in a "November to Remember," and it was a team that put themselves in a position to max out when it mattered the most.

The 2009 season showed me that with enough engagement I could make an impact on a team. One of the other lessons I learned

was that a coach, or anybody in a leadership position, can feel isolated, and it can be somewhat lonely in the role; my being able to
provide perspective and support to Coach Cook was something that
he appreciated and valued.

What I didn't know at the time—but made much more sense in
retrospect—was that some of the problems Coach Cook was having,
especially early in the 2009 season, were in part due to his struggles
with stress and burnout, created partly by his wiring but also because
of the expectations he put on himself to be perfect. In June 2009 he
had a "breakdown" and had no explanations for what his mind and
body were doing to him. In a *Lincoln Journal Star* story on May 8,
2010, Cook said, "There were doubts about whether I could coach
last season in the summer. I was worried, asking myself, 'Do I need
to get out of coaching?'" He reached out for help with the expertise of
physicians and mental health providers, and he had a conversation
with Coach Tom Osborne. Coach Osborne revealed that in 1985 he
started to meditate daily as part of a treatment plan following surgery
for a blockage of an artery in his heart. He also suggested Coach Cook
read a book called *The Spectrum*, and he read it in one night. He
started to get the proper amount of sleep and made a commitment
to exercise and meditate daily.

Coach Cook's issues were not all that different from Urban
Meyer's in December 2009. Meyer was Florida football head coach at
the time, and his wife made the infamous 911 call in the middle of the
night when she thought he was having a heart attack. She couldn't
get him to talk, as he had taken Ambien for sleep. That year, Urban
had lost thirty-five to forty pounds during the season, wasn't sleeping
well, and was racked by the anxiety of trying to repeat as national
champions. The night of the 911 call, his team had just lost in the
SEC championship game to Alabama.

As part of the process of reinventing himself, Coach Cook opened up to me about his struggles. We then spoke to Paul Meyers (head of Athletic Development at the time) and others about getting the word out to other men in high-pressure jobs. Coach Cook said that while doing research that year for his own issues, he found out that many other high-performing men shared some of the same struggles. Coach said, "Their bodies are always on edge, and at some point you just can't do it. But men don't talk about it; that's the thing. Women talk about it . . . Men never talk about it, and we need to get into an arena when men can talk about it." Even Nick Saban, Alabama head football coach, told reporters before the national title game in 2009, "The worst part of being a coach is you live in a state of constant anxiety, every day, every play, every whatever. And when the game is over, you have these brief moments of relief where you're not anxious anymore. Before I get home, I'm worried about the next game, so the anxiety starts all over again."

If Nick Saban, Urban Meyer, and Coach Cook have all struggled, it just points out the realities of the mind-body stress reaction and the importance of finding ways to manage it. Let's remember that when Coach Cook was feeling his worst, his record at Nebraska was 307-26 with two national titles in his first nine years at Nebraska! High levels of success do not prevent these issues and may actually make them more likely to occur for a variety of reasons.

We put on a Team Wellness program called "Competing with Stress and Aging and Winning" in May 2010 for many of the top athletic department boosters in the state. Mostly men attended, but a few women came as well. We brought in experts on wellness from the Cooper Clinic in Dallas, Texas. Coach Cook, Coach Osborne, and many others spoke that day. In his address, Coach Cook said, "I have as much passion as I've ever had for coaching, but I have to manage myself, and the test will be when we get into the heat of the season. Can I continue with the reinvention of how I manage myself of my time and my emotions and my energy? It's the same thing we ask of our players: discipline every day."

The word *courage* came to my mind about Coach Cook after the Team Wellness program. Courage to take over a program that had been in the hands of a legend, Coach Terry Pettit, and courage to share his struggles in such a public manner. It does not usually end well for a coach in the former situation, and it is rare for a person, particularly a man, in the latter situation to be that open about struggles such as those he described.

Coach felt like the team was on solid footing heading into 2010. The team went on a summer trip to China that helped hyperdrive relationships on and off the court. His daughter Lauren transferred back to Nebraska from UCLA, and a six-two system, meaning the use of two setters, was used with Sydney Anderson returning and Lauren. Other than working with some individuals on the team, Coach had not asked me to do anything with the team or leaders in the off-season or the start of the season. However, I did come up with a couple of team exercises that Coach approved. First, during August camp, I showed them an hour-long video I had put together with a series of movie clips, each with a message, and the first video footage of their trip to China, including their climb of the Great Wall. Each lady received a volleyball and each week passed it around so another team member could write something positive on the ball. It was my first foray into the Power of Appreciation. Finally, we had the team make a video in which each lady had a "Power of Positive" phrase for herself. The team liked it so much that they chose to watch it before every match that year. Besides these activities, I had no other role with the team itself that year, other than working with individuals one-on-one.

Coach did ask me to start observing body language and verbal/nonverbal communication at the games, both the ladies' and his own. I communicated with him quite frequently concerning my observations while at the same time continuing to build a relationship where he began to trust my suggestions for some of the individuals on the team. As a byproduct of going to the games, I started to observe his mannerisms in good times and under stress. There were a couple of things I noticed that year. First, he didn't always model for the team what he wanted from them: composure and positive communication. He would chirp at them in a negative fashion when they came out of the match as they ran by him, for example. He would pace on the sidelines at times. During time-outs, especially when he called the time-out, his body language and nonverbal cues sometimes came off as being angry. Second, he had a short leash when one of the players made an error and would often pull her out of the game. I made mental notes and shared my observations.

As our relationship strengthened, I also tried to support him, given what I knew about the issues he was still working through. In addition, I continued to recognize how easy it could be for a head coach or, for that matter, people in any leadership position to feel a sense of isolation and loneliness. We talked about the concept of having a "team within a team," and while that didn't come to fruition for a few years, its genesis was in 2010.

The 2010 season was generally successful without the ups and downs of 2009. I believe that Coach may have underestimated some of the challenges of running a six-two system—both technically and emotionally—on the ladies. There is also the challenge of introducing a family member into the team, which creates some stress for all parties. Coach asked me to meet with leaders unexpectedly once during the season. Keep in mind that I had not met with them collectively all year. When I walked into the room, one of the ladies said to me, "When we heard you were coming, we said to each other, 'We must be in trouble, because Doc is coming to talk to us.'" I felt terrible, and I told them that this would be the last time I ever met with them if I wasn't around the team throughout the year—in good times and in bad. Without mutual trust, which takes time to build, it is not fair to anybody involved in the process. We had a good meeting, addressed their issues, and did not have a follow-up meeting that year. I did tell Coach Cook my concerns and the comments made by his leaders.

The team advanced to the regional finals, was defeated by Washington, and finished the year 29–3. It is hard to see the cracks that develop in a team and its culture when a team is that successful by most people's measures. It was the second straight year of not making the Final Four. Just like a highly successful business that may have slowed profit growth but is still doing extremely well by industry standards, it's easy to get complacent or just not recognize that some erosion is occurring. In retrospect, I suspect Coach Cook also wished he had redshirted Lauren that season.

Coach and I had talked about implementing a year-round program to incorporate working on mindset, leadership, communication, and team chemistry. However, after the season, both of his assistants moved to other jobs, one as head coach at Georgia and the other to a similar position at Texas. Coach Cook's focus changed to replacing his staff. He hired Dan Meske, who had been the volunteer assistant. The second coach, Dan Conners, had come from the West Coast. This was a big change from the stable, seasoned staff he'd had for the past few years. It was the start of a series of challenges that never ended that year. For whatever reason, Coach did not utilize me at all that year in the team setting. When he asked me to speak to the team the night of the NCAA selection show at the end of November,

I turned him down, having learned my lesson from the past year. I just didn't see how I could make an impact at that point of the year. The season ended like no other team had before, falling short of even making the second weekend of the tournament. It was proof that if there are enough interferences on a team, it's virtually impossible to max out, no matter the talent level.

As you can imagine, Coach Cook was in a dark place after the season. He knew some changes had to occur, but he was still not committed to having—or didn't know how to implement—full engagement from sport psych. We did a couple of things in the off-season that suggested he wanted a different level of engagement. We started meeting weekly during the winter/spring with identified leaders for the 2012 season, and Coach Cook participated every week. Some big breakthroughs were made regarding communication, working through conflict, and building better relationships among the leaders. In retrospect, we made the mistake of never including the rest of the team at any point, and there is no question that many of them felt left out. We also held a coaches' retreat out of town over part of two days that went very well. The problem, however, was that Coach Conners left abruptly for another job at Illinois just prior to the season, and Coach Cook had to scramble to find his replacement. He did well to lure Coach Dani Busboom Kelly, a former player on his 2006 national title team, back to Lincoln.

Coach and I had ongoing dialogue about how important he thought the role of sport psych could be for his program and how much he valued the role of the mental game. I told him that to do it right, we would need consistent visits of at least thirty minutes per week with the entire team. He shook his head and said that he didn't believe that was possible. When I asked him how often they did yoga, he said that the team did it once a week for an hour. And when I asked him why they did it weekly, he told me that it was very important for the team. I then asked how often they did other things, like postpractice ice baths or working with the strength trainer, and I think he finally got the point. I told him there was a disconnect between what he said he valued and the time/effort he was giving to what he valued—in this case, sport psych involvement. Then I suggested that he contact me when he was ready to commit to sport psych similar to his investment in yoga or other endeavors.

I worked with more of the athletes individually in 2012, and I did a couple short exercises with the team during the course of the season. The team had a pretty solid year, but given the talent on the team, most people would say they underperformed, losing in the regional finals again to Oregon in Omaha.

The same issues that I'd observed about him and his team in 2010 remained following the 2012 season. It was also the fourth straight year his team had not made the Final Four. His teams could not find a way to beat Texas or Penn State; the latter was now in the same conference and had won four national titles in a row from 2007 to 2010. After the 2012 season, his focus narrowed and his competitive fire kicked in. I could tell, however, that some doubt entered his mind on how to go about solving the issues he identified. That being said, he wanted to assess every part of his program with the goal of finding a way to be two points better than Texas and Penn State. He was finally ready to implement a year-round sport psych component. The evolution of a coach was about to begin.

Here are the components that he identified as being critical for me to help his team:

- Help our players deal with failure, self-esteem, and communication.

- Measure and record feedback within practice between coaches and players.
- Assist with goal setting.
- Provide insight and suggestions to the coaches on observations with individual players and special needs.
- Observe body language and player interactions, and provide insight and suggestions to keep them positive.
- Debrief coaches after practices and matches.
- With such a big team, and understanding the importance of everyone feeling connected, identify players that might start feeling disconnected.
- Help create the ideal performance state with the team and coaches.
- Observe players and coaches during matches with regard to body language and emotions.
- Help create and nurture a positive environment for a team that is committed and believes in success.

Wow! I had to give Coach credit—when he made the decision to incorporate sport psych, he went all in! He also picked an incredibly challenging year to do so. He had seven new freshmen and two transfer players from Tennessee to add to the roster. Only eight of the seventeen players remained from the previous year's team. Given all the youth, it was a great time to start incorporating many of the components that Coach Cook identified. We started in the off-season by meeting as a team (without the coaches) on a weekly basis just to get to know each other, start the communication process, set goals, and so forth, but most of the freshmen didn't come until summer.

I started coming to practice a minimum of three times per week during spring practice and again during fall camp, with the primary focus of monitoring Coach Cook's mannerisms and interactions with the team. As you can imagine, with seven freshmen team members, there would be a large learning curve to understand how to practice, train, and play Husker Volleyball. Mary Pollmiller was a junior setter but had transferred in from Tennessee. Similarly, Kelsey Robinson, a senior outside hitter, also came from Tennessee. It took them less time to understand what was expected, and the year would not have been nearly as successful without them.

The year started off slow, with an early loss to a senior-laden team in Auburn. The Huskers team was high in errors in early matches but consistently improved during the season. One of the monitoring tools we devised was a simple positive-communication scoring system; the expectation was for a player between every point to give some type of positive communication to a teammate—a high five, a smile, a positive verbal comment, a positive body touch, or eye contact, for example. The purpose of monitoring this behavior was twofold: to increase awareness of the importance of positive communication and to train positive communication. It was a simple scoring system: one point for a positive communication and zero points for anything else. For one athlete in particular, after tracking her for twenty-eight sets over several matches, there was 100 percent correlation. During winning sets, this athlete had positive communications 62 percent of the time and during losing sets only 38 percent of the time. The most exciting finding was that over time—through awareness and training—positive communication improved overall from the beginning of the assessment until the end, from about 50 percent positive communication to 70 percent positive communication during wins. Even during losses, positive communication increased from 30 percent to 50 percent. When this one athlete looked at the data, she told us, "When I communicate in a positive way with my teammates, we win!"

Of course, I was there to monitor Coach Cook as well. He struggled at times with negative body language and frustration and would often yell at his assistant coaches from across the gym. He was also harder on some ladies than others. On the positive side, it was clear that everything in practice had a purpose and that no team was ever going to be better prepared physically, technically, and tactically. Many of the ladies committed to work on mindset in one-on-one meetings. However, growth still needed to occur with regard to relationship building between Coach and his assistants, and between Coach and his players.

The challenges on the 2013 team were mostly due to lack of experience and learning how to play together, since there were so many new starters on the court from the prior year. The team improved dramatically and made a run in the postseason that fell short at home against one main nemesis, Texas. Kelsey Robinson had a phenomenal season in her one year as a Husker. She is currently a member of the US Women's National Volleyball Team and has played a prominent role in the success of her team! I believe that the 2013 Huskers came close to maxing out and were playing their best volleyball at the end of the season. That being said, in crunch time, when it mattered the most, there appeared to be some apprehension or fear within the team.

During the 2013 season, another event developed that took Coach Cook's evolution to another level. Jack Riggins, Navy SEAL, started to interface a little with the team that year whenever he came back to the US on leave from Germany where he was stationed. I had been preaching to Coach that you build great teams though love, that teams need to have fun on and off the court and play with joy—but he bristled at that to some degree. He started his career in coaching as a football coach, and he had played for a coach who did not share my philosophies! He also loved the way the Chinese national volleyball team trained and played, and he honestly wanted players to be nonemotional killers on the court, like the Russian character Ivan Drago in *Rocky IV*. Drago was trained to compete like a machine, like a robot. Drago, however, didn't make deep interpersonal connections. Under stress, he fell apart in the ring and had no ability to handle adversity. While he was a fictional character, Drago, like the brick wall that was built by the University of Florida softball team without the mortar, was not nearly as sturdy as he appeared. In the end, Drago was not able to be fearless when it mattered the most.

When Coach Cook first met Jack, I know that he thought Jack's view would be more similar to his own rather than what I had been articulating. Coach had the perception that a Navy SEAL was a cold, calculated killer. In a 2019 podcast in which he was interviewed by Jack, he admitted that his first perception of a Navy SEAL was "a bad-ass dude, mean, stealth." But Jack told him the same thing I was telling him: that it was a brotherhood with a focus on love and building deep relationships that led the SEALs to assemble the best teams in US military history. Even with that knowledge, it would be a couple more years before Coach Cook was able to internalize completely what Jack told him.

In January 2014, the first Performance Team was created at the University of Nebraska. Conversations between Jack and me with Coach Cook imagined the 2014 and 2015 seasons as part of a two-year plan, considering that virtually the entire team other than Mary Pollmiller would be back in 2015. Essentially, all of the critical support staff met in one room with each player: athletic trainer; nutritionist; strength/conditioning coach; biomechanics expert; Jack (leadership on Skype from Germany); me (mental/mindset/sport psych); our director of operations; and the coaching staff. We then devised a comprehensive plan for each team member. The ladies already had a detailed goal setting sheet they filled out, encompassing such things as academic goals, nutritional goals, wellness goals, off-court team goals, and skill goals. The Performance Team Profile that Jack put together also gave them a word for the year and a couple of challenges specific to each athlete. In these player meetings, I witnessed a caring side to Coach Cook, a depth to him that I had not previously observed. He was thoughtful but very clear about his expectations.

Geno Auriemma is one of the most successful coaches of all time as head coach of the University of Connecticut women's basketball program. He has said, "When you have great relationships with your players, you can coach them as hard as you want to coach them, and they love it." I intentionally asked Coach Cook to attend a game when Geno's team came to play in Lincoln, Nebraska, in the NCAA tournament in March 2014. I knew Coach Cook had great respect for Geno, so I wanted him to observe Coach Auriemma's demeanor and mannerisms during the game and the way he interacted with his players. The lesson: nobody prepared a team like Coach Auriemma, and he trained them in a deliberate way, but it was also evident that his players connected with him in a favorable way. Coach Auriemma communicated in a positive manner with his team and maintained his composure, even when his team faced an early deficit. Coach Cook left the Pinnacle Bank Arena with more validation of how the best coaches model love and accountability.

The Performance Team had a follow-up meeting in the spring with each member of the volleyball team to review all aspects of their training and to adjust goals and expectations as necessary. There was an accountability plan inherently built into this model, and it served the ladies well in the off-season, especially since the team was headed to China in the summer. We put together a mental boot camp in the weeks leading up to China to help with mindset training and prepare them for the stressors associated with going on this long trip, since they would be taken out of their comfort zone. High-performance mental skills training was done with the team for the first time ever, and I introduced mindfulness training as well. I asked their yoga instructor (because the ladies liked her voice) to make an audio recording from a script I had written that included deep-breathing exercises, visualization exercises, and meditation. It was hard to get the team in 2014 to buy fully into doing mindfulness exercises, in part because I did not do as good a job then as now in explaining all the benefits and the WHY behind doing it on a consistent basis.

Jack was able to go with the team to China, and it gave him a vantage point that helped us come up with a much more defined plan for Coach. Jack also built relationships with the ladies that were critical for trust since they didn't get to see him as often, making it much easier to reconnect with them when he came home on leave.

Upon their return and with the start of fall camp, a couple of things were observed. One, because the freshmen didn't go to China, they felt left out, since Coach and the ladies referenced the trip so often. Second, Coach still got frustrated very quickly and tended to take it out on certain players and on his coaching staff. Some of the ladies on the team shared their frustrations during one of our team visits. They felt that if Coach wanted the team to have positive communication with each other, he should do the same with his assistant coaches and with all of the players on the team. They gave a specific example: if somebody made a mistake in a drill, Coach would often scream across the court in a negative manner at the assistant in charge of that position to fix the issue. When Coach was made aware of this, it made sense to him, and we discussed a couple of options. He could walk over and make the correction himself, or he could pull the assistant coach aside and share his concerns about what needed to be fixed. When he made that change, it had a big impact on the mindset of the ladies.

One of the cool things Coach came up with before the start of the season was his five-year vision. His pillars were tradition, education, pursuit of greatness, and careers. He wanted to show everyone—the team, administration, fans, and boosters—what his ultimate vision was for Nebraska Volleyball with the foundation built on the tradition of the program. These were all ingredients that he wanted to enhance and certainly not take for granted in the years ahead.

- The **tradition pillar** referred to the sellout streak, being number one in attendance in the nation, and thirty-eight All-Americans, which also led the nation.
- Coach was most proud of the **education pillar** with twenty-four Academic All-Americans, a 3.3 GPA, and a 100 percent graduation rate.
- His pillar of the **pursuit of greatness** reflected on areas of focus such as training the complete athlete, mind-body balance, leadership development, and life skills.
- Finally, he was also proud that many of the ladies went on to have **careers** playing professionally, on the women's national team, or both.

Now, back to the beginning of the season. They started off with two home losses to seasoned teams, Stanford and Florida State. There were challenges early on in having to replace Kelsey Robinson, who had graduated. The team was still very young with only one senior, Mary Pollmiller, on the team. Kelly Hunter made the decision to redshirt that year as well. We tried to stay process focused, as the preseason and Big Ten season were brutal.

I started a "Coach's Monitoring Sheet for Match or Practice," which Coach and I filled out, with most questions rated one to ten. The score would be based on how he handled himself during critical moments, after a controversial call, after a mistake by one of his players, and during emotional moments. There were also a few questions about what he did to support the team and to demonstrate confidence, and what he would do differently given the chance. It was a great self-awareness tool for Coach, and it started to get him more into a solution-focused mode. I also had a "Weekly Coach's Monitoring Sheet" that he and I filled out, but I also asked assistant coaches and other support staff who were there every day to do this as well. We rated the following areas from one to ten: composure, confidence, encourager, enforcer, and overall score. Everyone had a chance to identify what went well that week, what didn't go so well, and what Coach could do differently. They also were able to reflect on how the team was doing with regard to focus, confidence, unity, physical state, and if they were having fun. Since Coach is data driven, it was very useful information for him, and he was also able to see how other members of his staff observed him. Early on, he tended to rate himself higher in areas as compared to his staff, but as the season progressed, both Coach and his staff identified overall improvement, and there was alignment in the ratings.

At the midpoint of the season, I did a checkup with each class separately. Three questions were asked of the ladies, each with two parts:

- What does the team do well? What do the coaches do well?
- What are a couple of things the team can do better? Same for coaches.
- What are the action plans for the things the team can do better? Same for coaches.

While there were a number of common themes with regard to the team—both good and in areas for improvement—the most enlightening information came from the comments about what the coaches could do better from the team's vantage point, and specifically the action plans they suggested.

## COMMON THEMES

- Coach gets frustrated after one mistake.
- Coach makes comments that are personal.
- Coach blames the team during time-outs.
- When Coach is in a good mood at practice, we do so much better.
- Coach needs to show more interest in all of us.
- The coaching staff needs to be more cohesive, and Coach needs to be more positive with them in front of the team.

## ACTION PLAN SUGGESTED BY THE TEAM

- Have awareness that we are twenty-year-old women and we already know what we did wrong, so don't get so frustrated after one mistake. That leads to being afraid to mess up and playing with fear.

- Make comments more specific on how to get better, and make fewer personal comments, especially during time-outs.
- Be louder with positive comments.
- SET THE TONE. When you're positive and in a good mood, we do so much better!
- Get to know us better.
- Coach needs to model positive communication for us with his coaching staff.

On the positive side, the team felt that Coach Cook always had them well prepared, held them accountable, and had good insight, and they craved the times he gave positive comments after a good play.

To Coach Cook's credit, he internalized what he learned from the midseason checkup and used the information to make positive improvements in the second half of the season. Even though the team had a tough weekend the last week of the regular season, it was evident that great progress was being made. The team had a major challenge in the second game of the postseason against a very mature Utah team and found a way to win a close one in five sets. The reward was a Sweet 16 battle against number three–ranked Washington in Washington. On December 12. I sent the team an email to help put in perspective the season, the areas where I saw the most improvement, and the reasons they had a right to be confident even with the odds stacked against them. I ended the message this way: "You can all go out this weekend and play with fearlessness, with love for each other, and for the joy of playing your sport. You have nothing to lose. You've earned this opportunity." The team lost the first set but then took over the match, decisively winning in four sets! It was by far their most complete match of the season. Afterward Coach said, "Our team just really did a great job with the game plan. I thought at the end we handled the crowd really well. It was a tremendous effort by our team against a great opponent, especially on their home court. It was a huge effort by our team. This team's been getting better and better as the season goes on. We played really well last week, and we've been training really well. I expected us to play great tonight, and I told them that yesterday at practice—with the effort they put in and their focus and how hard they worked, they should expect to have a great effort tonight. And they did."

Unfortunately, they couldn't keep the momentum the following night, and a red-hot BYU team won and advanced to the Final Four. The drought was up to six years at this point in not making a Final Four. While great progress was made in the 2014 season, based on what we learned during the midseason evaluations and with my overall assessment, there was still much more to do. You may have noticed that Coach Cook's comments after the Washington win were all about the game plan and preparation, not about relationships. That was about to change!

Coach Terry Pettit said this about the importance of evolving: **"The heart of a great coach is his or her ability to adjust after recognizing patterns in their own behaviors and decisions that keep a program from moving forward."**

The work we all did preparing for and in the 2015 season was some of the most gratifying of my life. Coach started out with thirty-two areas where the team program needed to improve following the loss to BYU. Most of the items had to do with what he saw Penn State being able to accomplish and how they went about doing it. Thus, the list really reflected the things necessary to beat Penn State.

Coach had finally fully bought into how we were incorporating working with the team leaders, implementing exercises to help train specific skills, and continuing to come up with individualized plans for each athlete. In January 2015 we narrowed the Performance Team down to Lindsay Peterson (director of operations), the coaching staff, Jack, and me. At that moment in time, Coach identified us as "his team within a team" (including his wife, Wendy). That is, persons, often of different backgrounds, who can provide support, honest feedback, willingness to share the hard truths if necessary, and offer perspective to a leader. This is one of the first areas in which I saw Coach evolve. He allowed others into his "inner circle," whereas in the recent past there were not many people he ever allowed in. As mentioned before, it can be very lonely at the top of any organization, and Coach's creating his "team within a team" was something that helped him take his coaching to a higher level.

Coach Cook had a way of showing his human, caring side in these meetings better than ever, and we needed to leverage these interactions during the year, especially when the stress of the season hit. The ladies developed great action plans for improvement in the off-season. There were a few ladies we identified in these meetings who had to make some changes and show a new level of commitment if they wanted to remain a part of the team.

The 2014 team taught us that positive communication needed to be worked on by all parties, that the coaches needed to be more cohesive, and that the ladies wanted Coach to get to know them better. We also challenged the ladies to take it to another level.

In February 2015 we devised a team exercise in which each player and coach had to come up with one or more movie scenes that were meaningful to them and share with all of us why they picked those scenes. We felt it was a safe way to start practicing vulnerability since it wasn't something this team had done before. Coach was able to show vulnerability when he explained why movies were so important to him, including how many move him to laugh and cry.

His explanation of the movie scenes he picked allowed the ladies to see his human side and get to know him just a little bit better. Many of the ladies went deep and shared insights with the team that set the foundation for building stronger relationships with each other over the course of the year.

Concurrently, we started a book club just for the coaches and selected *Win Forever*, by Pete Carroll. We felt Coach Cook would relate to Coach Carroll since they shared similarities in their desire to compete. We wanted Coach to see how Coach Carroll evolved over time regarding several things, including the formation of his values and philosophy. Coach Cook's philosophy that he came up with included a part about coaching with love. It was the first time I had ever heard him talking about coaching through love, so I knew he was starting to internalize our conversations even more. He had also watched or rewatched the movie *Lone Survivor*. The brotherhood and love displayed by the Navy SEALs struck him in a way that made him finally realize that a SEAL was willing to fight so hard for the man to his right and for the man to his left because of the love and connection they felt for each other. It's where the genesis of deep trust begins and ends.

In March and April 2015, we did an exercise that we hoped would build upon our past positive-communication exercises, partly through awareness that others would be monitoring them. Think of the behavior change that occurs when a policeman is driving next to you or is monitoring a road in the open for those going over the speed limit. We asked everyone associated with the team to write down any positive or negative comments that they heard from coaches or anybody else on the team. We wanted to know what was said, where it was said, who said it, and how it made them feel. The comments were written anonymously on cards and placed in a lockbox. Initially we learned that 62 percent of the comments were seen as positive, 36 percent were negative, and 2 percent were neutral. We learned something really valuable: that it didn't take much to pick folks up or shut them down. A simple compliment in the weight room about effort, a smile, a high five, or a question about how things were going all elicited positive emotions. We learned that nonverbal cues from coaches were also powerful, especially if they were seen as negative. We shared the data with the leaders and encouraged them to continue to model what positive communication looks like for the rest of the team. We shared the data with the team and gave shout-outs to teammates who were deemed the most positive. We continued to show Coach the types of communication the ladies loved, and vice versa.

During this time period, changes occurred that shook the team to the core, but I believe this was also one of the reasons they became such a tight team. On April 1 it was announced that three ladies (eventually four) were leaving the program, all for different reasons, but in the age of social media, Coach Cook and the program were taking some hits on the message boards. It was a time for the ladies who remained to rally around each other and Coach. Interestingly, we recalculated the positive-communication data, removing the four players from the results, and we learned something helpful to the team as it worked on moving forward: a high proportion of the negative communications came from some of the ladies who were no longer on the team. This let the team know that positives can also come with change and that the cohesiveness of the team would likely greatly improve.

Another major change occurred when Dan Meske, our longtime assistant, took a head coaching job at another school in early May 2015. I was asked to be part of the interview process to hire a new assistant, and there were wonderful candidates. When we did our first interviews over Skype, I knew within minutes whom I thought would be the best fit for Coach Cook. Ultimately, Coach Cook agreed with my observations and hired Chris Tamas at the end of May. His wife, Jen, who had been part of the US Women's National Team, became the volunteer assistant and what I called "the hidden ingredient or X factor" of the team, given her knowledge, credibility, and personality. Chris had a rare combination of confidence without coming off as cocky, and it was clear that he would be able to complement Coach Cook and Coach Dani Busboom Kelly.

> It is during our darkest moments that we must focus to
> see the light.
>
> —Aristotle Onassis

I always think of this quote when remembering the phone call I received from Coach Cook one evening in June 2015. It was a low point for Coach Cook when Molly Haggerty decommitted from Nebraska. The whole situation was upsetting to him, but the details are not important. It is during these times that I am the most helpful to a coach or leader—in the dark times. Sometimes just to be a sounding board, to give advice or perspective. These are the times one remembers that make the successful moments later on so great to share together. These are also the moments when one feels the most connected to another human being. I still will never forget a couple of his phone calls to me, late at night, when I was suffering the effects of the shingles that attacked my facial nerve in the fall of 2014. The humanity he showed and the empathy he had in those moments not only helped me through my dark times but also gave me hope that he could show the ladies the same level of connection that he showed to me. That phone call to me after Molly decommitted represented the low point for Coach, but luckily, other than a few bumps in the road, it was an upward trajectory from that moment in time!

Around that time, Jack Riggins moved back to the United States, which made it easier to coordinate with the team leaders as we headed into summer, when we often asked the team leaders to give input on different ideas or if they agreed with a team exercise at all. Coincidentally, the US Women's National Volleyball Team (USWNT) would be playing in the World Grand Prix Finals in Omaha, Nebraska, over several days in July. It is always good when lessons can be learned by watching others you can relate to, want to emulate, or even idolize. It is more powerful than hearing me talk about the same concepts. I wanted our ladies to observe the coaches and their demeanor when the team was playing well and when they were stressed. Of special interest was Karch Kiraly, who was a two-time Olympic volleyball gold medalist, a coach, and an announcer. I wanted them to observe the bench energy and the huddles between points. We agreed to get back together to discuss what they had learned. There were also three former Huskers on the USWNT: Kayla Banwarth, Jordan Larson, and Kelsey Robinson. Before our team met to review what they learned, I found a video of Coach Cook meeting his former players after they had won the championship against Brazil. It was the first thing I showed the team. I wanted them to see the warmth that his former players showed him and the genuine, loving hugs that they shared. It was powerful for the team to see yet one more side of Coach Cook, especially as a new team was still forming with the newly arrived freshmen.

Here is what they learned from observing the USWNT:

- Coach Kiraly always had a calm demeanor, even when they were behind. They liked how he listened intently during time-outs but let the assistant coach do most of the talking.
- They noted how tight the huddles were between every point.

They pointed out that the huddles lasted a little bit longer and would be even tighter when the team was under stress. The ladies also commented that Brazil had the most energetic, tight huddles and celebrations when things were going well but completely broke apart under stress.

- They identified how energized the bench for the USWNT was throughout the match. The USWNT had dances and certain moves they made depending on the circumstance. They noted that Courtney Thompson, who was their serving specialist, took control of the bench energy.

- They noted how the ladies on the USWNT played with joy but also fearlessness.

- They commented on the fact that Coach did not pull players after they made errors.

The reason for the exercise was that I wanted the team to decide what they wanted to emulate from the USWNT. Of course, this information was meant for Coach Cook as well. Two-a-days were about to start, and he asked me a question that he had asked a few months earlier. When he asked it the first time, I didn't know the answer. I had a lot more confidence that I could answer it now, but it was just as important that he could come up with answers. Here's the question:

### HOW DO I GET MY TEAM TO PLAY FEARLESS AT ENDGAME?

I asked him what he thought the reasons were that they sometimes played with fear at endgame (since 2009). He gave me several answers, all of which had some merit. I then asked one of the few questions that have probably ever stumped him:

## *WHAT'S YOUR CONTRIBUTION TO THE PROBLEM?*

In other words, what role did Coach play in their playing with fear? He initially couldn't come up with any answers. I told him to sit on it for a day, and then I devised a plan to ask a few of the ladies to help Coach Cook discover the answers. To this day, it is one of the conversations I believe has had the most impact on the Coach's evolution. The following day I asked him a series of questions, then after he gave me his answers, I asked one of the ladies to share what they were thinking.

- What do the ladies think when you get up and start pacing the sideline?

  ⇒ Coach Cook's answer: I think the ladies love it; they see me as engaged and fighting for them.
  ⇒ Team answer: When you get up and start pacing, it makes us anxious on the court, and we think you don't trust us.

- Why do your athletes look over at you on the sideline after they make a mistake?

  ⇒ Coach Cook's answer: They are looking over at me because they are looking for a correction and they know I will have the answer.
  ⇒ Team answer: We look over at you to see if you're going to pull us out of the game, because you pull us a lot after we make mistakes.

- Why do the athletes try to avoid running by you when they are naturally coming out of the game or especially if they are being pulled?

  ⇒ Coach Cook's answer: They are just trying to get over to their team where they stand.
  ⇒ Team answer: You usually have something negative to say to us, and we already know what we did wrong.

- What does the team think when you get fired up during a time-out, at times slamming your clipboard, especially late in a match?

  ⇒ Coach Cook's answer: I think they like it, as they know how much I care and I am just trying to motivate them.
  ⇒ Team answer: When you get angry or mad or anxious, it makes us feel the same way, and we don't remember anything you told us during the time-out.

- What does the team think when you get frustrated with an official, to the point at times of getting a yellow or red card?

  ⇒ Coach Cook's answer: They love that I am fighting for the team for what is right.
  ⇒ Team answer: We appreciate that he is fighting for us, but it really just gets us uptight and anxious, and sometimes even embarrassed.

At the end of the meeting, I went over each question just with Coach alone to see if he understood what his contribution to the problem may have been with regard to playing fearlessly. I then asked him to do four things, which he agreed to do:

- He agreed not to pace the sideline or even stand up for very long unless he needed to communicate with the setter.
- He agreed to not pull a player unless she was absolutely discombobulated or if she broke team chemistry on the court.
- If he needed to make a suggestion or correction when a player was coming off the court, I asked that he stop her, look her in the eye, and give a positive correction. Otherwise, don't say a word, or have her sit and talk with one of the assistant coaches.
- I asked him to be aware of how his emotions impacted the team during time-outs and even when he talked to the officials.

I promised him that if he did these tasks better and we continued to work on individual issues and team trust, the team would learn to play fearlessly during matches, particularly at endgame.

As the second scorecard for measuring himself, I planned to give him a mantra at the beginning of each season over four years. His 2015 mantra: **"model the behaviors you want."** Since his number one goal was to have his team play fearlessly, he knew he needed to model that for the ladies—and if he followed through on the plan noted above, he would put his team in a position to do so.

Another exercise, having the team define what ultimate trust meant to them, ended up becoming a much bigger factor with this team than I would have imagined. We obviously wanted this team to fully trust in each other, but they went on to own this phrase in a way that I had not seen before. I am going to explain what we did in the following chapter.

Of course, the last project we did before the season started in August was the exercise previously reviewed about the team contacting past members of the 2000, 2006, and 2008 teams—the three teams that had maxed out under Coach Cook in the past. As you may remember, only a couple of common themes were noted. The teams that embraced their roles, committed to building deeper relationships, and found a way to love each other were the teams that succeeded. We were about to find out if all the lessons learned from the prior year and during the off-season would pay off for the 2015 team.

Right after our meeting in August, I found out that the University of Nebraska Athletic Department made a decision to no longer allow part-time help or outside consultants to work with athletes in the department offices. The Athletic Department eventually determined that outside consultants couldn't help in any capacity, even if the coaches requested it. However, at that moment in time, I was told that I could continue working with the team but not one-on-one with the ladies. After consulting with Coach Cook, we both felt it was in their best interests to have somebody who could do both. My role was to continue working with him and work on the problems he gave me. By this time, Jack and I had spent so much time with the team that they were ready to roll. And of course, the university could not tell athletes what to do if they wanted to visit in a private setting.

I still came to practice several times a week, continued to observe Coach and the team and give him feedback, and would give my input on performance to the ladies with whom I had built relationships.

Kelly Hunter had been biding her time to take over the starting reins at setter, even taking an unusual redshirt year after she played as serving specialist her freshman year. Kelly had worked hard to develop a relationship with Coach Cook, and she was the beneficiary of his willingness to build relationships better than ever with his players this year. There was a "once in a generation" type of trust between Kelly and Coach Cook, although one could argue that he'd had a similar relationship with his daughter Lauren when she played for him.

Teams that go on special runs usually have several role players who impact the team. Alicia Ostrander fit that bill. She was from a small town of about sixteen hundred people called Gordon in western Nebraska. Alicia had played a variety of positions in her career and made fourteen starts her junior season. Despite her relatively small playing time, she was named a captain her senior year. She had a quiet but powerful way of leading the team, and she was a big factor in how cohesive the team was that year. It shouldn't surprise you that when the team members all took a test that measured grit, she had the highest score on the team. She had lost her starting spot to Kelsey Fien at the midoint of her junior season and never got it back. Alicia said, "It wasn't easy at the beginning of the year, because everybody wants to be on the court. It was especially hard not being the leader on the court, but I try to give kids that are coming in and out of the game tips on what I'm seeing, or just finding different leadership roles that I can fill outside of being on the court. Playing isn't as important to me as I thought it would be. You can find important roles off the court. I use it as life lessons. You don't always get what you want in life, and you have to make the best of it." It had to be rewarding for her to see how the fans embraced her. Whenever she came into the game or made a kill, the fans would all make a big O with their arms.

We have already touched on Kelsey Fien and her rise up the program. She worked hard to gain the trust of her teammates and coaches. Early in the season, she said, "It's great having the coaches know they can trust me in big-time matches, and they do trust me to take those big swings."

The team had strong middle blockers in Cici Hall, who was one of the ladies who kept it light on the team, and Amber Rolfzen, who moved to middle in the off-season. The right side was taken over by Kadie Rolfzen. Both were playing at an All-American level. Mikaela Foecke emerged as a freshman powerhouse, which is very rare in a program run by Coach Cook. The back row was incredible with Justine Wong-Orantes as libero and Annika Albrecht and Kenzie Maloney as back row defenders. Sydney Townsend, a walk-on from Lincoln, Nebraska, was the serving specialist. You never know how much the ladies on the team internalize the concepts you talk about, but a tweet from Kadie Rolfzen in October let me know it was affirmative:

*TIGHT HUDDLES AND ULTIMATE TRUST IS ALL YOU NEED.*

The season was going along smoothly until the weekend of October 23–24, when they played Minnesota and Wisconsin at home. Team chemistry was solid. Play was crisp. Coach was doing better on all the elements identified for him to do. Nebraska lost both matches! Past teams may have tanked, but this team had worked on their resilience. Jack Riggins showed the team a photo of their time-out huddles that indicated they were breaking apart in the Wisconsin match. Lauren Carlini, their All-American setter, made a couple of plays that nobody else in the country could make, and it rattled the team. The one element we identified was that the visiting team had won the energy battle both nights, something the Husker team had not lost all year. Jack had a discussion with them about what the team had full control over—not a great set or two by Lauren Carlini, but their attitude, effort, and, in this case, the energy level of the team.

Jack coined the phrase "Bring the E," and the team agreed that they would give themselves an "energy" score the rest of the year as a second scoreboard. The team felt that if they won the energy battle in all of their remaining matches, the outcome would take care of itself. Now, the team had no idea they would run the table for the rest of the regular season, but that is exactly what they did.

In the postseason, they lost set number one to Harvard University, an orthodox team to play, but took control of that match and the next one to advance to the Sweet 16 tournament. They went to Lexington, Kentucky, to face BYU and then Washington, handling both of them fairly easily to advance to their first Final Four since 2008—and they were going to play in Omaha, Nebraska, in front of a sold-out home crowd! And by the way, the team (along with their very active bench) won the energy battle!

During the week leading up to the Final Four, Jack and I received a call from Steve Sipple of the *Lincoln Journal Star*. He told us that Coach Cook asked him to contact us about a story Steve was doing regarding his evolution as a coach. I was always cautious about speaking to the press and actually had never done so up to this point of my career, but Coach Cook confirmed the request when I called him. Over the years, I'd loved reading Sipple's column and always found him to be authentic with his thoughts. He called this column "Cook's Evolution Put Huskers on Brink of Crown." He started off the column with a phrase that Coach still uses today:

*THE LONGER I COACH, THE LESS I KNOW.*

Coach went on to say, "Some of the feedback I got in the past was our girls maybe were not getting all they needed from me and my coaching staff."

Sipple shared that Coach wanted to address his shortcoming, then commented on leadership: "Don't underestimate Cook's desire to improve, and the lengths he's gone to do it ... Excellent leadership involves both an art and science. Cook long has had the science part down. You know, the technical side of the sport, the physical training, the tactical elements ... Cook hasn't always been deft when it comes to the art element behind good leadership—which involves an intuitive feel for what players might need emotionally and mentally."

Sipple noted that it was at Coach's urging that Jack and I played a consulting role for him and his players. Then Sipple went on to praise Coach for not deciding he had all the answers given his past overall record of success.

As I read Coach's comments, it was easy to see how much he was evolving: "When you talk about evolving, I think student-athletes fifteen years ago, even ten years ago, were much different to coach than they are now. I don't think we've lowered our expectations as a program, but I've had to adapt in many, many ways. The big thing is, I listen to my players better and I surrounded myself with a team within a team ... I bounce things off of them, and I ask about situations—how I could've done it better. I actually have them observe me during games."

Sipple noted the picture of the wide huddle we showed the team, and that our goal was to have the team tighten the huddle during times of adversity.

Cook states that he has learned from us the value of the following:

- Cultivating trust through the program
- Building relationships
- Maintaining open and honest communication

The CenturyLink Center in Omaha was wild, with over seventeen thousand attendees mostly clad in red, as Nebraska faced off against Kansas in the semifinal match. The Huskers used the "energy" in the building to provide them an additional spark in the four-set victory! Steve Sipple, in his next column called "Huskers Bring the 'E,'" discussed the role of the crowd, or what he called "urging energy" from them but was quick to point out the team did its job as well and learned its lesson from the Wisconsin loss. Sipple wrote about Jack Riggins's message to the team after the Wisconsin loss and his reminder, "You always control attitude and effort—and the big 'E' Energy."

Nebraska now had to face Texas, who had defeated Nebraska five straight times. Jack had made a promise to the ladies way back in China that if they made the finals he would wear a special robe that he made for them. He added a big red $E$ on the back as well. As his battle buddy, we added to the back of one of my medical jackets the words ULTIMATE TRUST. Coach Cook was stoic and calm. The team "played fearless" and had control for most of the match. It was surreal. It was joyful. It made one feel proud to be part of something bigger than just oneself. In the end, Coach Cook did so many things better, but the first thing he said to Jack and me back at the hotel was, "I don't even feel like I coached tonight." What he did do was follow the plan that we gave him before the season to help the team play fearlessly. He stood up only once and started to pace, and I will tell you what happened in that regard in the next chapter. He let players work through errors on the court. He gave the ladies instructions when they came off the court. He was much calmer and quieter during time-outs. He allowed the team to have fun and learned to play along. He made only one comment to the officials the entire night (and it was a bad call). The team trusted him, and he learned to trust the team.

It was rewarding to hear from Coach Cook in the press conference about the impact he thought the "mentoring" from past players had in this team's winning the national championship. While Lindsay Peterson helped organize the project, I had come up with the project myself in the spring of 2015 and had run it by Coach Cook. I created the questions, discussed them with Coach, and then asked Lindsay to reach out to the former players. As Coach said: "I think it gave us confidence and the courage to be able to go for this, knowing that they had done it before, and they gave us the secrets to success."

In 2016 there was a lot of pressure to repeat—and we all know how difficult that is to do. Coach Cook was feeling fairly anxious in the preseason, as he felt the pressure also. I gave him the mantra **"calm is contagious,"** based on a short video from a Navy SEAL in which he identified the single most important piece of advice his superior had given him. The SEAL went on to share that anything was contagious, mirroring the lessons we talk about as related to modeling the behaviors you want for others. Coach was at a point where it was much easier to model the behaviors that he wanted from those he led. He was doing yoga once a week and that year told us about the yoga instructor: " . . . talked about the Japanese always having a 'beginner's mind.' Once you're an expert, you already know all the things that can go wrong. You know what can't happen and what possibly could happen. And maybe you think you know it all. But if you have a 'beginner's mind,' you're open to learning new things." I know he did his best to prepare the team for the expectations and the pressure, and he had a veteran team that won the Big Ten Championship that year. Coach Cook honestly believes it is tougher to win the Big Ten than it is to win the national championship. He proved to be correct that year, although they did find their way back to the Final Four for the second consecutive year. In listening to Kelly Hunter talk near the end of the 2017 season about the 2016 season, you got a sense that the pressure was physically and mentally exhausting. In reference to the 2016 team, Hunter said, "Last year [2016] we were a great team on paper and we won a lot of tough matches, but it wasn't easy for us to win those matches because we had people butting heads and stuff like that." Interesting and honest words, no doubt.

The 2017 team had an entirely new staff, as Chris Tamas took the head coaching job at Illinois and Dani Busboom Kelly took the head coaching job at Louisville. Bring on Kayla Banwarth, former Husker whom I have shared so much about already. Bring on Tyler Hildebrand, a younger coach who brought energy and insight, which Coach Cook valued. Kelly Hunter was named the lone captain, and to this day she is the best student-athlete leader I have ever been around. I intentionally kept the mantra the same that year—**"calm is contagious"**—and asked Coach Cook to pair it with the 2015 mantra.

The team suffered an ugly loss to Northern Iowa early in the year, which helped to be a turning point for the team. There are some challenges that every team has to work through, and Kelly Hunter was the perfect leader for this challenge. She had a way of using her humor to lighten Coach's intensity. She pulled off the perfect Halloween prank, dressing up exactly like Coach, including having the practice plan folded and tucked into her waistband. Keep in mind that this was taking away from practice time. How did Coach Cook react? Hunter said, "I have never seen him laugh so hard in my five years here. So, total success."

Coach recognized fairly early on that this was a special team to him, and he was going to enjoy them and find a way to have fun! It also sounded like someone who really was learning to coach out of love. After the team won a share of the Big Ten Championship, he gave a very emotional speech to the home crowd, letting everyone know how proud he was of the accomplishment. It wasn't the first or last time that season that he displayed his love and showed his emotions to the team. In the era of social media, many of the fans also saw it on Twitter and other platforms. When the team advanced to the Final Four after beating Kentucky, he said, "I'll tell you what—I don't know if I've ever had so much fun coaching. So let's go to Kansas City." Coach Cook's explanation as to why he had shown much emotion that year: "It's just the connection that we have with them, and the relationships that we have as a team and as a group. When you have teams like this, you've got to enjoy every moment. That's when everybody I surround myself with kept telling me, 'You've got to enjoy this team every moment.' The quirks, they are fun, they mess around, they play practical jokes, but they know how to win, and they play great together. It's just been, like I said, really fun and rewarding. I don't know how to put it in words. I will at some point."

Former Coach Dani Busboom Kelly was asked prior to this Final Four what was different about Coach Cook since she had played for him. She noted that he is softer and makes an effort to make positive connections to the player. She went on to say, "I think those who have watched John through his career, the way he does approach mistakes by the team has definitely changed. He's got great body language and he's been very consistent, and that's the one thing I've noticed the last few years, is the players aren't playing with fear."

Kelly Hunter said, "For someone who has been in the business that long and coaching for so long, seeing him grow and change, too, has been really cool. Just the way he's helped me find myself and stuff like that has been really awesome."

The Final Four was held in Kansas City, virtually a home match for loyal Husker fans, and it was filled to the brim with mostly fans in red again, like in 2015. The match against Penn State was very tight, and it appeared they may fall short. Late in game four, with Penn State appearing to have a shot to end the match, two of Penn State's players collided and the ball dropped to the ground. That was one of two set points Nebraska fought off on their way to winning game four, before taking over the match in game five to reach the national championship game against Florida. It was fairly uneventful in the championship game, with Nebraska dominating in four games to secure Coach Cook's fourth national championship and the second one in three years! Kelly Hunter summarized it well:

> Team chemistry took us farther than any other team, and it's just because we have genuine love and care for each other and good communication out on the court.

At the year-end volleyball banquet, there was one thing Coach told the crowd that was one more sign of his evolution. He told us it was the first time in his career that he had not received a red card or a yellow card during a season!

I continue to be available to Coach, and we share thoughts and ideas all the time. His mantra that I gave him for 2018 was **"own the moment,"** and his 2019 mantra was **"count your blessings."**

What I do know: In the ten years I've known Coach Cook, through the highs and the lows, there is nobody who has worked harder to evolve as a coach! I am grateful for all the relationships made with his past coaches, teams, and athletes. To be around the best and to help the best has been very rewarding, so I thank Coach Cook for giving me the opportunity to enter his world, and I am glad I was able to make a difference. He continues to use the Performance Team model that Jack and I started with him before the 2014 season, and it is the model now used within his Athletic Department.

If I were a reporter today and asked this same question to Coach Cook that was asked to Bill Belichick, I firmly believe he would answer in a similar way. When asked, "With all you have accomplished in your coaching career, what is left that you still want to accomplish?" Bill's answer: "I'd like to go out and have a good practice today. That would be at the top of my list right now."

As Coach Cook so often says, "Complacency comes to collect."

We all need validation on occasion that we are making an impact in whatever endeavor we are undertaking. When Coach Cook told an audience, in my presence, that "I wish I had learned to coach out of love instead of anger earlier in my career," I smiled and said, "Job well done, Doc!"

# EXERCISES

## TEAM WITHIN A TEAM EXERCISE

- Identify who is currently on your "team within a team."

- Be honest with yourself and determine if you have enough or the right people on this team.

- What do you need from each member of this team?

- Is there anybody not currently on this team that you would like to ask to join the team?

# EVOLUTION EXERCISE

- Identify three areas in which you want to evolve as a coach.

- Write these down and come up with an action plan for each of these areas.

- Identify who can help you evolve, and reach out to those persons.

# 12

## THE POWER OF ULTIMATE TRUST

IT IS WELL KNOWN that trust is an important component in any group, team, or organization. Trust is at the heart of all great cultures.

Companies spend millions trying to figure out how to keep the employees engaged—and they are certainly on to something.

In the "Neuroscience of Trust" article, Paul Zak found that trust is the most important strategic lever in business. "Employees in high-trust organizations are more productive, have more energy at work, collaborate better with their colleagues, and stay with their employers longer than people working in low-trust companies. They also suffer less chronic stress and are happier with their lives, and these factors fuel stronger performance." The specific data for high-trust organizations as compared to low-trust organizations follows:

- 74 percent less stress
- 106 percent more energy at work

- 50 percent higher productivity
- 13 percent fewer sick days
- 76 percent more engagement
- 29 percent more satisfaction with their lives
- 40 percent less burnout
- 11 percent more empathy
- $6,450 more a year in earnings, or 17 percent more

There is even a brain chemical, oxytocin, that plays a role in humans trusting one another. In rodents, oxytocin signals to another animal that it is safe to approach. Experiments in humans have shown that having a sense of higher purpose leads to an increase in oxytocin production, similar to how trust increases oxytocin production. It is said that "trust and purpose then mutually reinforce each other, providing a mechanism for extended oxytocin release which produces happiness. So, joy on the job comes from doing purpose-driven work with a trusted team." That implies to me that you should just make sure those you lead enjoy their job.

Leaders fundamentally understand the importance of trust but have done little to promote it. Why is that? It seems that most don't know how. Zak, through his research and surveys of companies around the world, revealed eight management behaviors that foster trust:

## 1  RECOGNIZE EXCELLENCE

It has the largest effect on trust when it occurs immediately after a goal has been met, when it comes from peers, and is unexpected, personal, and public. As we always tell our coaches, "Praise in public; criticize in private."

## 2  INDUCE "CHALLENGE STRESS"

This means to assign the team a difficult but achievable job, which in turn induces stress, which then increases the team's focus and strengthens social connections. In the athletic world, we call this "shared suffering," such as what occurs during two-a-days, during challenging conditioning workouts done as a team, or in practice drills that teams need to work through together. The key is that the goal is attainable and has a concrete endpoint—in other words, the "stretch goals" we have addressed.

## 3  GIVE PEOPLE DISCRETION IN HOW THEY DO THEIR WORK

In other words, give people the training they need, and then let them execute. Coach John Cook was guilty of micromanaging his staff for a long time. Similarly, Urban Meyer said, "When I first became a head coach at thirty-six years old, I would have long team meetings. I just didn't trust my assistant coaches, because I didn't train them. Now, I put in so much; I coach the coaches as much as I coach the players." Autonomy also promotes innovation. A 2014 Citigroup and LinkedIn survey indicated that around 50 percent of employees would give up a 20 percent raise for more control over how they do their work.

## 4  ENABLE JOB CRAFTING

This means giving those you lead the choice to choose what projects they will work on whenever possible. It leads to increased productivity and job satisfaction.

## 5  SHARE INFORMATION BROADLY

Open communication about company goals, tactics, and strategies leads to increased work engagement. Conversely, not knowing the company's direction leads to chronic stress and undermines teamwork. Project Aristotle at Google found the exact same elements: clear direction and open and honest communication are some of the keys to building trust.

## 6  INTENTIONALLY BUILD RELATIONSHIPS

Studies have repeatedly shown that when one builds social ties at work, performance improves. Google found that managers who "express an interest and concern for team members' success and personal well-being outperform others in the quality and quantity of their work." When social connections are built, people don't want to let their teammates down. This is one of the open secrets that are a key to the bonds seen with Navy SEALs. In fact, it wasn't until Coach Cook saw the movie *Lone Survivor* that he fully grasped the backstory to how SEALs develop a level of trust that can only be described as ultimate trust.

## 7  FACILITATE WHOLE-PERSON GROWTH

Make sure that the people you lead continue to develop personally as well as professionally. It is how people on your team evolve. It is done through a growth-mindset approach. It is done by having personal growth discussions with those you lead. It is done by thinking about what one needs to do as a leader to prepare those they lead to "get the next job." The best coaches I know have a coaching tree that has developed due in part to the time spent preparing their assistants to be head coaches one day.

## 8 SHOW VULNERABILITY

Leaders who create trust ask for help from their colleagues instead of just telling them to do things. Many leaders and coaches are concerned that if they ask for help, they may be seen as less competent. I love this quote from Daniel Coyle:

> *Vulnerability doesn't come after trust; it precedes it. Leaping into the unknown when done alongside others causes the solid ground of trust to materialize beneath our feet.*

Now that we understand some of the key ingredients and strategies that can be used in any organization to build trust, it is time to talk about what it means to have ultimate trust.

I had the 2015 University of Nebraska women's volleyball team complete an exercise that was based on the USWNT from an article called "Cultivating the Ultimate Trust" in jamthegym.com by We Serve First. The story struck a chord with me because Jack and I agreed that our top team goal was always getting them to play with ultimate trust. The article was written in regard to the USWNT winning their first world championship in sixty-two years in 2014. The ladies on the USWNT talked about the ingredients that led to having this level of trust on the team. There were many nuggets in this article that the Nebraska team could relate to—especially with the work they did in the off-season with vulnerability, positive communication, and the lessons they learned from watching the USWNT in person. The exercise involved having each person read the article and then define what *ultimate trust* meant to her. Some wrote out a definition, and others found pictures or other ways of showing it to the team.

The article starts off by talking about when athletes don't handle things the right way, especially during adversity, and the breakdown in trust that occurs as a result. In contrast, when observing the USWNT in the gym and during matches, there was a different feeling. Christa Harmotto, USWNT captain, talked about knowing your values, your goals, and what your leadership role is on a team.

Tori Dixon, the youngest player on the team, said:

> When something doesn't go our way, we embrace it. Karch calls it "embracing adversity." Karch went on to comment in a blog, "One of my goals is to prepare the team for as many speed bumps as possible, both in volleyball and in life ... Its mission will be to condition ourselves—players and coaches alike—to handle adversity so it doesn't detract from what we're trying to accomplish on the court."

To build on this, Nicole Davis, the longest-tenured player on the team, said:

> Yes, complete trust is a learned skill; it is talked about, worked on, and revamped often. Our team has had a history of dysfunction in such a way that has prevented us from reaching our true potential over the last decade. We ... decided to do it differently ... We are fully committed to be the best human beings we can possibly be to each other ...

Cassidy Lichtman, said the following with regard to bad behavior that she has seen on other teams:

> I think the people who yell and scream and hit things when they mess up or blame their teammates/coaches often believe they're just being "competitive." But they've misunderstood. Being competitive means wanting to win, and that behavior is not conducive to winning. I think what you're seeing in our team has a lot to do with the mindset we've collectively adopted. The constant goal on our team is to do everything we can to win the next point. Getting upset generally does not help us reach that end. Poise wins matches ... That's where trust comes in. We have to trust that the people around us are all equally invested in that goal of winning the next point. We have to trust our teammates want to succeed. We have to trust that they care about us as athletes and as people. And we have to trust that nobody on our team holds themselves above anyone else. I think it is important, finally, to note that the mindset and the culture of our environment starts at the very top. Karch is a big part of this, and we have a brilliant sports psychologist, Michael Gervais, who helps us navigate through these areas.

The article concludes that when a team develops this "ultimate trust," there is a sense of calm that makes them hard to beat. As Tori Dixon concluded as well:

As a team, we definitely present "cool, calm, and collected." This is practiced on a daily basis. We treat every match like a gold medal match. Because of this mentality, I think that is why you don't see any one of us acting out in a dramatic manner. We work on positive body language, we don't yell at other teams when we get points, and we also don't react to teams that yell at us when they make big plays. The best mentality is taking every point one at a time and resetting after every point.

The Nebraska team identified with the following key elements:

- Know what you stand for, and live your values.
- Figure out how to lead in your own way.
- Embrace adversity.
- Trust is a learned skill.
- Be the best human being you can be, and be that to each other.
- Do everything in your power to win the next point.
- Cultivate a positive mindset. Poise wins points.
- It starts at the top.
- It takes practice to stay cool, calm, and collected.
- Maintain a one-point-at-a-time mentality, and reset after each point.

Coach John Cook showed the team videos of crosswind landings where pilots have to trust their training to land. In a 2019 podcast with Jack Riggins, he talked about the ultimate trust the man who tested the first bulletproof vest in the 1920s must have had!

During the 2015 season, there were many examples of how the coaching staff and team demonstrated ultimate trust—a higher level of trust between coaches and players, between players and players, between coaches and coaches:

- Coach moved Amber Rolfzen from right-side hitter to middle blocker in the off-season.
- Three weeks into the season, after a loss to Texas, Coach moved Kadie Rolfzen from left-side hitter to right-side hitter and moved Mikaela Foecke from right-side hitter to left-side hitter.
- For Kelly Hunter, it actually happened in 2014 as a result of her trusting Coach Cook's recommendation to redshirt after already playing in her freshman year.
- Coach listened to the team's observations and suggestions about the elements that he could improve to put the team in the best position to play fearlessly when it mattered the most.
- For Cici Hall, it was about trusting Jen Tamas, volunteer assistant coach, who talked to her right before the Final Four about hitting the ball as hard as she could and trusting her swing. Hall had two of the best matches of her career in the Final Four.
- Coach Cook let his assistants do more of the coaching and trusted them with their roles; he micromanaged way less than any other time in his career.
- Coach allowed much more leeway for this team to show off their personality and have fun, from goofy group text message chains to prepractice joking around and pranks. He resisted tightening the screws after the loss to Texas in the regular season but met with Kelly Hunter and trusted her to "Let us try this our way." He also didn't seem to mind being the target of a joke. Kelly told me of a time at the Final Four where he accidentally put shampoo (a gift they received at the Final

Four) on his legs, mistaking it for body lotion—and how the bus filled with the smell of shampoo!

- In the championship match against Texas, he didn't say as much as usual, and Kelly Hunter said, "I think it just comes down to ultimate trust. We trusted Coach, and he trusted us. He said that last game he didn't talk that much. I just think he saw what we were capable of and saw that we could bounce back. He says all the time, 'It's up to you guys to make this happen.' So I think he seriously put it all in our hands and just let us go."

- Coach talked about Kelsey Fien in his 2016 book *Dream Like a Champion*, in which he referred to her as an "RM," a recruiting miss, meaning they made a mistake in having her come to Nebraska because she didn't appear to be good enough after she was here for a while. He admitted he learned a great lesson from this experience: That one should never give up on somebody. That it's important to stay committed to that athlete, and eventually it will click. That's exactly what happened. Kelsey, a junior at the time, took over as a starter midway through the Big Ten season and was named All-Big Ten at the end of the season. The growth in her senior year continued, and it was fun to watch. Coach found ways to reach her mentally and emotionally that had failed him earlier, and he drew up a play for the final point in the national championship game for her, showing ultimate trust in her abilities. When the game was on the line and it mattered the most, she came through with flying colors!

I am going to leave you with the best example I have ever seen when it comes to describing ultimate trust. As you will remember, the team told Coach Cook that they played much better when he sat down in his chair as opposed to standing and pacing on the sidelines. (Whether he started to do this due to an initial back injury or not is a point of contention with me!) He had followed through with their wishes for the bulk of the season, and it was paying off. He had developed the most trusting relationship of all on the team with Kelly Hunter, for a variety of reasons, but in part because of her role as captain and setter. I communicated with Kelly, telling her that human beings often revert to previous behaviors when they are under stress and that it was possible Coach Cook could revert briefly to his prior behaviors during the national title game—it's just part of the human condition. Then I asked if she would have the courage to tell him to sit down, knowing that is not an easy thing to do in any unequal relationship, and she told me she could do it. I also prepped Coach about it and made him aware from a behavioral standpoint how stress can cause us to regress. Coach finally told part of this story on a podcast with Terry Pettit in 2019, so I feel comfortable sharing it. During the Texas match, there was a questionable call by the officials, and Coach Cook did get up to discuss it, but he continued to stand and then started to move about. Sure enough, Kelly came over to Coach and said, "We've got this; sit your ass down!" And you know what? He never got up again until he went to hug his coaches and shake hands with the losing team!

I knew Kelly had told him to sit down, but not with that much emphasis! If that isn't the most powerful example of ultimate trust in sport between athlete and coach, I don't know what else it could be!

# EXERCISES

## ULTIMATE TRUST EXERCISE

- Identify at least two ingredients that Zak shares as the basis of building trust, and commit to improving in these areas.

- Come up with your action plan that will put you in the best position to build trust with those on your team.

# EPILOGUE

## SHINING MOMENTS AND
## HEARTBREAK IN 2020

THE YEAR 2020 WILL always be known for when COVID-19, the disease caused by the novel coronavirus, caused medical and economic hardships the likes of which the world has rarely seen. By the time the story has been fully told, everyone will have been affected in some way. In the world of sport, I want to share a couple of shining moments and a couple of heartbreaks, the latter due to the impact of COVID-19 shutting down most activities in the United States, including all NCAA sports.

Lexi Zeiss was thirteen years old when I met her in the spring of 2019. She had been part of the sport of gymnastics since she was two years old. Lexi had a big dream in sixth grade to reach Junior Elite status, which would allow her to compete nationally and internationally in her sport. That has happened for a Nebraska native on just a couple of occasions over the past twenty years. One of those persons was Coach Heather Brink.

I actually met with "Team Zeiss," which included Kelley Green (her coach) and her parents, Jess and Dana. Lexi decided that she needed to elevate her mental game to put herself in the best position to reach her goal. In order to do so, she would have to train for up to thirty hours per week and develop much more difficult skills on each apparatus: uneven bars, floor exercise, vault, and balance beam. She also wanted to continue maintaining a 4.0 GPA, which is just a great reminder of the level of commitment required for student-athletes. I didn't know if I could help her, nor did I know if she was capable at her age of working on mental skills and mindset to the degree necessary. After our first meeting, I had no doubt that she had the capability and would fully immerse herself in working on her mental game. She worked extremely hard improving her mindset, and yet there is no way to replicate the pressure of competing in a National Elite Qualifier. I thought it may take her several times before she qualified, and she did fail to qualify once in 2019 and again in January 2020. Each time, she learned more about how to compete in a pressure-packed environment, what helps her get into the right mindset the night before and the day of the competition, and how to stay composed, focused, and positive during the competition. She grew from discomfort and learned from failure. On February 7, 2020, in Las Vegas, Nevada, she put it all together and became just one of twenty-two gymnasts in her age bracket at the time to achieve Junior Elite status! As her coach stated about Lexi, "It is grit . . . she is definitely gritty." She is now fourteen years old, and her dreams have only become bigger—to get a Division I scholarship and compete in the 2024 Olympics! What a joy to be a part of "Team Zeiss!""!

Performance Mountain, our mindset/leadership/team dynamics consulting company, had an opportunity to work with the Creighton University men's basketball team in 2019–20. They were picked to finish seventh in the Big East Conference. After meeting with all the key personnel, it was clear that Coach McDermott had a special culture and a group of young men who wanted to elevate team performance. The team did a great job of being honest and identifying what they needed to do better. The number one value they wanted to be known for during this season was "sharing the ball." They wanted to be known as the team that made the extra pass to set up an even better shot. Anybody who watched them play knows how well they lived this value!

The team had a couple of setbacks in the preseason with injuries to a couple of key players. The team suffered a bad loss to San Diego State in November and suffered a late-game loss to Villanova in January at home. Like most great teams, they learned from the setbacks and chose to commit more than ever to the style of play, even late in games, that gave them the best chance to win. They paid back Villanova on the road, and they found a way to beat conference leader Seton Hall on the road as well. On the final day of the regular season, at home in front of a sold-out crowd, Creighton defeated Seton Hall to get a share of the Big East Conference championship. They got the number one seed in the conference tournament, and their first game was canceled at halftime due to COVID-19. We will never know how the postseason would have turned out, but what an experience to be around this group of men this year! Oh—by the way—the team did finish seventh like predicted in the final season poll, but it was seventh in the nation rather than seventh in the conference!

Due to existing connections on these two teams—LSU Women's Beach Volleyball and University of Florida Women's Gymnastics—I was able to witness the shining moments in what were becoming very special seasons. Taryn Kloth, who had played for Creighton, was still eligible to play beach volleyball since Creighton does not have a beach team. LSU was 12–2 and was ranked number one after defeating previous number one team, UCLA, two weekends in a row, when the season was terminated. Taryn was thrilled to be a part of this team, led by head coach Russell Brock, and was equally devastated when the team got the news that the season was canceled. Similarly, Florida was ranked number two in the country and had just won the SEC Championship. Coach Owen Field, assistant coach for the Florida team, and I talked several times after the season-ending heartbreak in 2019 that had kept the team from reaching their goals. His team worked hard in the off-season in the areas of commitment and building deeper relationships. They were competing at an elite level, under the leadership of head coach Jenny Rowland, when the season was canceled. Both LSU and Florida were in position to win national championships in their respective sport. The athletes and coaches on both teams had minimal closure due to the abrupt nature of the season cancellation, and the grieving process was real.

As I often say, life and sport are not always fair, and in this case it turned out to be true on all accounts. In the end, all I ever ask individuals and teams to do is to put themselves in a position to max out when it matters the most. In 2020, Lexi Zeiss, Creighton Men's Basketball, LSU Women's Beach Volleyball, and the University of Florida Women's Gymnastics did just that!

I am going to finish by coming full circle both with the philosophies I've discussed at the beginning of this book and by talking about my alma mater. I was supposed to be the keynote speaker for Westside High School at their Scholar Athlete and Spirit Banquet on April 29, 2020. In lieu of the event, a program was sent out to everybody noting the award winners and recapping the year. Here is what I included in the program:

To the 2020 Scholar Athletes at Westside High School,

Life and sport are not always fair—you've experienced this firsthand over these past few months. That being said, what you have accomplished this year as student-athletes can't be taken away from you. You've earned the right to celebrate your successes even in these challenging times. My message to you at the Scholar Athlete and Spirit Banquet was going to be about the powers you can control within you. If channeled in the right manner, these powers will always help put you in a position to max out in life and sport when it matters the most. Powers such as attitude, effort, positive mindset, appreciation, gratitude, relationship building, practicing vulnerability, and trust will continue to be attributes that will take you further in life.

I'd like to share two quotes from Dr. Viktor Frankl, who is a Holocaust survivor:

Between stimulus and response there is a space. In that space is the power to choose our response. In our response lies our growth and freedom.

Everything can be taken from a man but one thing; the last of the human freedoms—to choose one's attitude in any given set of circumstances, to choose one's own way.

These are unusual times, but your choices and attitudes of how you respond will help define your lives moving forward. As your journeys continue, I challenge you to spend as much time mastering your mindset as you do working on your physical, technical, and tactical skills. When you commit to working on these skills, you give yourselves the best chance to perform in any endeavor in business, sport, or life.

Go Warriors!

Dr. Larry Widman
Class of '82

# READY TO START MAXING OUT WHEN IT MATTERS THE MOST?

First things first. Pull out your phone and subscribe to the *Max Out Mindset* podcast. It will only take you ten seconds to search on your favorite podcast platform.

You can follow Dr. Larry Widman on all social media platforms: @doc_elitemind

If you would like to talk to Dr. Larry Widman and Performance Mountain, feel free to email us: info@performancemountain.com

Did you know if you post your goals where you can see them every day, your chance of success increases by 40-100 percent? Download a free SMART Goal workbook and webinar to help you Max Out:

## WWW.PERFORMANCEMOUNTAIN.COM/SMART-GOALS

Dr. Larry Widman is the co-founder of Performance Mountain. Performance Mountain empowers teams and groups to:

- Maximize Potential
- Minimize Frictions Points between coaches/players and players/players
- Communicate at the speed of trust
- Optimize Performance when it matters most

With over fifty years of experience in high-performance psychiatry, Navy SEAL leadership, and the NFL, we have dedicated our lives in the pursuit of elite. We have a proven track record of teaching how elite skills and dynamics work for you and your group.

# WHAT WE DO FOR YOU

## 1. PERFORMANCE SEMINARS

Educating on what the best leaders in the world do and how they do it through Leadership, Mindset, and Team Dynamics.

## 2. ELITE MINDSET TRAINING

The best in the world across all sectors use their most powerful weapon, their minds. Learn to maximize yours.

## 3. LEADERSHIP & CULTURE ASSESSMENTS

Have our team interview and assess your leadership and culture and provide proven solutions.

## 4. KEYNOTE & MOTIVATIONAL SPEAKING

Let one of our team help motivate and inspire your team.

## 5. EXECUTIVE & PERFORMANCE COACHING

We have made a career out of climbing our mountains. Let us help you climb yours to reach your peak.

# PERFORMANCE MOUNTAIN WEBINAR/ZOOM/ KEYNOTE SEMINARS

## "HIGH PERFORMANCE MENTAL SKILLS" – DR. LARRY WIDMAN

Mental Skills Training used by elites across business, military, and sport that increase focus and resilience in the individual and team when it matters most.

## ELITE MINDSET AND GRIT TRAINING – DR. LARRY WIDMAN, CDR JACK RIGGINS (SEAL)

Proven strategies for increasing confidence and fortitude within the work/life balance dynamic and crafting an elite mindset that works under pressure.

## NAVY SEAL LEADERSHIP LESSONS – CDR JACK RIGGINS (SEAL)

Lessons of leadership from teams inside America's most elite fighting force and how they translate to clarity and alignment for mission focus for your team.

## CHARACTERISTICS OF CHAMPIONSHIP TEAMS IN BUSINESS AND SPORT – DR. LARRY WIDMAN, CDR JACK RIGGINS (SEAL)

The best teams in any sector have characteristics they do extremely well. Learn what they are and why they matter to your group or team for optimization.

## "OUT OF NOWHERE: DANNY WOODHEAD'S JOURNEY" – DANNY WOODHEAD

How did a kid overcome being rejected at every turn get to the NFL? Hear what he learned from playing with the best organization in sports, the New England Patriots.

# ACKNOWLEDGMENTS

THE WRITING OF THIS book has been one of the most challenging and rewarding endeavors in my lifetime. As with most accomplishments, there are many people to thank who have been instrumental in supporting me not only with this book, but in life.

My life changed forever on October 13, 1998 when our son Bennett came into the world. Sophie followed in 2002. I hadn't fully learned to be selfless until they were born. They are my inspiration to model and teach the behaviors that are important for a healthy life. I will always love you both unconditionally.

My mother, Carole, is in a long line of females who have had a major impact on my life. Mom, my maternal grandmother, Mimi, and my sister, Cheryl, have all shown me what it is like to be kind, selfless, and fun, and how to be a wonderful human being. Cheryl also helped me with early editing of the book. My mother suffered a stroke late in 2017, and she has shown all of us what a positive attitude can do when recovering and dealing with adversity. This book is for you, Mom. You're the one who gave me life, always believed in me, and gave me the name Lawrence because you said it would look good on a diploma when I was a doctor! My love and admiration for you are off the charts!

My brother, Alan, has been by my side for over fifty years now. We share many interests, and not only has he been unconditionally supportive of me, but he is one of the most honest people I know. When you read about Ultimate Trust in this book, it is something that I have with Alan.

My father, Stan—who is deceased and suffered for years with Alzheimer's disease—taught me about hard work and honesty. He gave me a quote that I've never forgotten: "Don't step on people on the way to the top, because you will run into those same people on your way back down." He taught me to be humble and to treat people with kindness and compassion, no matter their circumstance. I know he would be proud of me.

My uncle, Marshall Widman, is one of my favorite people in the world. He is a writer himself and has been instrumental from the start of this book in helping me with every aspect imaginable. I value his creativity, intelligence, sense of humor, and his life experience. Mostly, I value our relationship.

Papa Phil Wizer has been in my life for as long as I can remember and has been married to my mother since 1997. He is a father figure to me, and I have loved our relationship. My mother was meant to be with him, and he has been incredible since she suffered her stroke. Love you, Papa.

Alina Weinstein has been a blessing to our family. *B'sheret* is our word. Enough said.

There are several people whom I asked to read an early version of this book and give me honest feedback and suggestions. Rod Jewell, a sports enthusiast and businessman, is someone I've known for nearly thirty years. We have built a trusting relationship. Bill Eckstrom, whom I have tremendous respect for and have collaborated with in the high-performance world, recently co-authored his own very successful book. Jolene Frook, who is highly intuitive, is a wonderful nurse and human being from Fillmore County Hospital in Geneva, Nebraska, where I work part-time. I knew all of them would be brutally honest and make the final version better because of their input.

Dr. Lonnie Albers, Associate AD, Athletic Medicine, for the University of Nebraska Athletic Department, gave me the opportunity in 2007 to help the student-athletes, and it fundamentally changed the direction of my career. His gentle manner and commitment to his craft is something I've always admired. As part of a team exercise on gratitude, I wrote him a letter in 2014 that let him know how I feel about him. While we don't cross paths often today, I still feel the same way.

Dr. William Burke was my supervising physician at UNMC during my residency training and became my mentor in the early stages of my career. While I was still in medical school, he gave me positive feedback after completing a rotation with him that were "the right words at the right time" and changed the direction of my medical career. He normalized the field of psychiatry for me with his native intelligence, compassion, and attention to detail.

Marilyn Bader was my senior administrator in my first career job in Minot, North Dakota. She showed me unwavering support at a time that was very important to me in developing confidence in my craft. She showed us all how to be a confident, empowered woman in a field often dominated by men, and this has helped me teach young women how to move in that direction.

My battle buddy and co-founder of Performance Mountain, Jack Riggins, Retired Navy SEAL Commander, has had a huge impact on the last several years of my life. Jack and I have healthy debates at times! We will have to agree to disagree with this one as well: Jack is a HERO to me.

The rest of my team at Performance Mountain—Scott Papek, Danny Woodhead, and Lauren Cook—have all inspired me in different ways. Scott, for your talents and unwavering belief in Performance Mountain. Danny, for your inspiring story to overcome all obstacles to reach the pinnacle of your sport and the fact that you are a great person. Lauren, for your ability to overcome adversity, developing your mental game, and watching you grow into an empowered, healthy adult.

Thank you to all of the coaches, athletes, and other high performers that I have had the privilege to collaborate with over the years. More than forty of them gave me permission to use their stories in this book. For that I am eternally grateful, as teaching about life through the lens of sport can be very powerful.

To Dr. Tom Osborne, who was a mentor to me years before we ever met, and who has supported me in ways somebody of his stature has not needed to do, and for the blessing of writing the Foreword of this book for me. Thank you for your support and guidance, including with Performance Mountain. I am honored to call you a friend.

To Daniel Yaeger, my cover design person, who was very patient in helping a novice in this regard.

To Mary Lou Reynolds, my editor. She does her job with efficiency and professionalism.

To Jon Rennie, for guiding me to those who could help me with all the non-writing parts of this book.

To Joshua Medcalf, for graciously taking the time to visit with me about the challenges of writing a book and getting it to market.

To Mike Cassling and Kyle Salem for your wisdom, for your belief in what I teach, and for support of Performance Mountain as a means to help optimize people, groups, and teams.

To Warren Buffett, a lifelong mentor of mine (whom I've never met), who has shown the world what it is like to be ethical, disciplined, and humble. He taught me investing principles that also apply to high performance in sport and life.